THE CASU/

PRI

THE EARLY
PLANTAGENETS

Alan McLean

Foreword by
Stewart Binns

Chiselbury

Copyright © 2021 Alan McLean

Published by Chiselbury Publishing, a division of Woodstock Leasor Limited
81 Dovercourt Road, London SE22 8UW

www.chiselbury.com

ISBN: 978-1-908291-75-2

The moral right of Alan McLean to be identified as the author of this work is asserted.

This is copyright material and must not be copied, reproduced, transferred, distributed, leased, licensed or publicly performed or used in any way except as specifically permitted by the publishers, as allowed under the terms and conditions under which it was purchased or as strictly permitted by applicable copyright law. Any unauthorised distribution or use of this text may be a direct infringement of the publisher's rights and those responsible may be liable in law accordingly.

Chiselbury Publishing hereby exclude all liability to the extent permitted by law for any errors or omissions in this book and for any loss, damage or expense (whether direct or indirect) suffered by any third party relying on any information contained in this book.

Cover design and illustration by Jeremy Leasor
www.jeremyleasor.com

To my beautiful wife Laura…

…Because she said I had to.

Table of Contents

Acknowledgements

Thank you to my wife Laura for her support during the writing of this book. Thank you to early readers Ben and Adam for their kind feedback and comments. My Illustrator Jeremy, who managed to bring to life a vision we never knew we had, know that it is appreciated.

Thanks go to veteran author Stewart Binns and his wife Lucy who when contacted unsolicited by a wannabe author asking for assistance, decided not to ignore the email, but instead to help by introducing me to my publisher and even writing the foreword. Binns' "The Making of England" series is a must read for any aspiring Casual Historian.

A special thank you goes to Stuart Leasor and his team at Chiselbury Publishing, their professionalism, diligence and dedication has decoded the world of publishing and made this book a reality.

Foreward by Stewart Binns

You will be fascinated by this new and, in an adventurous and spirited way, unique book.

On the blurb of this epic, we are teased by a quote from a rejection letter: "*We would never consider publishing this, it is completely unclear as to whether it is a work of fiction or non-fiction.*" There have been many ill-judged rejection letters from narrow-minded publishers. This is one of them. Rather than be a weakness, Alan's innovative approach to telling history's stories is fresh, stylish and compelling.

It is particularly clever in that its intimate approach to the characters and events makes its non-fiction narrative read like a novel. Publishers often say that they are looking for new ways to write history. Well, that's exactly what this new account of the Plantagenets does.

The story of their dynasty is indeed a huge canvas, but Alan fills it with a precise attention to detail. However, it is not dry detail, it is rich, powerful and delivered with a highly readable style laced with humour, drama and pathos.

A good illustration of the book's engaging style is some of the lively Chapter headings: *Chapter 31: No pigs were harmed during the writing of this chapter. Chapter 32: Who the Hell is Edward Morris?*

Another insight into the merits of the book can be found in the author's brief biographical notes: '*A Casual Historian presents The Early Plantagenets' is a book for people who like to buy History books but never normally finish reading them.*"

Read on; you will really like this book and certainly won't put it down.

Introduction

The Plantagenets remain the longest serving dynasty of any to have ever sat upon the English throne. Their reign spanned three centuries and was defined by blood, betrayal, and on occasion, periods of great prosperity. Though The Plantagenets may wear the weighty crown of longest tenure within England, it is highly unlikely the earlier generations of the family identified as English.

The Early Plantagenets' focus was largely fixated on Western France, for this was both their homeland and where they drew the majority of their revenues from, England was a nice bolt-on. In opposition to the Plantagenets, were the Capetian family who ruled Eastern France. In the twelfth century, when we will join our story, The Plantagenets eclipse their rivals across almost every conceivable metric; land mass, wealth, annual income, sons, you name it.

Not only were The Plantagenets not English, they weren't even really called The Plantagenets. They would come to be known as such due to the *planta genista* flower worn by early members of the family in their hats. For those not familiar with Latin per se, *Planta Genista* refers to the common broom plant that can be seen across European moorlands today.

This strikingly bright yellow flora has been described as resilient, mildly poisonous and the possessor of an aggressive tendency to invade neighbouring soil beds. Plantagenet was a good name for the family and it stuck. Europe had never seen a ruling dynasty on the scale of the Plantagenets. They were vast, highly organised, wealthy and brutal.

But how much trouble can one dysfunctional family possibly cause?

Quite a lot it turns out, especially when they are the resident Royal Family for all of England and half of France. It's time for you to meet The Early Plantagenets.

There'll be some characters you've heard of before and some strangers that will no doubt become friends. Don't fret though, we'll introduce you to everyone slowly and keep it simple, we're here to have fun after all. I am sorry to say though that before our tale is complete there will be a ton of squabbling, quite a bit of treachery and it might get a bit stab-y in the middle. At least one Archbishop will, unfortunately, be very much harmed during the reading of your new book.

We'll jet about too so I do hope you're comfortable travelling. Whilst our story will begin in Northern France, we'll ride back and forth across Europe and even sail to The Holy Land on Crusade - there'll be a nice stay in Cyprus too for those sun worshippers.

I hope that you enjoy the ride…

Chapter 1: The Plantagenet family host a rather un-peaceful peace conference

Our story begins in a picturesque, homely, Medieval French town. It is Winter and the scene before us looks like a Christmas card. Giant snowflakes, each as uniquely individual as the characters we are soon to meet hang suspended in the air. They neither float sky bound on an updraft nor are they pulled sedately down to earth, for this is a moment frozen in time forever, it is a fork in the road.

The 25th February 1173, is one of those rare days that though feels mundane and routine, will in fact set in motion a chain of events that will forever change the course of European History.

As your eyes wander across the small settlement below, you are charmed by the smoking, chuckling chimneys, the intricately woven thatched roofs and the hardy limestone walls. Your gaze is lazily drawn to the centre of this snow globe and your breath catches in your throat. There, in the middle of the town, you spy a stunning cathedral. It is so great in magnitude and craftsmanship it would stir reverence in even the most committed of atheists.

You study this House of God a little closer and feel the first tugs of something more sinister begin to pull at your heartstrings. The illumination of a thousand candles flickering within the walls of the cathedral, spill light out of the stained glass windows to the darkness beyond. This glow dances, causing ominous and menacing shadows to look as though they are patrolling the perimeter. The demons wish to get inside.

A door opens from one of the larger cottages a short walk from the cathedral. An unassuming man of average stature, slowly emerges from the dwelling. Before he draws his hood closely about his face to shelter him from the swirling snow, you catch a fleeting glimpse of chiselled cheek bones, youthful eyes and locks of long red hair the colour of fire. The man walks with a dignity and poise that marks him as a member of the upper classes. As the gentleman strides with purpose towards the cathedral, he is followed obediently by a hulking, giant of a soldier. This great behemoth is fully armoured in plate mail and has a long broadsword buckled to his waist. You are in no doubt that he knows how to use it.

As the pair reach the cathedral doors and throw them open, they are hit by an explosion of noise, warmth and light. The Plantagenet empire has, at this point, reached its pinnacle. It stretches from Ireland, down through England and across most of Western France. The empire is the greatest of its kind in Europe and tonight, we have been invited to a leadership meeting hosted by the Plantagenet family themselves.

The hooded gentleman seems bowled away for a moment, he is facing sensory overload. The cacophony of sounds, smells and outfits in the nave before him are explosive. From the threshold of the cathedral the hooded gentleman can hear subjects conversing in Latin, French, English and Arabic. In the same breath he can smell both Middle Eastern spices and cheap French wine. Some are dressed in simple tunics, others ornate robes whilst still more, stand stiffly in full armour. The gentleman freezes, he seems unsure how to enter the chamber. The giant knight behind him pats him heavily on the shoulder, "Come on Kingling, these are your subjects, best make a good impression," he mutters quietly.

Throwing back his hood, the Young King Henry dramatically leaps into the cathedral announcing himself loudly, "The King has arrived." Embarrassingly, over the din, he cannot be heard. He tries again, "I said...I said...that the King has arrived!" Still nobody turns around or

8

disengages from their conversations. The Young King Henry looks desperately at his house knight, Sir William Marshal. Marshal thinks on it for a moment before nodding slowly. With catlike grace and fluidity he unsheathes his blade, swiping clear a table laden with fine golden goblets and ornaments. The resulting crash echoes about the stone chamber cutting over the noise. Finally, the hall falls silent.

"The King has arrived," announces Sir William Marshal. This time it is heard.

Hundreds of heads turn and The Young King can hear his own heart beating in his chest, his ears glow bright red. He hears somebody say, "Oh, it's *that* King! Never mind." The conversations start back up and the din returns to its previous roar. William Marshal shrugs at his master. Both men take a seat at the front of the church.

The Young King Henry was, technically speaking, King. He had been crowned three years previously at a ceremony in Westminster Abbey, but Young Henry ruled in name alone. He had been crowned to reign alongside his father, The Old King Henry. Whilst it wasn't unprecedented for a father to crown his son whilst he was still alive, it was unusual and hadn't been done for some time.

There are positives to crowning your son whilst you are still alive. It sends a clear dynastic message out to the Court, "this is my heir, do not mess with him, do not challenge my lineage. Should I unexpectedly die there will be no opportunity for chancers to try it on amidst a power vacuum, my son *will* become the next king". Thrones though, for all of their luxury and ornateness, are but single seat armchairs. They are not sofas and do not lend themselves well to sharing.

Just as The Young King Henry is not as much of a King as you would have expected, neither is he as young as his name would suggest. At this point in our tale, he is eighteen years old. Were he alive today, expectations of his achievements may have been fairly modest, for the period though, these were considerably higher. Take his father for example. By age fourteen, The Old King was the anointed Duke of Normandy, commanding all legal matters and revenue for the region. The Young King Henry by contrast has no income. He relies on handouts from his father and possesses hollow titles of leadership at best. No wonder his subjects ignore him, they are not waiting for this king to arrive, they are waiting for The Old King.

Thinking of his father, shocks the Young King out of his self-flagellating reverie and he begins to take into account his surroundings once more. Gathered beside him today are his immediate family.

His mother is there, the infamous Eleanor of Aquitaine. Eleanor is a formidable lady of exquisite beauty. You would be forgiven for making the mistake of assuming that she is a show bride for the Old King, a nice accessory to look good on his arm, this is not a mistake she would permit you to make twice.

For Eleanor is dangerous, her family have ruled the tumultuous region of Aquitaine that stretched across Southern France for generations. She would keep the notoriously troublesome barons in line using both the carrot and stick adeptly. She understands the psychology of people and knows intuitively when she should be kind and when she should be cruel. Those residing in the Aquitaine region, on paper answer to The Old King, however it is Eleanor they are loyal to. They are fiercely proud of their mistress.

Eleanor has more on her side though than just a fortuitous birth, she has demonstrated her competency in leadership repeatedly. She had even ridden in The Second Crusade, commanding men and fighting on behalf of the Pope and all of Christendom for the Holy City.

Eleanor smiles, oh so sweetly, at the Iberian general she is conversing with. She tosses back her head, exposing her slender neck and laughs musically. To a casual observer, this seems like a pleasant enough exchange. The Young King knows differently though, he knows that behind his mother's eyes a thousand calculations are being made at lightning speed. How could she use this man to her advantage? Was he important? If so what is his weakness? Eleanor is a master tactician and she sees every interaction as an opportunity to further her interests.

Sat beside Eleanor is the Young King's brother, Richard. Richard is stuck in a conversation with a leading member of a merchant's guild from England and he looks very unhappy about it. Richard would prefer to be talking to just about anyone else right now and there are three main reasons for this.

Firstly, Richard finds the important but routine operations of running a region uninspiring, we can even go so far as to say he finds it boring. Conflict, now that's where it's at for Richard, he loves it. Having troubles with King Louis of France or rebellious barons in the Aquitaine region? Richard is all over that…concerns over arable practices and taxation for goat herders, less so. Richard's penchant for assertively addressing issues had even caught his father's eye. Old Henry rates Richard, perhaps more so even than his crowned eldest son and heir apparent.

Another reason Richard would prefer not be stuck talking to this boring man, is that Richard does not care about England. Richard loves Southern France, namely Aquitaine, the ancestral land of his mother. It is there he resides as Count and it is the azure glass like lakes with wildflowers that splatter colour explosively across the countryside that he calls home.

The third and final reason Richard would prefer not to be trapped by this absurd English man who won't stop talking to him, is that Richard doesn't speak English. Not a word of it. The short time he has spent on the soaked, mud filled icy outpost of his family empire certainly has not been long enough for him to pick up the dialect. He has had neither the inclination nor the opportunity to learn the confounding language.

The Young King watches as Eleanor of Aquitaine skilfully and seamlessly switches between flirtatiously manipulating the Iberian General with one ear, whilst translating for her son Richard with the other. Eleanor loves all of her sons and her sons love her, but there is a special relationship between herself and Richard.

Eleanor's name is rarely spoken without her title, "of Aquitaine". Eleanor is inseparable from her homeland, she is the heartbeat of the land. Is Richard's love and loyalty so fierce for his mother because of his love for the region? Or, is it the other way round? Is his love for the region so ingrained because of his unquestioning disposition towards his mother? Nobody truly knows, but we do know this, challenge his mother, question her or insult her and you will see that Richard is not the soft boy of sixteen years his youthful looks suggest. Richard is a vicious wolf and he will not hesitate to bite you. This mummy's boy is very much his father's son.

Next to Richard is another of the Plantagenet brood, John. John's feet dangle a full foot from the ground and he swings his legs kicking out first the left and then the right, in a never ceasing cycle. The seven year old is excited to be sat at the front and for so many eyes to be upon him. John has a big smile on his face and hums softly to himself, it is passed his bedtime and he is still awake.

Sat next to John is the final Plantagenet son, Geoffrey. If Richard is Southern France than Geoffrey is North. He loves the pageantry of the Parisian Capetian court and wishes to create its doppelganger in Brittany. He lacks the relative status bestowed upon Young Henry by his birth, he does not possess the magnetic charisma of his mother and nor does he command the sheer ferocity of Richard. Consequently, Geoffrey finds the Plantagenet court a very difficult environment to navigate. He has been caught out many times. Though still young, he is already gaining a reputation for being treacherous and unworthy of trust.

Young Henry, Eleanor of Aquitaine, Richard, John and Geoffrey, meet the Plantagenets. They are quite possibly the most dysfunctional family in all of Medieval Christendom, but they are still a family and in some ways they are just like any other. They will squabble and reconcile, they will love and they will hate, they will celebrate new additions and they will mourn their losses, however, this is where their similarity to us mere mortals ends.

When we bicker with our loved ones, there will be things said that are regretted and doors may be slammed in frustration. When The Plantagenet family row though, that is something else entirely. The Plantagenet temper is legendary and over the course of this book, hundreds of thousands of men, women and children will die as a result of it.

If this family portrait seems incomplete to you, that's because it is. The patriarch of the Plantagenet family, The Old King, has not yet joined us. Though he is absent, his presence permeates throughout every inch of the cathedral. The entire royal family may be sat at the front of the hall, but the gathered subjects can't help themselves. They keep furtively glancing over their shoulders at the great oaken doors. Soon, The Old King will come, soon he will be here.

Why this feverish anticipation for his arrival? The Old King is not a particularly popular monarch, he is not a chemically charismatic leader nor is he the greatest military mind across Europe for the period - to be honest, he probably isn't even the greatest military mind that will sit in the room here today. Despite his shortcomings though, there is not a subject that resides in his empire that does not respect and fear him in equal measures. For one thing, unlike other Kings, everyone gathered in this room have actually laid eyes on him, that's a big deal for this time period.

For the Old King travels... a lot. He travels like none before him ever have, his roaming is extensive and constant throughout his kingdom. He imposes himself on the hospitality of lords, barons and earls indiscriminately. The speed he traverses these great distances is unfathomable, it is even described as supernatural. The Old King, in a matter of days can somehow and inexplicably complete a ride that would take other men weeks. It is both awe inspiring and terrifying for subjects, who are constantly looking over their shoulder, painfully aware that he could arrive with his terrifying smile and fixing stare at any moment. That he had been reported on a different continent only yesterday, meant nothing to this Old King.

Accompanying him, is one of the greatest courts the land has ever seen, hundreds of subjects travel with him. They clutch desperately at the King's coat tails and hold on with bleeding fingers as though their lives depend on it as he speeds off once again. This is no show court that travels with him either, it is purely functional and has evolved of sleek efficiencies. The court consists of house knights, judges, legislators, scribes, courtiers, advisors, earls and facilitators. Entertainers and prostitutes are kept, relatively speaking, to a minimum. The Old King's court is one of the wonders of the medieval world, both vast and completely baffling.

It is baffling, for what is the benefit of being King if you cannot command others attend you whilst you live it up in the lap of luxury being fed grapes? Who wants sores from travel? What is the point of spending night after night in a separate bedroll from the beautiful Eleanor of Aquitaine? The point, as The Old King sees it, is that the subjects gathered here today know him, or at least they feel like they do. They have got drunk next to him, their servants have wiped the sweat from his horses' flanks, they have seen the Old King commit horrendous atrocities in his family's name to those who have thought to betray him. They remember his acts of generosity, they fear his displays of malice.

The Old King is a shark. He will never stop moving forward. His eyes are always fixed on the horizon and he relentlessly spurs his horse towards this mark, never sideways, only forwards, faster and faster. The resulting court the old King has cultivated is frenzied, frantic, evolving, exhilarating, exciting and deadly for those that fall into his slip stream. Subjects that can't keep up with the relentless pace will drown in the waves of change The Old King kicks up in his wake.

The Old King will soon arrive, somehow, all gathered, know that his presence is imminent long before the cathedral doors will be thrown open. The hall falls silent and the temperature of the chamber drops perceptibly. A smattering of candles in the hall unexplainably go out in a hiss and plume of smoke. The doors fly open, smashing heavily against the wooden floor buffers. A shiver shoots down Young Henry's spine.

Anticipation is greater than fulfilment in many settings. This can be true of drunken lovemaking, overly indulgent deserts, or, unfortunately, The Old King. When you fix your eyes on the Old King, should you contrast him directly with his legendary reputation that he has built, you may find him a little wanting. There's nothing wrong with his looks *per se*, it just doesn't quite add up. The crown that sits atop his head is an old, Aztec relic which is largely hidden by his overgrown and wild, curly red hair. His nose is bulbous, he has a slight paunch, he is short of stature and walks with a hunch. He isn't even particularly old like his title would suggest, he is just older than his eighteen year old son with the same name.

The Old King charges up the aisle of the cathedral with his head down. When he reaches the end he turns sharply on his heel without even a nod of acknowledgement to any of his gathered family members. Eleanor of Aquitaine's mouth thins a shade, otherwise she does not acknowledge this slight.

"Thank you all for coming, I appreciate a number of you have travelled some distance," The Old King began. If we're going to continue picking faults in the Old King, which seems to be the theme of the last few paragraphs, he isn't a great orator either. His undiagnosed ADHD causes him to pace relentlessly back and forth across the stage whilst presenting. This both distracts from the message he is trying to deliver and makes it look as though he needs to visit the toilet.

This unfettered energy also means he talks far too rapidly for somebody presenting to a multilingual audience. A lot of the people gathered find it very difficult to understand what it is that he is saying.

The Old King enjoys a short speech though. No doubt he will reach his point quickly. "Enough of these flippant frivolities," The Young King wasn't sure what "flippant frivolities" his father was referring to, "I am here to announce the marriage of my son. The great swordsman, cunning strategist and holistic thinker, John, to the Count of Maurienne's daughter." Everybody gathered cheered, who doesn't love a wedding?

Young Henry looked at his seven year old brother John. *The great swordsman, cunning strategist and holistic thinker* was humming quietly to himself whilst picking his nose and kicking his legs. If John seems a little young to be married, he is, but you can relax a little. Whilst betrothals of toddlers in this period was not necessarily uncommon, actual marriages generally were not performed until the bride to be had reached child-bearing age. Don't get me wrong, marriages are still conducted at a horrifyingly young age when considered contemporarily, equally though, life expectancy wasn't great either. There were no guarantees that you would grow old enough so getting on with securing your lineage as early as possible was important.

"A marriage is much like the meeting of an unlockable lock with a master key, or the tree snake with the wild weasel, I'm sure you all know what I am saying?" continued The Old King raising his eyebrows provocatively.

Nope, thought Young Henry, I do not know what you are saying. What I do know though father, is that securing the marriage of Count Maurienne's daughter into our family for the small price of your youngest son, is an absolute coup. At seven years of age, John possessed no castles, he managed no revenue streams, he was not idolised as a military general, as fourth in line to the throne, John would never command any of these things either, he was a no hoper. Young Henry could hardly believe they had gone for it.

For Count Maurienne belonged to an important family that held sway across the empire. Securing their loyalty meant a lot to the Plantagenets. She was a nice enough girl too, Young Henry had known her since she was little, they were related somehow, cousins maybe? It didn't matter too much, the ruling elite across Europe during this period had a gene pool that ran about as deep as a puddle. A donation to the Pope would nullify any concerns on that front. It was a very tidy wedding. Young Henry doesn't love his father, he certainly doesn't like him, but akin to all gathered here today, he respects the hell out of him, "nice move father," he mutters distractedly, "nice move."

"We can now, with luck, go to the next item of business," the Old King continued, "A kingdom is much like a pig, fantastic to have, but to eat a whole one alone? Unmanageable. Even for a man of my voracious appetite. It is therefore time to pass the plate, to slice the pork as it were."

It was strange to hear his Father talking in metaphors for he was usually explicitly direct. Young Henry knew though that this speech was not easy for his father. Today was the day that The Old King was to surrender some of his lands, to hand over some of his responsibilities. Today The Old King was to begin the phasing over of power and Kingship. The twenty-fifth of February 1173 would forever mark the start of what would be the mighty reign of the Young King Henry and the beginnings of The Old King's retirement.

Young Henry hoped he would not always be referred to as the Young King. *Henry the Wise, Henry the Sage, Henry the Brutal,* Young Henry mentally tried on different titles like a newly betrothed practices her signature.

"I will be handing over all military, administrative and financial responsibilities of the four great castles of Anjou, Chinon, London and Mirebeau to my fine son."

Young Henry didn't realise he had been holding his breath, but he lets out a great whoosh of air at this point. That was more than expected, these were not ceremonial castles of inconsequence, this was real power, this was real responsibility, this was a ton of money, revenue and prestige. Young Henry felt something akin to affection for his father wash over him for the first time. His heart hammers with pride.

"I will be handing over all of this and more to my fine son, to congratulate him on the day of his betrothal," announced The Old King.

Can you see what has happened? Even Young Henry doesn't see this sleight of hand just yet even though it has been performed right in front of him.

My betrothal, Young Henry wonders? What on earth could my father mean? Does he not remember that I am already married? A significant slice of Young Henry's inheritance has just leapfrogged him and landed squarely in the lap of his youngest brother, who remains sucking his thumb and kicking his legs.

"I give these castles as a wedding gift, I gift these castles, to my son, I give these castles, to John!" grandly declares The Old King.

The room is cheering, people whoop and clap wildly, some stand on pews to express their elation, everybody loves a wedding after all. Eleanor's face betrays not a flicker of emotion. Richard wasn't listening so his face remains blank, he was lost in a daydream where he was drowning peasants for amusement. John continues to smile and hum, his swinging legs are a perpetual motion machine.

Only Young Henry truly reacts, he looks aghast, his mouth hangs open, frozen in a comedic, silent scream of which the entire hall can hear but choose to ignore. All colour has drained from his face, his hands ball into fists and his youthful heart pumps battery acid through his veins.

Young Henry begins what can only be described as an out of body experience. His perspective shifts from within his own head, to sitting high above the gathered nobles, residing amongst the rafters. Young Henry watches communion wine being cracked open below him and passed around the revellers to toast the upcoming nuptials, he sees his mother, Eleanor of Aquitaine, elbow him surreptitiously in the ribs.

This peaceful, out of body, floating-in-water like experience, is broken for Young Henry when he hears a shrill, high pitched voice scream, "You are no father of mine!" the hall gasps in shock. Young Henry looks around for the culprit, who has dared to challenge The Old King in such a public setting? As Young Henry searches the hall, he is shocked to see all eyes are staring at him. Each gaze that meets his own is a pin prick, the thousand tiny piercing barbs that are set upon him has his skin crawling. Slowly, realisation dawns on Young Henry. The high-pitched voice that screamed had been his own. The Old King turns slowly to confront him.

"You are no father of mine," Young Henry shouts it again, "I am the Count of Anjou. I am the crowned King of England. I demand proper lands. I demand, something...Father...Father." His voice broke with his final words.

The Old King was furious. His son was making them look foolish. If it had been anybody else, they would have been arrested and killed on the spot, but it was unclear what the correct response was in this rather unique situation. If in doubt, stick with what you know. The Old King fell back on his classic course of action and fixed Young Henry with an icy, unyielding stare. He drew himself to his full height, bared his teeth and snarled. The Old King looks more wolf than man.

Young Henry is hit with the force of The Old King's menace. He both shivers and sweats, melts whilst being internally frozen solid. Young Henry's lip begins to tremble. In front of his entire family and the gathered crowds, Young Henry runs down the central aisle and out of the cathedral, those gathered laugh and jeer.

The giant knight, Sir William Marshal, walks slowly out behind his master.

Chapter 2: How could The Old King possibly imagine that it would go down any differently?

In what world was Young Henry not going to be angry about this? The castles of Anjou, Chinon, London and Mirebeau were *his* legacy. Casually leapfrogging these to John and simply hoping Young Henry would be okay with it, was a plan doomed for failure.

In The Old King's defence though, he may have viewed the announcement as largely symbolic. After all, John was seven years old, the wedding would not *actually* be conducted for some time and wouldn't be consummated for even longer, a lot can change over that sort of stretch. Who even knew if it would go ahead? Rumours persisted that the Pope planned to declare their matrimony illegal on the grounds of consanguinity as they were first cousins.

The whole thing, in The Old King's mind anyway, may just have been a ruse to bring the girl's father to the negotiating table and get his hands on their family money. If so, it was an adroit political strategy. At least it would have been, had he actually taken the time to explain any of this to his own family.

Another theory that is floated about, is that The Old King is a control freak and an eternal hoarder of power. The act of releasing his iron grasp on the reigns of the kingdom causes him a physical stab of pain to the gut. Whilst The Old King faces growing pressure from his family to begin a phased handing over of kingship, it is also undeniable that he is too young to retire. By relinquishing control of key seats of government to his seven year old son, who is clearly in no position to administer these governances himself, The Old

King gets the best of both worlds. He can publicly pass the mantle whilst simultaneously retaining control. The Old King will get to have his cake and eat it.

Tempting though it is to follow the narrative that Young Henry has been so terribly wronged and The Old King so very cruel, this is a difficult argument to support. The Old King has, after all, already relinquished some of the hold he has over his empire. Both Geoffrey and Richard hold titles of significance. It could have just been that The Old King doesn't rate his oldest son, Young Henry. The Old King may not have believed he was capable of leading and unifying such a diverse and geographically separated empire, which is certainly an apt description of the Plantagenet nation.

By no certainty at this point, could the Plantagenet empire even be called a nation. The continuity of these until-recently completely separate states, was a totally new concept. North-Western France had unified with Southern Aquitaine just twenty-one years prior with the marriage of Old Henry and Eleanor, England had only been tacked on two years after this. The Old King's empire was a patchwork one, erratically stitched together by a drunken madman that put the bitterly cold Yorkshire Peaks, alongside the semi-tropical wine growing counties of Southern France. There was no unity or archetypal understanding that existed across the residents of this nation.

There wasn't even complete clarity on whether these regions would remain as one indefinitely. Carving the counties up piecemeal and splitting them across his sons may have been an appealing notion to The Old King, particularly if he did not believe Young Henry was up to the challenge. After all, what else could The Old King do? His only alternative would have been to watch the family business, and his own legacy, collapse under the stewardship of the second generation.

The Plantagenet Peace conference of 1173 will result in a war, but as with any good story, there is more to it than that. To the casual observer, or even to The Old King himself initially, it appeared that the war was a result of a characteristic loss of control from Young Henry. This is not the case though, for this is a tale that began many years earlier.

Our next two chapters will see us winding the clocks back to a time when Young Henry was younger and ironically, somehow, the Old King was older. This was due to the ever-increasing weight of the crown he wears. The Old King was facing the greatest challenge of his reign to date, this challenge had a name and that name, was Thomas Becket.

Born the son to a minor knight and lady, Becket had once been as close a thing to a friend as The Old King had ever known. Becket had learned his politics by living at the heart of the beast, he had travelled with The Old King's great court as an administrative clerk. He performed tasks such as grain stocktakes, financial audits, the kind of routine and mundane work that would send most of us to sleep.

Becket loved it though, not just that, he was seriously good at it. He attacked this work with a conscientiousness and diligence that made The Old King sit up and take note. For Old Henry was of the belief that the exemplary execution of fundamental tasks, were the foundations any great organisation was built upon. The Old King likes Becket, he likes him a lot.

With this personal interest from the King, Becket's career was written in the stars. The promotions came thick and fast. The Old King both admired Becket's ascent from afar and gave him a leg up along the way whenever he was struggling. Finally, Old Henry even lobbied the Pope himself to appoint his friend Becket into one of the most prestigious offices in the land. The Old King will score his friend Becket the gig as Archbishop of Canterbury.

The Pope wasn't sure about this and had needed convincing. Whilst monarchy, state and religion were intrinsically interlinked in Medieval times and Becket did have considerable experience across all of these fields, his career was not defined by a commitment to God. It wasn't just that though, The Archbishop of Canterbury had traditionally acted as a spy for Rome and a counter balance to the King's all-encompassing power. Becket got on a little too well with the current administration to be the other side of the coin that bore the crown.

Eventually, after a series of donations from The Old King to the Crusader Coffers, Becket was approved and anointed as The Archbishop of Canterbury. It should have been a match made in heaven, The Old King could not have been more excited to have marched his pawn to the end of the board and transformed him into a beautiful bishop. Becket though, felt that his station in life had changed. He was now a man of consequence and power, he wished to be treated as such. Becket started to push back on everything The Old King was doing.

This is why we begin our foray into exposition not with The Old King, for he is away on business trying to deal with Becket, but with his wife. We will begin with the beautiful and cunning Eleanor of Aquitaine. Her fourteen year old son Richard won't be far away either, he rarely is. The Old King will return in the following chapter and when he does, he will be very different to the composed man who opened this tale.

Chapter 3: Eleanor of Aquitaine plucks a rose and hosts a secret meeting

Eleanor of Aquitaine smiles contentedly as she walks the rose gardens. Eleanor loves the city of Poitiers and the city loves her in return. Like an owner who has begun to resemble their dog, the very buildings themselves seemed to be transforming to mimic their mistress, inspired by her elegance and beauty.

Even in modern times, Eleanor's mark is stamped all over the place from the grand courthouse of justice to the cathedral she personally commissioned so many centuries ago. She is even immortalised within the stained glass windows of city hall, this vantage point allows her to watch over those who possess offices of civic responsibility and ensure they are safeguarding her ancestral land. In this stained glass likeness, she wears a crown atop her head and robes of pale blue, she looks simultaneously regal and biblical.

Born to the elite ruling classes, Eleanor of Aquitaine was one of the most eligible bachelorettes across all of Europe. She was always going to end up wed to a man of power. Her story could have been very different though to how it will be written, for she could easily have spent her time with handmaidens, doilies and display cushions. She could have lazed away afternoons sipping tea in the sun gardens whilst nights were dedicated to embroidery. She could have been defined by the act of servitude to her husband. Each day could have blurred into the next so as to be almost undistinguished from one another. Her sole function on this earth could have been to pop out children, many queens of this period existed in this manner, but that isn't the road

Eleanor wanted to walk. Eleanor is an adventurer and was born to rule in her own right.

Her first marriage, prior to The Old King, had been to his arch nemesis and rival, the Capetian King Louis VII who occupied modern day Eastern France. The ceremony was held in 1137 and had all the pomp and grandeur any fifteen year old bride could ever have dreamed of. The celebrations lasted for over a week and reflected the shared interests of the happy couple. There were debates on Aristotle, hunting, jousting, Aquitainian fashion parades, the education of chauvinistic Norman knights on showing proper respect to women. It was a festival of culture and lit a torch for all that was good, it heralded the dawning of a new age of enlightenment. Eleanor even held a competitive poetry recital, big burly French Knights would dress in their finery and read poetry to the gathered ladies, who would judge their delivery of these classics. When we think of chivalric knights and Arthurian legend, to some degree, it is Eleanor's court that we are thinking of.

Whilst the newlyweds enjoyed a brief honeymoon period, underlying tensions surfaced swiftly. Though only two years separated the bride and groom, their sexual appetites could not have been more polarised. To understand the reason behind this, you must first understand King Louis himself. Louis you see, was never meant to be King, he never wished to wear the crown. He had been born the younger son to his father and was sat forcibly sat down upon the throne after his elder brother Philip died falling from the saddle. Although Philip had been a competent rider, his horse had unfortunately and unexpectedly tripped over a small pig whilst riding through a Parisian market.

Prior to becoming King, Louis had been training for a life of devout servitude to God. Eleanor on the other hand, was raised a troubadour who delighted in courtly love poetry. She was said to possess a sensual grace and has been openly quoted complaining about her husband's lack of vigour in the bedchamber.

On the rare occasion that Louis could be drawn into hanky-panky, he wanted it to be over swiftly and to result in a son. After all, if sex with his wife did not successfully secure his legacy, then what the hell was the point of it? Whilst Eleanor proved herself to be fertile, she succeeded only in siring two daughters, Louis was not best pleased about this. We can only imagine Eleanor's reaction at her husband's dismissive attitude towards his own children just because they were born female.

That being said, the King *did* need an heir and that heir probably *did* need to be male. As was often the case in Medieval times, it was decided all of this was most likely the woman's fault. Alongside needing to produce a son for the Capetian realm of Eastern France, other pressures were coming to bear upon the couple.

Firstly, there was the upstart Duke of Normandy, Henry (The future Old King). He was growing in both power and influence across the continent. There were even rumours he had a claim for the English throne and that he intended to make a play for it. Whilst this wouldn't necessarily impact The Capetians directly, it would create a menacing and powerful wolf that was living next door. He was certainly one to watch.

Secondly, The Pope was causing problems. The county of Edessa in Palestine had been a crusader state until very recently. In 1144 it had fallen into the hands of the Saracen Muslims. The Pope wanted Edessa back and had formally requested that Louis led The Second Crusade personally.

It's hard to say no to a Pope, it's even harder to say no to your wife. Eleanor of Aquitaine wasted no time on making her thoughts on the matter abundantly clear to all. She publicly announced to anyone who would listen that she absolutely believed her husband should take the cross and lead The Second Crusade. When Eleanor really believes in something, she goes for it. She advised the Barons and Earls of the Capetian court that she would be throwing all of *her* family resources into the campaign… That's right, *her* family resources. Louis had married so that these assets would be his. Eleanor seemed to hold a different interpretation on the wedding vows she had taken with Louis to the viewpoint he held.

Eleanor wanted to push forward with The Second Crusade so she organised a ceremony in Northern France to formalise the swearing over of thousands of Aquitainian soldiers to the Pope. Louis found himself on the back foot. He wasn't sure that she was allowed to do this. He was, after all, her husband. Any lands and resources should be *his* to command or pledge to the Pope as he saw fit. Equally though, it would be extremely unpopular to withdraw support from such a publicly praised cause.

Louis realised that his choice was, in fact, not a choice at all. He decided to "let" the ceremony go ahead. Even here though Eleanor had to steal the show. She arrived on a fine white horse, dressed from head to toe as an Amazonian warrior woman, some accounts even depict her as bare breasted. Her horses' hooves thundered up and down the cobbles of the city as she called for yet more men to enlist in the crusade. A summons that was met with cheering and further conscription.

"So that's it," sighed Louis, "I'm going to Jerusalem then I guess."

On the day Louis was set to depart, he was somewhat bemused, as were the rest of the soldiers, when Eleanor turned up with three hundred of her ladies in tow, bags fully packed.

"Well of course I'm coming Louis, somebody needs to lead this army!" Eleanor explained in an exasperated fashion rolling her eyes. In reality, Eleanor did not lead the army. That being said though, she came closer to combat than perhaps any other queen consort ever had before or will since. The soldiers detailed to protect her are recorded as having direct contact with the Saracens. Eleanor was prepared to get close to the action and potentially even die in support of this cause.

Not that it did much good. The Second Crusade was a resounding failure. Eleanor found herself at odds in strategy meetings with her own husband throughout the campaign. The two will return home unsuccessful and on separate boats. The cracks in their marriage are by now visible for all to see and The Pope wished to proactively prevent a high profile royal separation. He set up a series of marriage counselling sessions at a mountainside retreat, hosted by himself. The exact reconciliation methods employed by The Pope are not recorded but they were clearly effective, for it is over this period that Eleanor fell pregnant with yet another daughter. Disaster had been averted, for now.

It was also around this time that Henry, Duke of Normandy, the man who will become The Old King, first laid his eyes on Eleanor of Aquitaine. He was visiting Louis' court to discuss something so routine and mundane that the records of these conversations have not been documented. Even so, this meeting will change not only Henry and Eleanor's lives, but everyone residing in Europe.

When The Old King first spoke with Eleanor, he cocked his head to the side like a dog trying to comprehend what is before him. For The Old King was able to see past the charming, even flirtatious small talk they were engaged in. He could see the calculations burning behind her eyes, he could smell her ruthlessness and ambition and what's more, he liked it.

Though the arrival of a new daughter applied pressure to the gaping wound that was Eleanor and Louis' marriage, it only delayed the inevitable. Louis and Eleanor have both by now individually lobbied the Pope for separation. This was eventually granted on the grounds of the couple being third cousins, in reality though, it is carried through because

Louis does not believe Eleanor capable of bearing him a son.

Just like that, fifteen years of marriage were over. Eleanor found herself once again one of the most eligible bachelorettes on the European stage. She doesn't have time to enjoy this new found freedom though. Almost immediately, she was kidnapped by the Duke of Anjou who intended to force her to marry him and thus take control of Aquitaine. Eleanor managed to escape his clutches but this served as a reality check for her. She needed to secure a union that would offer her protection and further her already significant European portfolio and fast. She thought back to the young, ambitious Henry, the man of whom she had seen so much of herself in.

Just eight weeks after her previous marriage was annulled, Eleanor found herself once more stood at the front of a church, her vision of those gathered obscured by the white veil she wore. The modest ceremony was conducted in Poitiers cathedral. Her husband to be, Henry, paced restlessly throughout the service. His speech was a little marred by talking too quickly and shuffling on the spot, but Eleanor didn't mind. With the command of both Aquitaine and Normandy, should Henry realise his ambitions of England, the Plantagenets would be one of the greatest powers on the European stage.

The next few years, saw Eleanor's second husband achieve all that he had said he would and more. He made his claim for the throne of England, wrestling it from King Stephen, he clashed with Eleanor's ex, the Capetian King Louis of Eastern France and expanded his empire's borders. Eleanor and Henry had created the union of nations across all of Europe. On the home front things were going well too, with Henry, Eleanor will have eight children, four of which are boys. This assertively dispelled Louis' claims that Eleanor was incapable of bearing sons.

The twenty-two year old man that she had married, could and frequently was, described as brutal, decisive, assertive and aggressive. If Eleanor was completely honest, it was these very qualities that attracted her to him. But let us not make the mistake of thinking this was a marriage of love. Both Eleanor and Henry entered this union in the full knowledge that theirs was a marriage of status and ambition. There was a fundamental belief that the assets owned by the other, would complement them both.

In the years running up to the public outburst from Young Henry that opened this very book, it would seem that their marriage had lost some of its shine and more than a little of its convenience. There are suggestions that an understanding had existed between the ambitious power couple. Once Eleanor had finished her maternity leave, she seemed to be of the belief that the responsibility for governing Aquitaine would return to her. If indeed this had been the agreement, it was a deal that The Old King reneged on. Unsurprisingly, he found it difficult to relinquish this control.

To further compound the brewing bad blood between the two former lovers, The Old King also had a string of rather public mistresses. Two of his affairs of particular note were Mistress Alys of France and Mistress Rosamund Clifford.

Rosamund was a great beauty at court, she was more beautiful even than the enchanting Eleanor of Aquitaine. Rosamund was nicknamed, "*The Rose of the World*," poets and bards composed works of such perfection that people would weep in her honour. Perhaps Eleanor could have forgiven her husband, had she believed it was just the Rose's young, nubile looks that her husband was enchanted with, but it was more than that and Eleanor knew this. The Old King was in love with Rosamund Clifford.

To keep his affair a secret in the early days, it is said that The Old King had a complex maze constructed in the Oxfordshire parklands of Woodstock. The maze was designed with no pattern, rhyme or reason so as to make it completely unsolvable. The only way to the centre was to know and memorise the route, prior to entering this fiendish labyrinth. At the centre of this maze, is where The Old King would meet with the Rose of the World.

Eleanor suspected something was up when her husband, rather uncharacteristically, began spending hours each day hanging out in a maze. Eleanor would walk the hedgerows for hours calling Henry's name. Whilst physically she was close to him, emotionally they had never been so far apart.

The maze was undoubtedly a challenge, but unsolvable is a bit of a stretch. In all honesty, no maze is unsolvable, for there is a trick to any that will render it beatable. It is not so much a trick as it is a labour of persistence and commitment. Should you place your hand on either wall of a maze, keep it there and continue to walk, you will eventually solve it. This strategy will ensure that every passage is traversed, every corridor is followed and every aisle explored. It is not a quick method to solve a maze, but it is one that will work.

Upon arriving at the heart of the maze, Eleanor found a straw mattress. She waited, for surely this must be the rendezvous point for her husband and his promiscuous lover. When The Rose of the World arrived, it was not to see Henry, but instead, Eleanor of Aquitaine. Eleanor sat calmly smiling sweetly. She is said to have given the young girl the choice of either a dagger or a poisoned chalice to end her own life. Rosamund's choice is not recorded.

The tale about the maze almost certainly isn't true, after all, The Old King had castles up and down the land, it seems unlikely he would go to the bother of constructing a maze to conceal his infidelity. However, The Old King was indeed having an affair with Rosamund Clifford and she certainly seemed to be a mistress who enjoyed a lot of favour. The story also underlines quite neatly the fearsome, brutal reputation Eleanor had at the time. She is not somebody that things happen to, she is one that makes things happen.

Another mistress with both feet firmly in the world of reality and slightly closer to home, is Mistress Alys. She was the daughter of King Louis VII and his second wife. A political union had been formed and the young girl had been promised to Henry's son, Richard. The relationship between the Plantagenets and the Capetians was rocky at best, perhaps this marriage could assist in forming an alliance between the feuding dynasties.

Just as The Old King always had to eat first when seated at the table with his family, he also felt that he should sample his son's fiancée before Richard got a taste. Not only did he lie with the lady who had been promised to Richard, he may have also had a bastard child with the lady. Eleanor didn't like that, not one bit. She loved Richard more than any other in this world. This public humiliation of him was a cruelty she could not bear to witness silently. More than her own betrayal, she hated her husband for the mockery he had made to his duties of fatherhood.

As pleasant as this walk down memory lane has been, it is time for us to return to whence we began this chapter. It is five short years before the public blow up of Young Henry that opened this very novel and Eleanor is walking in the rose gardens of Poitiers. She is content and this is for a number of reasons. Firstly, Eleanor is always happy to be in the heart of her homeland, she is also pleased that her favourite son Richard is with her, the boy never fails to make her smile and finally, she is pleased because her husband is away on business. Apparently there had been some kind of issue with the Archbishop of Canterbury over in England, Old Henry had left in a whirlwind of energy and characteristic intensity.

Eleanor breathes deeply as she looks out over the rose gardens, "the rose of the world, honestly!" she mutters, "what a stupid title". Her thoughts are interrupted by the soft sound of cat-like footsteps behind her.

"Do not move Lady Aquitaine," a hushed and urgent whisper commands her, "there are bandits in the rose bushes".

Eleanor froze, time stood still, she felt the warm breeze brush lightly against her cheek. Breathing deeply, she fought off a smile, she knew what was to come…

Sure enough, her second youngest son Richard, lithely leapt from behind her into the middle of the field of thorns. His sword carves in mighty arcs tearing up rose bushes and sending field mice scattering for safety. His sword flashes at an eye blurring speed as he fights a thousand imaginary foes.

The entire time he keeps up his relentless attack, he shouts a string of challenges into the pleasant Summer air, "Have at you cur. You would challenge so fine a lady as my mother? Little did you know that Prince Richard, with the heart of a Lion, was awaiting in the wings to dance with you. And lunge. Stand back Mother, stay back, I will save you…"

Eleanor of Aquitaine is in stitches laughing by this point. She is considered to be a beautiful lady of poise and class, but right now she could not be more real. She is doubled over, her nose is running and her eyes are streaming as she watches her favourite son Richard save her from a field of roses.

"Stay back mother, it is not safe. Our family, honour and our Lord God has been challenged," he cleaved a hovering dragon fly in two before reversing his swing and severing a reasonable sized sapling at its base. Though he is young, Richard is strong.

"Richard, Richard, what are you like?" Eleanor says between sobbing gasps of mirth, "Stop, the groundsman will kill you!" Her chastising is somewhat undermined by her continued laughter as she struggled to regain her breath.

"I would like to see him try," her son had a fair point, even though he was just eleven, he was already becoming a force to be reckoned with. More impressive than his physique though, was his determination. He had to win, always, it was an obsession. The boy was insanely competitive. It was a trait he could have picked up from either his mother or father.

Finally, Richard stopped carving up the rose gardens and stood, panting heavily from his exertion, sweat pouring down his face, "Will Father be visiting us soon?"

The temperature dropped sharply at just the mention of The Old King. Eleanor felt a wave of not fear, just cool and calculated anger. She hated the man. That power crazed, micro-managing sociopath.

"Well?" asked her favourite son.

"We will not be seeing him for a long time".

Her son smiled, "good."

"Tell me again about the time you went on crusade mother?" begs Richard.

"I've told you that story a thousand times son and besides, there isn't time now, you need to wash and get ready for supper. We have guests coming to stay."

As they walked back to the palace Richard paused, suddenly concerned by something, "Mum, I'm sorry about the rose bushes, I just got carried away is all".

"That's fine my little prince. I think that roses are rather ugly anyway."

That evening shortly before dinner, Eleanor of Aquitaine enters Richard's chamber, she sits beside him on the bed.

"Now Richard," she begins, "tonight, as you know, we will be having guests for dinner." The way she says it leaves Richard certain that these guests will make interesting dining companions.

"Okay mum," Richard responds, his short answer invites his mother to elaborate.

"It's very important though, that you do not tell your father about these men that are coming to dinner. Even if he asks, which he may, even if he orders you to tell him, you must always hold your tongue and keep what transpires this evening an absolute secret. Can I trust you?"

"Entirely and completely mother," Richard swears solemnly and he means it. Richard would take any secret his mother asked him to keep to the grave. Eleanor smiled, what on earth had she been worrying about? There are few things in this world that she could depend on, but Eleanor knew she could always depend on Richard.

"We will be holding a meeting tonight and I would like you to attend."

"Okay," Richard does not miss a beat. Eleanor wants to cry, she would rather not pull him into this adult world but he was eleven, it was time for Richard to start growing up.

Shortly before the sun begins to set, our first guest arrives at the palace of Poitiers. He is a short man, Richard thinks, as he watches him ride up towards the stables against the setting sun. Bizarrely, he seemed to be wearing a skirt? Don't mention the skirt, mentally thinks Richard, as the man approaches him holding out his hand, don't mention the skirt.

"Why are you wearing a skirt then?" Richard asks immediately, unable to help himself.

The man begins talking but Richard has absolutely no idea what he is saying. Even had Richard been able to speak English, he would have struggled to follow what was being said, for the guest talks with a heavy, Glaswegian accent.

Richard's mother is giggling at her son's candour and translates on his behalf, "This is William the Lion, King of Scotland and he says, that you are a cheeky 'wee' bairn and that this innae nae skirt it's mae family tartan." Even with the helpful translation, Richard still doesn't have a clue what William the Lion is on about, he decides that he likes the man though. William walks off inside waving good naturedly to servants and muttering something about how Northumbria had once been under Scottish rule.

Next to arrive, was Richard's elder brother, The Young Henry. Richard was excited by that and confused in equal measure, why would he keep it secret that Young Henry had been here for dinner? What on earth would they be discussing tonight?

Geoffrey followed Young Henry, he arrived primly and barely acknowledged Richard. He hugged his mother, talked about the pageantry of the Parisian court before settling himself down inside and pouring a large goblet of wine.

Behind Geoffrey, is a distinguished older gentleman who although he dresses discretely, is clearly a member of a prestigious bloodline. The scent he wears portrays this, as does the diction with which he speaks. He is quite possibly the poshest man I have ever met, thought Richard. Upon his arrival, Richard's mother begins to blush, "It's good to see you after all these years," she begins, what's wrong with her, Richard wonders? Why is she behaving all giddy?

"My lady, I have never been more excited to receive a summons, your beauty has matured like a fine wine." The Capetian King Louis of France is overcompensating due to the awkwardness of it all, he has ridden half way across the country to participate in a meeting… with his ex. Inside he is cringing painfully. Eleanor tries not to remember the pet name she used to call him nor the face he used to make when she would… well, anyway, she ushers him inside the palace.

The final dinner guest arrives, "Philip of Flanders at your service my lady," this well-dressed gentleman bows preposterously low, grazing Eleanor's fingers with his lips. She giggles, the rumours were true, he was rather dashing. Philip of Flanders is a rising star in the European medieval world, he ran North Eastern France with a chameleonic diplomacy. Somehow, he seemed to command the respect of all and yet deliver none of the atrocities that were becoming more routine daily for The Old King.

The eleven year old Richard hovers in the doorway, he is a little intimidated. He can tell by the way that his mum is acting that she is too, although nobody else would be able to tell this. Eleanor is nervous for this was not your typical guest list, these men shape not just their own destinies, but that of hundreds of thousands of others across the continent.

The power harnessed at the dinner table tonight was unthinkable. Would it be enough though? Will we be able to overthrow The Old King, wonders Eleanor of Aquitaine?

"Richard, would you come and join us at the table please?" requests his mother.

Richard takes his seat as his mother begins speaking, "Thank you all for attending, no doubt you are wondering what it could be that such a diverse group of leaders has in common to discuss? The common problem that we are all faced with, is my husband. I want to kill Old Henry."

Richard's heart catches in his throat, Young Henry smiles, Philip of Flanders tilts his head imperceptibly, Louis nods slowly whilst William the Lion throws his arms into the air.

"About time wee lassie, your man is a monster we need tae cut down, but how? He's bleeding everywhere!" exclaims the King of Scotland in exasperation.

"The question is not how, William the Lion, but when, in this room is enough resource, power and know-how to overthrow him, we just need to choose our moment to strike," explained Eleanor of Aquitaine.

"Very well Eleanor," purrs Philip of Flanders, "Forgive me though if I ask for some reassurances. I find this more than a little unusual, I am sat in a room where we discuss the overthrowing of a man who is your husband and their father," Philip gestures at Young Henry, Richard and Geoffrey, "How do we know this isn't some kind of test to weed out the rebellious?" It was a fair question thought Eleanor, before she is able to answer though, her son Richard jumps in.

"Yes, The Old King is my father, but I am no son of his. I hate the man, he has made a fool of my mother, he has bedded my fiancée," Eleanor's heart shatters into a thousand pieces, she wanted to sob and hug her son but she remains composed. Richard continues, "I will fight any of you gathered for the right to cut his throat," states Richard. The table is stunned into silence, which is only broken by William the Lion slapping his thigh and cheering loudly.

"Well spoken wee prince, well spoken," William the Lion began, "You have a heart after my own, you have the heart of a lion Richard, I'm convinced." Philip of Flanders nods slowly, he too seems to believe that this is no test.

Chapter 4: Have you ever said something you regretted after too many glasses of red wine?

It is 1170, two years after Eleanor of Aquitaine burned midnight candles with a who's who list of her husband's enemies. The secret meeting had retired to bed long after Richard had fallen asleep on a sofa. Even when the participants eventually did head upstairs, neither Philip of Flanders nor King Louis of France could welcome the warm embrace of sleep. They were too excited at the opportunity that lay before them.

They were also worried though. All of the conspirators, with perhaps the exception of William the Lion who snored contentedly that evening after a skin full of wine, were crucially aware of the significant risks that the scheme posed. Stepping into the ring with The Old King felt like leaping into an alligator pit. Even had he not been such a competent, wily and vicious rival, the outcome of the endeavour would still have been far from certain. Pitched battles over this time period were avoided where practical. They were just too unpredictable. Whilst one side may command far superior cavalry units, it only needed heavy rain for them to be rendered useless. There were so many variables in open battle, it was often considered best to not even pick up those dice.

As we join the Plantagenet Christmas party of 1170, we are still three years before Young Henry will explosively pull the trigger on the rebellion. Young Henry looks across the great hall to his father, seated at the head of the table.

As he watches The Old King's face, scarred with an ugly drunken leer staring venomously into the middle-distance, Young Henry's resolution for the scheme is faltering. He has never seen his Father look so dishevelled and feral. The Old King gnaws at his filthy fingernails like a cornered rat. Messengers are constantly bringing him a stream of letters, each provokes further despair and outrage from The Old King. One of his fingernails starts bleeding. Eleanor of Aquitaine whispers something to her husband and squeezes his knee, it breaks him out of his mental torture for the briefest of respites. He manages to pull himself together enough to slur drunkenly a toast to the gathered guests. It does little to dispel the black cloud that has gathered above him.

Everyone is a bit annoyed, although none dare to say it. Whereas work Christmas parties of today can feel more of a duty than a privilege, this wasn't the case back in the twelfth century. Particularly for the wider concentric circles of the Plantagenet spheres of influence, this was meant to be it, their major blowout for the year. The fact that The Old King was in a bad mood, snapping and sniping like a wounded wolf, wasn't their fault. Young Henry listens to the deafening silence and scrutinises his father once again.

Does Young Henry have second thoughts about the rebellion because he is watching his previously unflappable father, the paternal figure that raised him, caught in a tempest of priorities and conflicting responsibilities that are tearing him asunder? Probably not, The Old King didn't really raise him after all and Young Henry feels no affection or loyalty to the man.

The reason Young Henry has doubts, is just six months prior to this party he had been crowned Young *King* Henry. Whilst it was unclear exactly what form his new royal duties would take, it was a public endorsement and one that Young Henry felt could represent the dawning of a new age. An unintended consequence of the crowning of Young King Henry, was that his father had been unofficially and unceremoniously forever dubbed, The *Old* King Henry.

Sir William Marshal felt a familiar buzzing behind his eyeballs that indicated he should probably slow down with his drinking. To hell with it, he drains another goblet. *If I am going to sit in attendance at the world's worst Christmas party, I'm going to do it pissed.* Marshal was a house knight for the Lady Eleanor of Aquitaine, whilst this position afforded him prestige, it was also one that was balanced by ridicule from the other knights.

"Does she make you read poetry in lace?" one had asked.

Yes once, Marshal had thought with glowing cheeks.

But that was beside the point, Marshal owed his life to Eleanor and she to him. A bond existed between them deeper than that of a normal servant-master. When Marshal swore fealty and declared he would gladly die for his mistress, he meant it and no shadow of doubt burdens his peripheries.

The worlds of Eleanor of Aquitaine and Sir William of Marshal had collided two years earlier, shortly after Eleanor had launched her plan to overthrow her husband. Eleanor was travelling on a routine PR tour through the hills of Poitier, spreading sunshine and hope with her dazzling smile. Suddenly, armed men hollering terrible war cries poured down the gentle hillside slopes and set upon the retinue.

It was a rival dynasty, the Lusignan (Loo-Sig-Nan) clan. The Lusignans, close to drowning in the inescapable and rising tide of The Old King sought to secure significant hostages of note to trade for increased independence throughout their own lands. It was an opportune attack, a cheap shot and one that the Plantagenets had not been ready for. Earl Patrick Salisbury led Eleanor's caravan guard and in a display of undisciplined complacency, Salisbury and his soldiers seem to have been enjoying the clement weather for they rode unarmoured.

Despite this lack of form, Salisbury recovered himself and acted swiftly. He commanded Eleanor to ride hard for the safety of a nearby castle. Salisbury and his band of unarmoured knights turned to cover their mistresses' retreat. As the Lusignans slammed into the defenders, their lack of plate mail rendered them vulnerable as a newborn babe to the attack.

Earl Salisbury was skewered by the attackers' leader, Guy Lusignan, as he tried to pull himself up into the saddle. This was a moment of shock for those in the skirmish. The Lusignan's objective in leading this ambush had been to secure hostages, to simply kill somebody as valuable as Salisbury was ludicrous. The rough and tumble with which the knights usually played with was entirely appropriate to allow for the capture of hostages, or the infliction of minor injuries, providing one was wearing their armour. The vigour of the assault on the unarmoured Plantagenet nobility was having a devastating effect. Eleanor's men cannot believe what they have just witnessed, it is tantamount to murder.

Overcome with rage at this atrocity, an unknown and minor knight by the name of Sir William Marshal had exploded against the Lusignans. Even when his horse had been cut out from beneath him and he could no longer use his lance, he carved great scything cuts, two-handed, with his sword, allowing none to get around him to pursue his mistress. Even with Marshal's best efforts though, it wasn't enough. One of the attackers did eventually sneak behind Marshal and wounded his leg deeply, by cunningly stabbing him through a hedge. Marshal was captured, but he had done his duty, Eleanor had escaped.

Hopefully, this was some comfort for Marshal during his period of captivity, for little else could have been. He was a lowly knight, with minimal value who had been seriously injured. He had lost his war horse, his armour and his weapons, he had no money available to him to replace these staple items of knighthood. Even if his leg did manage to heal and he didn't die of infection, the future did not look good for Sir William Marshal.

Eleanor had never heard Marshal's name before, but

once she was told how bravely he had fought to cover her retreat, Eleanor felt a sense of duty and responsibility. She also saw a chance to imbue complete loyalty in this clearly able soldier. Eleanor arranged both for the payment of Marshal's ransom and refurnished him with the tools of his trade.

Marshal couldn't believe either his fortune or the benevolence of the Plantagenet Queen. He happily swore an oath to do whatever she commanded, to be her protector. The only problem was, this had been a very unusual event and typically Eleanor didn't need much protection. Marshal was a knight in limbo. It may have been a nice assignment for an older soldier entering his twilight years, but for the young Sir William Marshal, it was torture. He longs for adventure, for glory, for campaigning and battle.

Thinking of the lance that pierced his leg, sends a phantom pain shooting through his calf that jolts him back to the banquet hall. Marshal looks over to his mistress, Eleanor of Aquitaine, she is deep in conversation with her son Richard. The Queen loved all of her children, but Richard was undoubtedly her favourite, thought Marshal. Eleanor threw her head back in genuine laughter, those close to her could identify when she was being real as opposed to playing politics. She looked beautiful when she truly laughed.

The Young King Henry approaches Marshal lithely across the great hall. Young Henry knows that dark days lie ahead and the success of leaders is often dependent on the pedigree of those they surround themselves with. Young Henry would like Marshal to join his household, "I saw you in the training yard yesterday. You beat three men in single combat. I was impressed."

"Thank you, Prince Henry," Marshal replied.

As part of Eleanor's entourage, Marshal had been present at Young Henry's coronation in France, his use of the word Prince was calculatedly antagonistic.

Young Henry takes the bait, "I am no longer a

Prince, I was crowned, I am the Young King."

"Aye, that you are."

"Are you scared of me?" the Young King asks the giant Sir William Marshal.

Marshal's shoulders shake with laughter, once he manages to recover himself he responds, "There is but one man who scares me and that is your Father."

The Old King is swaying in his seat by this point. Eleanor whispers something in his ear and The Old King goes to strike her. At the last minute, he controls himself. Marshal's hand rests on his dagger, his eyes are upon his mistress, she shakes her head slowly.

The Old King was not usually a big drinker, it didn't fit in with his whole, "*get up at first light to ride across the empire and assert authority*" philosophy, but tonight, he is wasted. In fact, he has been so for the last three months.

A number of things have driven The Old King to drink. For one, there was the barons of Northern France. Whilst he initially thought he had succeeding in quelling this uprising, rumours were rampant that this storm had not passed. There was also the persistent pestering by some buffoon in Scotland, by the name of William the Lion. He just kept requesting Northern territories of England for his own. Not an invasion mind you, oh no, nothing so brazen, he just sent constant letters that needed replying to. He would send these incessantly, usually late at night and with many others cc'd in. It was exhausting.

Leave me alone William the Lion, I'm not giving you bloody Northumbria, back off. If you feel up to it, try and take it, I'll crush you – but this Lion was a kitten and would not attack, instead, he'd get straight back to it, writing letters again asking for the bloody land. LEAVE ME ALONE WILLIAM THE LION, is an internal monologue that accompanies The Old King on many a solitary ride or sleepless night.

Worse though than both of these bothersome, "flies in

the ointment," was Thomas bloody Becket. The mention of his name makes The Old King's heart race and blood pressure spike. From the Old King's perspective, he had taken this administrative clerk and ascended him up to an office of Godly elevation, only for Becket to betray him.

As we alluded to earlier, this isn't really Becket's problem, nor was it entirely unexpected. Becket had proven himself to be an insanely competent administrative manager who was obsessed with detail. That's kind of Becket's thing. As Becket had continued to develop professionally, he had eaten up any work placed before him. These were in fact the very qualities that attracted The Old King to Becket in the first place! They also spelt out though that he would not be an easy Archbishop to control.

"And why should I be?" wondered Becket.

Prior to taking the job of Archbishop, he had conscientiously read the job description a number of times. In his hand was a precisely measured 125ml glass of wine, his trousers had been pressed as per the label recommendations and washed at the prescribed temperature. Becket does not feel that the job specification before him, depicts a lackey who is answerable to the King. He envisions the role of Archbishop of Canterbury being an alternative power channelled through the church that worked not in adversity to the crown, but certainly in autonomy of it. The Archbishop should be able to cause great change for good for the people of our land, who can object to what I'm doing, wonders Becket?

"I object wildly to what he is doing," The Old King spits, frantically scratching at hives that have become visible on his neck. He looks furtively around the great hall. The Old King is not well, a vein throbs at his temple. A scribe brings The Old King yet another letter, "No William the Lion! I will not give you Northumbria you raving madman," screams The Old King.

Young Henry takes the opportunity, whilst his father

is distracted, to approach the promising young knight Sir William Marshal once more.

"One day, I want you to be part of my retinue. I want you in my service, together we will achieve greatness," the Young King tells Marshal.

"Well I want a wife with three breasts. Run along little Kingling, I work for your mother, I work for Eleanor of Aquitaine." Marshal was not one to play politics, although in time he will ultimately end up working for the Young King Henry and yes, together they will achieve greatness.

"I grow in power everyday Marshal, one day, I will be greater than even my father and at that moment I will strike, I will topple him and the people will cheer," Young Henry whispers in hushed tones, eyes wide as saucers.

"Now that sounds like treason to me little Kingling, I'll assume I misheard you, after all, a son should respect his Father." Marshal goes to turn away but Young Henry places his hand on the giant's shoulder, pulling him around sharply.

"Do you know what it's like to have a monstrous snake as a father?" emotionally demands Young Henry.

"I most certainly do," Marshal isn't exaggerating. In his own way, Marshal's father was more of a tyrant even than The Old King, though that is a story for a later chapter.

Marguerite of France, Young Henry's wife appears at his elbow and the Young King is forced to abandon his play for Marshal's loyalty. He introduces his lady wife, "Have you met my wife, Marguerite of France?" The Young King asks.

Sir William Marshal blushes, as does the lady Marguerite, "Aye, we have met," the lady giggled and Marshal lowers his eyes.

As the evening continues and the flaming torches in the stone walls are re-filled with fresh oil, Marshal's tongue is becoming increasingly lubricated. He finds himself rubbing his eyes as one Sir William de Tracy sits down beside him. Sir William de Tracy is a minor English knight and unlike

Marshal, he is very political, he just isn't terribly good at it. Though Tracy will tell people information is the currency that he trades in, he is famously ill informed.

"He plays the part of a great war leader, but does anyone actually know of any battles this *Old King Henry of the Plantagenets*, the second of his name, has actually won?" Sir William de Tracy throws his arms aloft as he declares in disbelief, "I mean he's not even English, he's bloody French!"

Marshal isn't the man to display French xenophobic tendencies to. Although Marshal was English born, a Berkshire lad to be precise, he spent his formative years in Normandy with the cousin of his mother. It was here that Marshal learned chivalry, horsemanship and how to whack someone very hard with a sword. Marshal begrudgingly fixes his blurred vision on the toy soldier before him.

"The story I have heard, the one that I believe sums up the Old King's unrelenting obsession with control and submission," began Marshal, "is when he first came over to England. People did not know whether this was a man to fear or to laugh at." Marshal pours himself a fresh goblet of wine. "Now a new monarch is always a time of great upheaval and change for everybody in the country, but this is truest most of all for the Barons of the land. They have to make quick decisions and judgements. The choices that they make will govern the relationship with their ruler for potentially decades to come, it will decide whether they curry favour under the new regime or awaken with a dagger between their shoulder blades."

William de Tracy leans in to hear the big knight speak, "One Welsh Baron, Rhys, decides early on that this Old Henry doesn't scare him and he is no leader to follow. When Rhys receives his invitation to come and swear fealty at the Plantagenet court, he doesn't even bother to write back. He scrunches up the summons into a ball and casts it into the hearth. Rhys knows full well that the invitation to come and pay homage is anything but, it is a demand, equally though, Rhys doesn't care.

He rules South Wales and although this upstart English King could probably best him militarily should he want to, it was highly unlikely he would travel all the way to South Wales just to posture. It would cost a lot of energy and resources whilst offering little in the way of reward. Old Henry had more important places to be and greater knees to buckle than Rhys', he had decided. Besides, no other English King had bothered that much about South Wales before, why would this one?"

"Past indicators are the best predictor we have for the future, until they are not," philosophised Marshal. "Old Henry surprises everybody, firstly by mobilising his entire army and readying for war with South Wales, and secondly, by attacking South Wales from… the South. He leads his men round in a wide arc halfway across the country to seize the initiative and attack the tender underbelly. A ride that should have taken him over a week, was somehow completed by Henry in less than three days".

Marshal continues his tale, "During Henry's approach to the castle, Rhys will have his sons carry out persistent raids against the invaders to protect their homeland. He tells his progeny to make these foreigners pay in blood for every step they take. They embrace this new role of guerrilla fighters and whilst Henry's men are willing to kill for South Wales, they are willing to die for it. Alas though, it is for nought, they are but annoying flies when up against Henry's endless resources. When Henry eventually captures Rhys' son, he does not hesitate, he has the man blinded and sent back crawling to his father. Upon completing this atrocity, Henry calmly returns back to England, he isn't even bothered about securing Rhys' fealty nor did he take the time to invade the castle."

Marshal continued, "Okay, so Rhys didn't bend the knee, but so what? The old Welsh baron can hardly have felt like he had won as his son and heir stared blindly at him from empty and infected eye sockets. Though Rhys did not swear fealty to Henry that day, he will later. Henry had a point to make, this point was that there was a price to pay for disobedience and the price was high. Old Henry will stop at nothing to make his point." Marshal drank from his goblet, pleased with his story telling though he may say so himself.

"So he went all that way and didn't even take the castle?" asked Sir William de Tracy in disbelief, somehow he had missed the point of the case study.

"Henry never wanted the castle! He wanted to be feared and after plucking out the young lad's eyeballs with a rusty dagger, you can bet that he was. Everybody in South Wales knew his name and that he was not a man to be crossed."

William de Tracy hears what he wants to though, "Didn't even take the castle… it's just as I was saying, I've not really heard of him actually being involved in that many big battles and winning."

Marshal decided to try once more, "Look, see over there, see Hugh de Mortimer, the tall fellow in the silly hat?" Marshal gestures across the room to a man wearing what appeared to be a stuffed peacock on his head.

"Aye, he is one of Old King Henry's most loyal subjects."

"That wasn't always so. When Henry first made landfall crossing The Channel and arriving in Dover, Hugh swore he would face him down in combat and win, he too underestimated this French King. Now, Hugh resided at Castle Wigmore, on the Welsh borders, he had time to prepare. Hugh could spend the next two, maybe even three weeks readying for combat before this challenger would darken his doors. He began preparations at once and yet again, Henry did the impossible, arriving at the castle in just over one week."

"The force he has brought to bear on Hugh is as infinite as the grains of sand on a beach and as thunderous as the waves that smash and grind them. There would be no siege here today, it would only take a slight nod from Old Henry and his men would pour over the walls like a tsunami. Hugh prepared himself to do the right thing. With a white flag held aloft, he led a procession of his men out of the front door and into the heart of the jeering, spitting Plantagenet army who cursed his name and grabbed at him. Hugh tried not to think of the stories he had heard about the Old King's cruelty, about the French bullwhip his entourage carry, reserved for traitors just such as he. Instead, he shuts his eyes as he tried to keep words such as castration, or blinding, out of his mind."

Marshal involuntarily crossed his legs as he continued, "Old Henry marched straight into the castle and the men began celebrating their easy victory. Hugh was locked up in his own dungeons and told he will be fetched at first light. Hugh will have all night to sweat about what is to become of him when the sun peaks over the oh-so familiar hills. He was even given an Eastern facing cell, so that his fate would not come to greet him unannounced. Hugh will not sleep that evening as he mentally tortures himself, wondering what the Old King intended to do to him. Do you know what the Old King did to him?" Marshal asked.

"Did he kill him?" asked William de Tracy.

"Did he kill – what? You can see the man over there we were just talking about him he's wearing a silly hat, he clearly didn't kill him did he?" William de Tracy was not the sharpest sword in the armoury, thought Marshal, "he didn't kill him, he gave him back the castle and all of his titles."

"Didn't even take the castle," De Tracy shakes his head in disgust.

"Again though, he doesn't want the castle, it isn't castles that rule kingdoms, it's people," Marshal pleaded with his eyes for De Tracy to get his point.

"Always nice to have a castle though, isn't it?" De Tracey raises his eyebrows.

Marshal has to concede that one and he nods, "Aye, it is, but the King wants the man. He wants to ensure that every time Hugh walks the battlements or hunts in the nearby forest, he is under no illusion that it is Old Henry that has given him all of this and it is he that can take it away again; whenever the hell he wants. That's why Hugh is loyal to Henry, Hugh is terrified of the man, he spent a whole night picturing The Old King doing unthinkable things to him." Marshal drained his goblet, he is confident he has made his point.

"Didn't even take the castle," William de Tracy shakes his head.

The two are interrupted by the scamper and scurry of a messenger handing a letter to The Old King. The Old King reads it slowly, calmly and in its entirety, his bloodshot eyes are bulging and he begins to hyperventilate. The Old King is apoplectic with fury.

"Breathe deeply husband, just ignore him, William the Lion gets drunk and sends antagonistic letters late of a night, it's what he does, don't let him anger you like this! He's only trying to wind you up," soothingly breathes Eleanor of Aquitaine, her hand on her husband's knee.

"It is not that insane Scottish mad monarch with a death wish, it is Becket, it is always Becket!" The Old King does not realise he has screamed this and the entire hall has fallen silent, "Who will rid me of this troublesome priest?" he slurs into the hall before storming out of the room.

We said earlier that William De Lacey was both stupid and ambitious. This is a very dangerous combination, for De Lacey's ambition far outstrips his aptitude for understanding or navigating the complexities of the Plantagenet court. De Tracy believes he spies an opportunity to curry favour with The Old King and he gathers up two of his friends. They ride for Canterbury cathedral.

Here, they will brutally cut down in cold blood the man The Old King had once called a friend. They will kill the Archbishop of Canterbury, Thomas Becket, as he stands alone and unarmed at his altar. They will make a martyr of the man and bring a storm down upon their master.

The sound of Becket's smashed open head hitting the marble lectern will echo across Europe. The clatter of his caved in skull will reach all the way to the Pope in Rome. If The Old King thought Becket was a problem alive, he will prove tenfold so now that he is dead.

Chapter 5: The Old King must have expected consequences

If ever you have awoken from a night of drunken debauchery with, "the fear," you will know exactly how the Old King felt as he stirred. *What did I say? Have I done anything stupid? Why am I still wearing my socks?* Typically though, you have probably not inadvertently ordered the murder of your once-friend turned irksome colleague, the Archbishop of Canterbury

The story of The Old King and Thomas Becket's friendship was a peculiar one, but not entirely unexpected, they had plenty in common after all. They could both, without a doubt, be described as committed workaholics and they inherited a nation that required plenty of work to be done upon it.

This may surprise you, but The Old King's big thing was justice for his people. Prior to becoming Archbishop, Becket and The Old King revamped the entire legal system together, changing how it was administered throughout the country. They declared that justice would be based on principles of fairness that, in some forms, still exist today. The two travelled extensively throughout the kingdom, listening in on cases personally and mentoring members of the legalese profession ensuring law was administered as the pair interpreted it should be.

The church, however, proved something of an irritation to The Old King in his goal of judicial reform. They had their own court for clergy members and this was completely separate from the crown. Should you happen to be a rapist that was also a Bishop, you would be tried by this kangaroo court and would probably be found innocent. This umbrella of privilege stretched further than just the bishops though, grave diggers, vicars, church cleaners, choir masters, no clear division was made and technically any of these could appeal to be tried in this lenient, separate court.

The Old King put pressure on The Church to give up this privilege, unsurprisingly, they said no. The whole judicial advantage the church enjoyed, was dark, seedy and grossly unfair. Equally though, this was the twelfth century and The Old King and Becket had a lot they should have been proud of. They had completely overhauled and improved the legal system for a significant portion of their subjects. Surely it was time for The Old King to pop the champagne corks? Who was really going to worry about this small minority that had not fallen in line with the rest of the country?

The Old King, that's who would worry about it. He makes a habit of worrying about *everything*, but especially anyone that does not fall into line behind him. So, when The Old King sees a chance to disrupt the papal establishment, he takes it. He appoints his old friend and extremely adroit managerial administrator, Thomas Becket, to the lofty echelons of Archbishop of Canterbury. This position was supposed to be filled by the Pope's right hand man in England and represent church interests. It was an unwritten rule that he should have, generally speaking, opposed the crown. The pre-existing exceptional working relationship The Old King and Becket enjoyed made a mockery of the counter weight Becket was supposed to have represented. On the plus side for the kingdom though, it was a chance to get things done and get rid of the church's dodgy courts.

Annoyingly, it had been at this precise moment Becket had decided to find God. Given the time period he was almost certainly already a believer, but it was now he decided to go next level. He gave away all of his worldly possessions, wore a lice-infested sack, drank only water and ate plain boiled rice. He became a parody of the pilgrim in the desert and though his disciples loved it, The Old King was less keen on these developments.

"Whatever," shrugged The Old King, weirdo, as long as you agree with my new initiatives that the clergy are not above the law of the crown, you can wear a sack with your little friends living in it.

Only Becket didn't agree with The Old King, he refused to give up the clerical courts and the privileges that they enjoyed. Old Henry was furious, he sent Becket into exile. It was probably a testament both to the weakness of the presiding Pope and the ferocity of The Old King that he didn't get into trouble just for doing that.

It took almost seven years for things to cool down enough for Becket to return. Over this time The Old King had been unable to overthrow clerical privilege. To complete this project, infuriatingly, he needed Becket's signature who was hiding away in exile. Old Henry had no choice but to invite Becket to return to England.

It will not surprise you to hear that The Old King had not been idle though. He had appointed a board of bishops to surround Becket that all sneakily reported everything back to the crown. With Old Henry's agents surrounding The Archbishop, he was confident he could overturn this latest challenge to his authority. By this point, it had become less about the nobility of the cause than it had about beating a rival.

1170, the morning of December 25th, around twenty hours before The Old King blew up and accidentally ordered the Archbishop of Canterbury's death, Becket delivered a speech. In this announcement he publicly excommunicated each and every one of the bishops that The King had surrounded him with. In this one act, he had purged his council of The Old King's shadow. Becket had never felt more free.

In celebration he supped from a warm glass of water, then chastised himself for inadvertently committing the sin of pride. His actions sent white rabbits running across the empire and these rabbits had a tale to tell. When a letter reaches The Old King telling him what has gone down...well...you saw what happened.

So, The Old King's goons had ridden hard for Canterbury and in front of trembling monks cowering in the cloisters, slashed down the great, the Holy, the pure, the disciple, Archbishop Thomas Becket. They made a martyr of him. This incident will come to define The Old King's career. When you think of Henry II today, if indeed you ever do, this atrocity will be forefront in your mind. Typically though, modern interpretations of this act tend to fade to credits with the murder of Becket, but this is not where our story ends, by this point, it has hardly begun.

Modern stories about the murder of Thomas Becket do not usually show The Old King hearing the news of what has transpired, they don't typically show him howling to the night sky or chewing his straw mattress like a feral dog in abject horror and terror, but these things happened. For the first time in this story, we have found The Old King paddling furiously in shark infested waters completely out of his depth.

His first act in damage limitation was to shut the English borders, every port, every harbour and every dock was closed for visitors. Nobody got in, nobody got out. If the Pope cannot send word to him then maybe, just maybe, it wasn't happening. Perhaps The Pope would forget that an Archbishop had just been murdered at the altar? This wasn't a long term strategy though, for The Old King has a cross-channel empire and needed directives to flow freely between England and Europe.

The Capetian King, Louis VII of France, was *very* interested to hear that The Old King had shut himself and his leadership team in England, far away from his continental interests and that no word could reach him. The Plantagenet barons are seriously worried about this, there are even rumours the usually level headed Philip of Flanders planned to side with Louis and attack Northern France during this period of instability.

"I'm just devastated about this," tearfully declares Eleanor of Aquitaine as she watches her husband pack his bags, "devastated!" she sobs dramatically holding the back of her hand to her forehead – am I overdoing it, she wonders? – no it's fine, she sobs dramatically again, "devastated". Eleanor of Aquitaine would like to thank the academy for her inspiring performance, for Eleanor of Aquitaine is not devastated at all, she is delighted at this turn of events. It was in fact *her* who had sent word to every leading dignitary in Europe about what had transpired at her husband's word. "I will tell Young Henry to prepare himself for travel to Ireland then, perhaps there we can withdraw graciously from the spotlight and take what we can. At least there we will be together," she squeezes The Old King's forearm, "forever".

Eleanor has no intention of staying with her husband, the first chance she gets she plans to return to Aquitaine with Richard and be away from this hellish nightmare and do you know what? If the dashing Philip of Flanders fancied calling in on occasion than why the hell not?

"You two aren't coming," The Old King mutters distractedly, "where are my black socks?"

The Old King leaves Eleanor of Aquitaine and Young Henry behind to face the music, whilst he completes a tour of the windswept country of Ireland. Over on this rain-soaked rock populated almost entirely by goats, Old Henry will be declared the King of Kings. If The Old King had a suspicion that politics worked a little differently in Ireland, it is not an inkling he has time to follow up on at this juncture. For whilst The Old King can race at inhuman speeds, even he cannot outrun his problems.

Old Henry has to, eventually, return and face his demons. Upon reaching his palace in Normandy, he finds every uncluttered surface piled high with post addressed to him. There is literally tons of correspondence. With a sigh, he reaches for the first one. A silhouette appears at the door.

"How was your trip to Ireland?" somehow Eleanor manages to make this innocent enough question sound accusatory.

"Amazing, actually, they declared me overlord and king of all their land," The Old King replies hollowly.

"You conquered all of Ireland in less than a month?" Eleanor hates herself for sounding impressed, but she is.

"I think so, I didn't fight a single battle, I guess they had heard of me."

"You need to talk to your son, you need to talk to Young Henry. He has had to deal with emissaries from Rome, a priesthood that think we are murdering psychopaths and a populous that are worried if they die during this period of excommunication, they will go to Hell. He has had so much he has had to deal with whilst you have been off gallivanting. How could you leave when there is so much going on?" Eleanor has been holding this inside her for weeks and the words erupt from her like lava from a volcano.

"So much going on…" The Old King mutters quietly staring off into the middle distance, "So much going on…" he repeats, "When isn't there, so much going on?" his volume climbs dramatically. "When is there not a war to win, a rebellion to quell, a Pope to pacify?" He is building up to a crescendo. "When is there not so much going on Eleanor? I'm sorry that my son, the crowned bloody king, had to deal with some old Italian vicars choked by their dog collars, whilst I was out braving the storms of Ireland. Everything I do is for this family, everything I do is for us," his eyes narrow as he fixes his gaze upon his wife, "I wonder why it is you do what you do, Eleanor?"

Eleanor of Aquitaine turns sharply and walks away, that isn't how The Old King had intended their reunion to go, he sighs and reaches for the first letter. It is from William the Lion requesting Northumbria, as is the second, third, fourth and fifth, the sixth he reaches for though, is from the Pope. Essentially and unsurprisingly, The Old King has been excommunicated, as have the knights who have committed the murder. The concept of excommunication terrifies The Old King, for all of his challenging of the authority of the church, he is actually a traditionally pious and devout man.

It is unclear how one should react if they are excommunicated by the Pope, but probably not like this. The Old King spends three days dressed in a sack and living in fire ashes. He refuses food and will drink only water, he cancels all social occasions in his calendar and writes persistently to the Pope begging for forgiveness. He tracks down the trigger man, William de Tracy, and his murderous men. He detains them on behalf of the Pope.

Interestingly, he also promises that he, or one of his sons, will take the cross and lead two hundred men or more in the Holy Land for a period of no less than three years. As a cherry on top, he also offers to embark upon a major construction project across England and France, throwing up churches like they were picket fences. The Old King is prepared to pay a heavy price for what true Christians believe comes for free, God's forgiveness. The Pope eventually relents and removes the excommunication from Old Henry. The people have not forgotten though, neither have Henry's family.

How do we know the magnitude of the church construction project that Old Henry launched? Because of a glacier. High in the Swiss Alps a frozen wave has been cutting a valley, hyper-slowly, through the mountains for millennia. Aside from being a natural geographical wonder, this glacier is also a frozen time capsule.

By drilling responsibly through the ice, historians can travel back in time and assess the chemical levels within the shards below to draw conclusions. Over the years of Becket's exile, lead pollution levels in the ice is close to zero and hardly registering on any of the scales, after his murder though, it explodes. The water is basically black.

Lead was a primary construction material in churches,

the roofs needed it, the walls did, if in doubt some lead would be chucked in. The construction project the King embarked upon to aid in his reconciliation with the church has registered on a glacier in the Swiss Alps. We all leave footprints as we walk this earth, some of these are deeper than others.

Becket's remains will be laid to rest in an ornate, decorative tomb. The Pope will posthumously declare the man a saint and this spot will become one of the most famous Holy sites of the Middle Ages. People will travel far and wide to visit the shrine and miraculous happenings are not uncommon for visitors who pay their respects here. Geoffrey Chaucer's fourteenth century collection of short stories, *"The Canterbury Tales"* features thirty-one pilgrims who are making their way to Canterbury. Why are the pilgrims travelling to Canterbury? To visit the tomb of Saint Thomas Becket of course.

If you don't believe in Holy miracles, you may by the end of this book. For we will revisit the Shrine of Saint Thomas Becket on two more occasions and unlikely happenings will follow both of these instances. If you find you are at a point in life where you yourself are in need of a miracle, unfortunately, visiting the shrine of Saint Thomas Becket is not an option that is open to you. The shrine was destroyed in 1538 as part of the dissolution of the monasteries by King Henry VIII, in the infamous break up between England and Rome.

It is almost time to close this chapter and return to our main timeline. We will shortly be revisiting the morning after Young Henry publicly renounced his father at the Plantagenet peace conference. Before we do though, let's close the loop and answer the final question, what happened to William de Tracy and his three companions? The Old King seems to have copped a lot of the blame for Becket's murder, whilst comparatively, de Tracy enjoys relative anonymity today.

The Old King hunted down those responsible for the murder and awaited word from the Pope as to what should be done with them. Statues of the murderers are erected just outside the hallowed grounds of Canterbury Cathedral and pilgrims visiting the site would take a detour to the stone likenesses and spit on them. The men themselves are sentenced to fourteen years on crusade, better than a death sentence…just.

Things are seriously heating up in the Holy Land, the Saracens are increasing the pressure on Christendom and a young commander, by the name of Saladin, is proving extremely adept at uniting his people. The Saracens grow both in number and organisation every day whilst volunteers from the West are drying up. Having four trained knights of fighting age simply killed, would have been wasteful of the Pope when they could be put to use in the sands of The Holy Land.

Though De Tracy was scared to stand on the front line of the Holy War, he at least would have a fighting chance there and would be one of the privileged few to cast his eyes upon the Holy city of Jerusalem. Unfortunately, he never even got there. He contracted leprosy en route somewhere in Southern Italy. De Tracy's men don't do much better, they are thought to have only lasted for a couple of miserable years in the desert before meeting their end. During this time, so shunned were they for their crimes it was said that even dogs would not accept food from their plates.

The men were buried beneath the main road into Jerusalem, ensuring that all who visit the Holy City have a chance to pay their disrespects by walking over their graves.

Enough exposition, it is time for us to shift our focus from The Old King, to the Young One. For Young Henry has just lit the fuse on a bomb that has been five years in the making. The best plans are always simple and the conspirators plan is anything but. It involves so many key players, which means there is an awful lot that can go wrong.

Let's recap, there is the beautiful, poised and deadly Eleanor of Aquitaine, the Wildman William the Lion, Young Henry's younger brothers Richard and Geoffrey, the hyper intelligent holistic thinker Philip of Flanders and the tried and tested veteran Louis VII of France. They had all said they would fight the fearsome Old King, but will they really? When they are put to it and the time comes, will they follow the Young King Henry into battle or not?

Chapter 6: Young Henry starts a rebellion and rather embarrassingly loses his socks

Young Henry didn't sleep well that night. The conspirators' plot has been so many years in the oven and talked about at such length from every conceivable angle, that it has taken on an ethereal, other-worldly edge. To touch it, as Young Henry just has, could render it real or make the whole thing blow up in a plume of smoke.

Perhaps for William the Lion, it was a drunken fantasy and nothing more. Maybe King Louis just enjoyed the chance to sit at the same table as his ex-wife? Philip of Flanders, the eternal strategist, could have been playing one of his political games. Young Henry has to consider all of this, for he is stood at a fork in the road. He could publicly and humiliatingly back down by swearing allegiance to his Father and prostrating himself at the feet of The Old King, or, he could follow through with what he has started, Young Henry could start a civil war.

When the sun cast its first feeble rays across Young Henry's chamber the following morning, it is to find the Young King already awake and fully dressed. Young Henry has not actually slept. Aside from mentally wrestling with the conundrum of what to do next long term, he is also worried about the here and now.

At first light, Young Henry imagined that he would be sent for, not by a courtier, a senior servant or even a household knight. Most likely, it would be one of the lowliest of his Father's household. A servant responsible for mucking out the latrines or scrubbing The Old King's gussets, it was unlikely Young Henry would even recognise the man or know his name. This would be a deliberate slight, everything that The Old King did was deliberate.

He would then, Young Henry predicted, be walked back to the church in the centre of the village. This walk of shame would be scored by the sound of shutters flying open and hushed laughter. The Young King would be permitted no entourage, no security would be in place, the aim of this would be to humiliate Young Henry in front of his subjects. Just imagining this ordeal has Young Henry's face burning and eyes pricking in anger and shame.

Upon entering the church, court would be fully gathered, it may even already be in session. The entire cathedral would fall silent as Young Henry enters. The Old King would be presiding over the room, his bright red hair would be matched only by the fire in his eyes. His mother, Eleanor of Aquitaine would try to show some kind of sympathy to him, she would cast a soft look or a comforting glance in his direction perhaps but she would be unable to do much more. Stood behind the thrones would be the rest of his family.

His father would begin to speak. There would be no introduction to the session, it would be straight to business. There would probably be a reduction in Young Henry's allowance, no surprise there. This would cause the Young King more than just personal embarrassment; it would also cause serious operational challenges. House Knights such as Sir William Marshal did not come cheap, neither did the lavish luxuries and practices a King was supposed to indulge in. Aside from the money, there may be some kind of house arrest. He would be detained with his beautiful wife Marguerite, possibly in their country house in Winchester, more likely though in one of the draughty, run-down castles of the Northern provinces.

Young Henry's stomach knotted as he continued mentally torturing himself with these dark and twisted fantasies. Behind the heavy oak doors of his house arrest he would not be a prisoner, as such, but he certainly wouldn't be free. His influence would wane. Courtiers would begin to forget about him. Letters that previously required his royal seal would now by-pass him completely. Perhaps, in his absence, his Father would begin working more closely with one of his brothers. The Old King may even learn how to delegate Young Henry feared, breaking up his birth right and carving the kingdom up like a Christmas turkey. This wouldn't be announced in the courtroom session, but it is what his Father would be thinking.

The Old King would probably conclude with a quick line about how much of a disappointment Young Henry had always been. The courtiers would chuckle. The Young King would be forced to apologise, to thank his father for his leniency, his mercy even. The Old King would stride out of the church without making eye contact with anyone. As usual, he would win, he always did.

As Young Henry sits alone in his bed chamber trying to predict The Old King's next ten moves, he decides then and there, that this is it, today marks the start of the rebellion. He will be celebrated as the greatest Plantagenet King who has ever lived. People will cheer him and his co-conspirators will fall into line behind him, for he is their King and they will be his subjects.

Young Henry is snatched from his thoughts by a knock at the door. He walks over it as if in a dream. He opens it slowly. Stood before him is a man he does not recognise who smells of stale crotches and latrines.

"I am a servant of your Father," the smelly, pox-infested man grunts.

"I understand. You wish for me to come with you to the cathedral?" asks the Young King.

The troglodyte creature looks confused, "No, your Father wants you to prepare yourself for travel. We leave in one hour. We are going hunting."

Young Henry's predictions about how his Father

would handle his outburst proved to be entirely incorrect. The Old King had tentacles wrapped around every facet of his empire. Following his son's outburst, he had reached out to his network of spies and informants, the information that had returned troubled him.

The Old King does not know all of the details, he does not know who is involved, but the burning pain in his gut tells him that something is definitely up. He suspects Young Henry's outburst is more than the churlish actions of an over privileged brat, it seemed more like a symptom of a far greater sickness. Until The Old King could ascertain exactly how far this cancer had spread, he needed to isolate the infection and prevent further transmission of, well, whatever the hell it was he was up against. The Old King needs to get his oldest son, Young Henry, as far away as possible from the rest of the family.

You will not be surprised to hear that The Old King is not taking Young Henry hunting. Instead they will ride North, as if pursued by demons with the entire Plantagenet court in tow. Young Henry spends the first day of travel constantly looking over his shoulder and awaiting a summons to ride alongside his Father to discuss the events that had transpired the previous evening, but the summon never comes. The Old King is not idle though, there are constant meetings the entire time they are travelling. Young Henry witnesses almost every member of management sent for at some point to ride alongside The Old King. Young Henry is not required at any of these meetings. Though he is glad to not receive a public and humiliating tongue lashing, he is also unnerved by this silent treatment.

There are other things the Young King is unsettled by, firstly, all of Young Henry's servants have been changed. As he rides, he is not surrounded by a single familiar face, even William Marshal seems to be being kept away from him. The travelling court of The Old King is one of the medieval wonders of the world. It is not dissimilar to the great barrier reef. It is vastly infinite, ever evolving and potentially dangerous if you are not paying attention. Somehow though, Young Henry finds himself at the heart of this organic, hyper-charged eco-system feeling both alone and lonely.

After three days of this treatment, Young Henry decides that he has had enough. He resolves himself to steal away in the dead of night. For the second time in the last three days, Young Henry vows that today is the day the rebellion will start. He sends word to those who he believes are loyal and asks them to meet him safely away from the main encampment at a clearing in a nearby forest.

Young Henry stands alone in the moonlit clearing next to a stream surrounded by great oak trees. The scene is washed in mercurial silver and Young Henry feels so far away from what he is familiar with, he may as well be on another planet. His heart is in his mouth as he awaits to see if anybody will join him. The first to arrive in the clearing is the giant knight, Sir William Marshal, he nods to the Young King.

"I wasn't sure you were going to come Marshal," says Young Henry, his eyes convey relief he has turned up, "Thank you."

"Hopefully we will not regret it," gruffly replies Sir William Marshal.

Over the next hour, people slowly trickle into the clearing like the babbling brook they stand beside. Young Henry greets each new arrival the same, whether they are a lord, knight or lowly servant. He earnestly shakes each arrivals' hand and thanks them profusely for attending. He is genuinely grateful for all that are prepared to stand with him against The Old King. Young Henry politely motions for one of the servants to come closer, "Please, arrange for these letters to be delivered to my brother Richard, my mother Eleanor, my brother Geoffrey, Philip of Flanders, William the Lion and Louis VII of France." Young Henry hands over the six letters.

As more people arrive in the moonlit grove, one person is noticeable by her absence. Young Henry's wife, Marguerite of France, has not come. Perhaps her letter did not arrive, perhaps she thought it safer to remain at the castle and not openly declare herself at war with The Old King. It is hard for Young Henry not to feel gutted by this. Young Henry needs to get over this personal devastation however, for he is a king and kings have responsibilities. Young Henry must address those who have gathered in the midnight grove to show their support, Young Henry must prove himself a leader.

"Thank you all for coming. The road we walk is not always smooth, it can often be fraught with peril. When we believe in a cause though, when we know that what we are doing is right, light can be shed on even the darkest of nights," those gathered are hanging on his every word, contrary to his father, Young Henry certainly can deliver a speech.

"I'm not going to lie to you," he continues, "Fighting my Father will not be easy, it will be dangerous. If you do not believe in this cause enough to give your life, I would suggest you turn around and leave right now, I will not punish you nor will I carry any ill will, but speak now for come morning it will be too late for you. Look deep within your soul and ask yourself, would I die to overthrow The Old King?" Young Henry pauses the pause of a man who is confident that nobody will speak, he goes to continue but is cut off.

"Actually, my liege, we'd rather not die," a voice nervously calls out from the crowd.

Young Henry scans those gathered trying to pick out who has spoken, finally he identifies the man, it is one of his baggage carriers. Young Henry is more than a little surprised, I mean why would you travel out in the dead of night to a secret meeting just to not join a rebellion? Young Henry doesn't know what to say, he settles with a simple, "P-pardon?"

"Myself and the other baggage carriers, we've been talking about it and we've decided, that actually, if it's okay with you, we'd rather not die, we think?" the Head Baggage Handler is clearly unaccustomed to speaking so publicly and explains his position awkwardly.

Young Henry is flummoxed and not at all sure what to do, he has, after all, just publicly granted amnesty to any who wished to leave. "Okay then, well, off you go I guess" Young Henry shrugs.

"Thanks Sir, best of luck with it all!" the baggage handlers shuffle off.

In what is an example of perfect ludicrousness and the randomness of the universe, they diligently continue to perform their duties to the very end. They carry with them, all of Young Henry's luggage as they depart back to the castle of The Old King. Everyone is too surprised that they are leaving and too accustomed to seeing them carrying the Young King's belongings to even think to stop them. It will be much later that night before Young Henry realises with no shortness of frustration, that he has just lost all his changes of clothes and finery. He will have to fight the rebellion wearing dirty socks and yesterday's underwear, it was not a good start to the campaign.

When the baggage handlers returned to the camp, The Old King listened calmly as they explained what had transpired in the woods. They were nervous to tell The Old King but he did not seem in the least bit surprised. He had pieced together most of what was going on from conversations he had conducted over the last three days. He is troubled by something though, he does not really want any son of his to be riding around Europe looking like a beggar in soiled britches. He sends the baggage carriers back to his son and orders them to return his suitcases.

Next, The Old King does something he would really rather not. He sets up a meeting with William the Lion of Scotland. William the Lion has been writing to The Old

King every day for the past three years, requesting that The Old King hand over Northumbria. At first, The Old King had wondered what leverage The Lion had against him, did he have legions of soldiers ready to thunder South, what gave him the audacity to think he could just demand these lands? It turned out, William the Lion had nothing of the sort, The Lion just thought, like a persistent toddler, that if he kept asking repeatedly enough he might just wear down The Old King.

It was an insane strategy from William the Lion, a ridiculous one and what bothered The Old King the most, was that it had worked. As much as it irked Old Henry to lose this land, he also did not want to fight a war on two fronts. Spies had sent word to him that his son, Young Henry, had been sighted riding hard South. Best guess, was that he intended to meet up with his Father in Law, Louis of France. The Old King could deal with his son and Louis, he hoped, he wasn't sure that he could do so with The Lion rampaging about his Northern borders.

"Thank you for finding the time to meet with me William the Lion," formally begins The Old King, nodding his head precisely.

"Aye, tis nae bother, the highland roads are passable in tae low season and taes nae a thing like feelin' the cold fresh air breath on ye bare knees aye?" William the Lion looks at him knowingly and winks.

"Yes, I should well imagine it is, a good feeling that is, on the knees, as it were." The Old King can get by with English, he prides himself on speaking passably every language within his empire, even so, he's finding it difficult to follow The Lion's unusual dialect. The Old King decides to take control, "Now, I'm sure you know why I was keen to meet with you William?"

"Nae," is the simple reply from The King of Scotland.

"Well, you must have heard about my son?"

"John?" asks William innocently raising his eyebrows.

"No, not John," snaps The Old King.

"Richard, is Richard okay?" William the Lion sounds genuinely concerned, "If taes anything the matter with Richard just'a tell mae?"

"It is Young Henry that I refer to," The Old King says, back to being overly formal to compensate for the strange direction this meeting seemed to be taking.

"I didn't know you had a son called Young Henry," lies The Lion with wide eyes.

"You've met him a number of times William, remember the feast of remembrance last Autumn, you made multiple toasts in his honour, do you remember?"

"Alas, I cannae. I had mae skins of those wee red wines ye wae servin' than I shouldae. I cannae remember the feast of remembrance." William the Lion shrugs his shoulders.

The Old King felt an irrational surge of envy for anyone who is able to drink to oblivion, without waking up the following morning only to discover that they have inadvertently ordered the murder of the Archbishop of Canterbury. Eleanor's words returned to him from the evening of that very feast, she spoke about William the Lion and said this, *ignore him, he is trying to wind you up, it's what he does.* The Old King breathes deeply and goes on calmly.

"My son, The Young Henry, is on the edge of leading a rebellion against me, now what I need…"

William the Lion jumps in explosively, "Ye own bairn is plotting to rebel against ye? If that is'nae the saddest thing I 'are hae tell'ae!"

"SHUT UP LION!" William the Lion seems to know he has gone too far, he feels The Old King's warm breath on his face as he is screamed at from the distance of a millimetre. "Shut up, just shut up. Now what is it, that you desire more than anything else in all of the land? What is it you have written to me requesting every day and every week for the past God knows how long?"

William the Lion's eyes light up, with reverence, he

says the four syllables longingly like he speaks the name of a lover, "Nor-thum-bri-a. Northumbria. Northumbria"

"Northumbria, I will give you Northumbria, in return for your allegiance against Young Henry, what do you say Lion, shall we unite?" The Old King holds out his hand and the ghost of a smile tickles the corners of his mouth. An eternity passes.

"Nae, I'd rather not!" William the Lion shakes his head remorsefully, it seems to be causing him physical pain to turn down this offer. He turns his whole body away from The Old King but cannot resist peeking furtively at the outstretched hand.

"What the hell is wrong with you? You have written, literally thousands of letters to me, requesting that very county, why would you not take it now?" The Old King is furious with this mad monarch who has wasted his time.

"I dinnae want tae fight against the Wee Henry."

"You couldn't remember who he was a second ago!" The Old King throws his arms in the air in disbelief.

"Aye, well, I remember it all now. I will nae attack ye Old King, just leave me out of your family feud. Leave me out of your war."

The Old King leaves this meeting having not got his own way, which is something he isn't used to. His courtiers can hear his teeth grinding over the thunder of the horses' hooves as they ride back for mainland Europe.

Chapter 7: The family that slays together, stays together

On the 22nd August 1914, something remarkable happened. Dragoon Guard Ernest Edward Thomas fired a shot at a German cavalry officer. Thomas hit the man who doubled over in pain. It was not a confirmed kill, even today we do not know if the soldier died or was simply wounded although this is something many have tried to determine.

Why have investigations been conducted as to the outcome of this particular bullet, when many billions of rounds will be fired in France alone over the next four years? The reason Ernest Edward Thomas' shot is one of such note, is that it is believed to have been the first British bullet of World War One fired in anger.

Interestingly, this shot was not taken until eighteen days after Britain joined the Great War. Prime Minister Asquith's sober announcement to The House of Commons was not scored by the sound of shrapnel shells falling or howitzers howling, but to a deafening and terrifying silence.

Similarly, the declaration of Young Henry's rebellion elicited nothing more than an ominous quiet. It was a quiet, but not quite a silence. If you listened closely, you could hear goblets being filled with wine, whispered conversations on dark castle ramparts and the spluttering spitting of midnight candles. What you can hear, is the sounds of diplomacy.

The Old King's best guesses proved to be correct. Young Henry was riding for his father- in-law and mother's ex, Louis VII of France. Upon arrival at the Capetian court, he began handing out titles, earldoms, baronies and spare bits of land to anyone vaguely influential in a bid to win their support.

It is worth bearing in mind that the cheques Young Henry is writing are post-dated, these could not be taken to the bank and cashed today. Young Henry would only be able to make good on his promises should his rebellion succeed. It was a hell of a gamble for those pitching in with him. After all, on one side of the equation was Young Henry, who was paying substantially above the going rate for allies but was untested, whilst on the other hand, there was The Old King, he would do no more than maintain the status quo but he had stacks of experience under his belt.

April of 1173 saw both The Old King and Young Henry ferociously riding throughout the Plantagenet and Capetian empires, drumming up support. This was a task The Old King was born to do. Everybody knows his face, he somehow travels at three times the speed of any of his rivals, people fear and respect him in equal measures. He enjoys a huge amount of success in subscripting local Lords to his cause.

Equally though, The Old King is an archetypal villain. People don't like him, they are scared of the man and they dare to dream of a brighter future could his demise be orchestrated. Once it becomes public knowledge that Louis of France, Philip of Flanders and Geoffrey are supporting Young Henry, a seismic shift begins that changes everything.

The Old King is now very much on the back foot. The prospect of Young Henry being both lead and followed by the Capetian old timers, whilst simultaneously supported by his youthful and ambitious brother Geoffrey is an unbeatable formula.

Had The Old King been anybody else and not already spent a lifetime riding the length and breadth of his empire exerting his will, he would have lost this war before it began. As it was though, even outnumbered and outgunned, he has something of a chance. He has met with a lot of influential people in the last few weeks, he has kissed hands and shook babies, he has both inspired and terrified.

Remember Baron Rhys of Wales, William Marshal told us about him earlier? The Old King plucked his son's eyes out back in the initial invasion of England. Rhys has his chance to rebel and enact revenge and yet, he doesn't. He doesn't dare. He has stood in The Old King's presence and is scared of the man, he even goes as far as to send soldiers in support of him. Similarly Hugh, the Baron who was imprisoned in his own dungeons stands shoulder to shoulder with The Old King.

Even so though, as the diplomacy round draws to an end and as first shots are fired, The Old King's war room is found wanting. He has clearly lost the pre-game. Messengers doggedly follow The Old King's travelling court and deliver damning correspondence detailing uprisings here, rebellions there, defections everywhere. The Old King's empire is erupting in flames all across the map, it is an impossible and insanely fast paced environment The Old King is called upon to operate in.

Perhaps a testament to his own unique skillset, is that The Old King manages to piss out a number of these fires, simply by turning up. He promises leniency to all who swear to return to his cause and a painful death should any continue disobedience.

The subjects in question have met him before, they know that he is serious. Where possible, The Old King would much prefer to settle things amicably. Deep down, he both hates and fears open battle. He is a complete control freak, he loves to manage every detail of every situation and a large scale war ground is a scenario where that is simply not possible. If The Old King is able to psychologically snarl people down beforehand, he would prefer to follow this course of action.

First blood is spilled in Normandy, homeland of The Old King. Philip of Flanders strikes from the East whilst Young Henry and Capetian Louis launch from the South. Their devastatingly synchronised pincer movement afforded them much advantage. The Old King's borders tremble and shake against these attacks, but ultimately, they hold strong. This is largely due to The Old King for he is everywhere and never far from the action. Whenever the night looks darkest he will ride in, clearly visible in gold lined armour, bellowing orders and charges, night would retreat and dawn would break.

This prolonged period of hyperactivity and hypertension is taking its toll on The Old King though. His eyes are heavily lined and he is breathing deeply, occasionally, during particularly heated strategy meetings, he grasps at his stomach in pain with agony lines framing his face. The Old King needs a rest but there is not time.

Further embers are smouldering in Southern France and The Old King must ride hard to lay siege to a strategically important castle there. No sooner has his vice like grip ensured all supply chains are cut off and moral derelict, than he receives another letter from one of his barons based in England. They are writing to advise that William the Lion has now changed his mind and decided he would actually like to join the war against The Old King. Unsurprisingly, he is riding for Northumbria.

Although the Lion secures Northumbria swiftly and efficiently, he is finding it very difficult to get past the Northern castles of Tyneside. William's army consists primarily of light infantry, he is not supported by the rumble of siege engines so taking stone fortifications was proving all but impossible.

This is some comfort for The Old King, but not much. He still has Young Henry and the leaders of the Capetian empire attacking him from the South and the Northern Wildman, William the Lion, shaking the tree up North. Breathe deeply, thinks The Old King, breathe deeply, you will make all of these traitors eat their own tongues, hearts and livers. The Old King is an unflappable problem solver who adamantly believes there is always a solution.

"Things could be worse," he says to himself with a dry chuckle. What would have been worse, The Old King thinks, was if my second youngest son, Richard, were involved in all of this. Richard's acorn had fallen a little too close to the tree for comfort. The Old King could see both his own ruthless determination in the lad and Eleanor's mathematical calculation in everything he did. Richard could not join the war anyway, for Eleanor of Aquitaine controlled the troops of the empire in Southern France, they reported to her, he was at least safe on that front.

"Sire, we have a letter to you from Eleanor of Aquitaine," a servant announced to The Old King.

The letter from The Old King's wife outlined that Richard had taken control of the forces of Aquitaine to join Young Henry's rebellion. Eleanor of course remained loyal to The Old King, though she would be staying away for a time and be difficult to reach. She wished him the very best of luck.

"She wishes me luck, wishes me luck, this is unbelievable… the barons of Aquitaine adore you Eleanor, they would not lift a finger without your say so…" The next letters to arrive with The Old King advise that his son Richard is conducting attacks all across Central France with vigour. These parchments depict that Richard is proving himself to be a highly adept general, competent in supply chain management, troop manoeuvres and inspirational leadership. Alongside a creeping stomach clenching of betrayal, The Old King can't help but feel a flush of pride for his son. Reports pouring in about Richard describe a devil with a crossbow, popping up in the thick of every battle, never missing, never losing his composure, evangelically arising wherever he is needed the most.

"Well Richard, there are still some tricks I am yet to teach you, let's dance my son." The Old King relishes the chance to play soldiers against Richard, the next letter he receives however, will put a stop to this ambition.

Young Henry, confronted with unyielding resistance at the Normandy border, did something entirely unexpected. He cast his eyes North. He set his crosshairs on England. None of the Plantagenet family have, to date, paid much attention to this rain-soaked island. Yes, it is a part of their empire and one that they did not wish to lose, but they do not have a passion for it. Young Henry's move is genius, with one action, he has completely undermined all of The Old King's defensive entrenchment.

Should Young Henry be able to safely arrive in England before his father, he will unite with William the Lion and provide the missing siege engines his Scottish counterpart so coveted.

"Richard can wait," thinks The Old King. He must travel North immediately, sail across the channel and deal with this very real threat.

Young Henry has a two day head start on his father but it doesn't matter, for The Old King rides like a demon. Both kings reach the English Channel at different crossings but on the same day. The Channel Sea is choppy, it is a churn of white, angry froth, both Kings watch the swell rise and fall ferociously, both narrow their eyes and suck on their teeth. Both have the same impossible question to answer, should they set sail or not?

As he stares across the heaving waters, Young Henry slowly shakes his head. His followers breathe a palpable sigh of relief, "It isn't worth it, we will wait for calmer waters," he declares. Young Henry's followers are left in no doubt that he has their best interests at heart and takes his duty of care seriously.

As he stares across the heaving waters, a glint appears in The Old Kind's eye as he slowly nods his head. His followers look uneasy. "We depart for England immediately, I have pissed choppier waters than this," The Old King's followers are left wondering both at the state of the Old King's sanity and kidneys.

The Old King and his men make it to England, of course they do, people like The Old King don't die in a channel crossing. Had a rogue wave dared to rise up out of the sea like a great leviathan to smash down upon his ship, The Old King would have stood upright with one foot rested upon the bow and shouted the wave into breaking. The Old King is a force of nature in himself equal to any tempest.

It is not hyperbolic to describe this moment in History as pivotal, not crossing the channel has not lost the war for Young Henry, but it *has* lost him a chance to win it. Had the Young King successfully beat his father across the channel, he would have united forces with William the Lion and it's difficult to imagine how The Old King could have recovered from this.

As it is though, The Old King arrives in England almost a week before his son and during his channel crossing, he has a lot of time to think. It is quality time to think too, time that is uninterrupted by the usual constant stream of letters he endures. It is time devoid of distractions and provides a chance for The Old King to reflect.

When he thinks of the rebellion, Old Henry isn't too bothered about the Capetian King Louis, or Philip of Flanders for that matter. Their actions were to be expected, they were rival dynasties and fighting them was an occupational hazard. William the Lion was a bit annoying because a truce had been agreed, again though, The Lion had made it perfectly clear in his mountain of correspondence over the years that given the chance, he would seize Northumbria. The Old King found it difficult to resent him for it.

His sons though, Young Henry and Richard, well that stung a little. Would I have done anything different though, wonders The Old King? Probably not. Watching his sons leading their first major conflict had stirred far greater pride within him than watching their first baby steps. The civil war had also thrown up some surprises. Young Henry had proven himself to be largely ineffective, losing his socks on day one of the conflict and not doing much better there on in, Richard on the other hand, there was something of The Old King in the lad, he felt that he could work with Richard.

What really hurt though, was Eleanor of Aquitaine's involvement, for she must surely be involved. Richard would not be rampaging around central France with an Aquitainian army had she not acquiesced. The barons of the region loved her and would follow her into the fires of Hell, or sit on the touchlines if she commanded. Why did you betray me Eleanor, what did I ever do to you? Was it the string of mistresses and Rosamund, the Rose of the World, my one true love? The public humiliation of my fathering multiple bastard children? Making a cuckold of our own son Richard, the apple of your eye? The cruelty I have inflicted on your people of Aquitaine and not handing back the land I promised to you? Actually, when you put it like that, The Old King surmised she might have a point.

Where did it all go wrong? The Old King searched back through mental photographs he has taken throughout their relationship, he scans each one for some kind of hollow smile or bitter face expression. He analyses every argument and each time they rolled away from one another in bed. He thinks back to the last time they had made love, had there been any indication they were actually strangers in one another's bedroll?

As far as The Old King can tell, the curse on his life seems to have begun at precisely the moment he and his old friend Thomas Becket fell out. The Old King can see that now, it brings tears to his eyes. I turned my back on my friend for just a little more power, I challenged the church and everything I believed in, I must make amends, The Old King thinks.

Upon arriving in Southampton, he rides hard, not to intercept his son but for Canterbury, he rides for the monument of the former Archbishop of Canterbury, he rides for the shrine of Thomas Becket. Upon arrival, The Old King pays penance and then some. He walks for three miles, barefoot through the slush and slime that sluices the streets of medieval Canterbury. He wears a simple brown sack, much as Becket himself favoured in his final days. He lashes his back repeatedly with a birch branch drawing bloody welts. To look at this filthy, sorry creature, you would not know he was the King of England and half of France, except, The Old King will avoid no humiliation in his bid to make things right. A crier walks behind him announcing his presence. People point, jeer and spit, for when else will they have a chance to commit such unkindness to a King?

Once The Old King arrives at the cathedral, he prostrates himself at the feet of the monks who were forced to witness the murder of Becket, they too whip The Old King. Though he tries to remain stoic, he is soon howling in agony like a banshee. He lies, whimpering on the floor, like a beaten dog as he receives three hundred lashings from the unforgiving holy men.

When The Old King tries to sleep that evening, he must do so on his front for his back is aflame. He does not know whether his penance will suffice for the Almighty and his old friend Becket, but he prays that it will. He also is aware that God moves in mysterious ways, he would have to look for the forgiveness of God in the abstract. He would need to see it in the smile of a newborn baby, the scent of a rose, the glow of a sunset. The Old King knows that any sign he receives, will never be concrete, nor will it clearly demonstrate that he has been forgiven.

A knock sounds at his door, "Sire?" His servant is almost embarrassed to look upon him in this state, "William the Lion, King of Scotland, has been captured, we have him in chains, we've caught the King of Scotland."

It was true, William the Lion had been racing South in a bid to meet up with Young Henry and seeing an armed force he assumed was his ally, he rode out to meet them. With growing alarm, he realised it was not Young Henry's men but The Old King's. Though he tried to turn and run, it was too late for him. He was hunted down and fettered in chains.

If that wasn't a sign from God than The Old King didn't know what was, his defining steel and fire returned, "we must ride to confront my son at once."

"Richard?" asked the servant.

"No, Young Henry."

Young Henry arrived on the sandy shores of England to an animated and breathless messenger awaiting him on the beach.

"Young Henry, William the Lion has been captured by your father," the messenger looks terrified to be delivering such devastating news to the Young King.

"Okay," Young Henry feels like he has been punched in the solar plexus, but he has learned from his father to accept bad news calmly. I am a swan, Young Henry tells himself, though I may be paddling beneath the surface I float with a grace and poise above the water.

The messenger continued, "Your father walked barefoot three miles to Canterbury whipping himself, prostrated himself at the shrine of Thomas Becket and is now considered by pretty much everyone to be an Agent of God on Earth."

"Okay…Right…sorry, my father did what?"

"Your father walked barefoot three miles to Canterbury whipping himself, prostrated himself at the shrine of Thomas Becket and is now considered by pretty much everyone to be an Agent of God on Earth," the house knight Sir William Marshal helpfully repeats to his master.

"Right," responded the Young King, it was getting difficult by now to not convey panic.

"Pretty much all of the lords of England have now switched sides again to stand alongside your Father instead of you."

"Okay. Very good."

"Your father is riding his horse as if he has stolen it to come and confront you, best guess is that he will arrive in two days," the messenger finished.

"Okay…Right…Okay." Young Henry is shaken but he is a born leader. He begins to address the gathered men, "Okay, two days. In war my loyal subjects, two days, may as well be two years." Young Henry's men gathered closer, they could feel a speech coming on and were ready to be inspired, "we have a blessing in these two days, we have something tangible with these two days, we will make every second count. We will dig trenches, we will ready the artillery. We came here with a job to do and by God we'll do it. Two days, in two days, why, we'll have these cliffs before you turned into a fortress," he motions dramatically towards the craggy white rocks, everybody turns to stare at the ridge.

"Sir, is that your Father and his army atop the cliffs we are to turn into a fortress?" William Marshal asks.

"Yes, I think it is. Back on the boats everyone, back on the boats!"

The Old King has some work to do in England to ensure his seat is secured, but he will not be far behind his son. Young Henry has one final roll of the dice; he makes for Rouen, capital of his father's homeland Normandy. Rouen is a charming little city, nestled between the lazy meandering bends of the River Seine. The colourful buildings and crooked streets could not be any more French. The city is beautiful. What makes it beautiful though, also makes it a challenge from an operational perspective to lay siege to.

The city straddles both the North and South banks of the Seine. Tributaries split off from the main waterway like the berserk veins of a drunkard's cheeks, offering both extra protection to areas of the city and additional supply routes. With The Old King not far behind them, Young Henry and William Marshal will need to successfully siege this city and quickly, if they are to have any chance of salvaging some kind of victory from the mess they find themselves in. Sieging

Rouen is difficult, but it isn't impossible.

Two hundred and forty four years later, Young Henry's great-great-great-great-great-great Nephew, will succeed in sieging the city of Rouen. Young Henry's great [6] nephew, will set up four different barricaded encampments encircling the city. He will erect a web of sturdy, cast iron chains blocking either side of the river Seine, these will be kept taught using a series of winches and pulley systems. The city will be choked off, no supplies will enter the city, no dignitaries will leave the war zone, fairly quickly the city will be gasping for breath and beginning to turn blue.

Four months after Young Henry's great[6] nephew's siege of Rouen began, the inhabitants were eating cats, rats and dogs from the city. Five months into the siege the poor had been evicted from the city as they were considered a burden and were killed by the invading army. The smell of their rotting flesh in the French sun permeated every crevice of the picturesque city. Young Henry's great [6] nephew won his siege in seven months.

Young Henry doesn't have seven months though, his father will soon have concluded his business across the Channel. Young Henry needs to nail this first time and quickly. Sadly though, he doesn't, he doesn't do a lot of things. He doesn't set up four different barricaded encampments, he doesn't string up a web of chains to prevent all maritime traffic from entering the city. Young Henry makes a lacklustre attempt at sieging the city, for deep down, he knows he has already lost.

"How long before my Father arrives?" asks Young Henry of his advisors in a deadpan voice.

"Best guesses would suggest he will be here within the month. He has a lot to do in England, there are barons to win over from Anglesey all the way to Durham, it will be no small feat and even for a man of your Father's undoubted talents, this will tie him up for a considerable time," pompously declares the lead advisor.

"You're sure about that?" Young Henry's voice is hollow, his eyes are lifeless.

"We are Sire."

Sir William Marshal coughed discretely and motioned to the dust clouds kicking up on the horizon indicating the arrival of The Old King's advanced outriders, "Come on Kingling, it's time, let's parlay with your Father, let's discuss peace terms with The Old King."

It is said that children that are not taught accountability for their actions, will grow up to become adults whom believe nothing they do is wrong, if this is the case, The Old King is facing a difficult parenting conundrum. What is the appropriate punishment, I mean consequence, to dish out to your children who have openly rebelled against you in civil war and caused the death of tens of thousands of men alongside untold damage to the national economy? It was a head scratcher. Best deal with the non-immediate family first, thinks The Old King.

Peace agreements were drawn up with Louis VII of France and Philip of Flanders. They were not punitive, for The Old King is unable to punish them without entering into a costly war which isn't something he is entertaining at this point. William the Lion is released from captivity, but not without cost. Scottish churches are now answerable to England and a number of castles on the Scottish side of the border are gifted across to the Plantagenets. It is a humiliating defeat for William the Lion and not one that he will forget soon.

What about Eleanor of Aquitaine? That one also required more thought too. It seemed almost certain that she had been behind the rebellion and this was a first for the Medieval world. She had been caught, disguised as a man, trying to sneak into Capetian France towards the end of the war which surely further demonstrated her guilt.

Whilst it wasn't unheard of for sons to fight their father for inheritance, a wife doing this was humiliation on a whole other level. It didn't help that her ex-husband had been involved. The Old King couldn't get it out of his mind, they had been involved, together…together…talking and plotting and scheming and laughing late at night, The Old King shudders. Publicly admonishing her though wasn't the answer. This would only add credence to the rumours and confirm to the populous that yes, The Old King had been betrayed by the lady who shared his bed. For now, Eleanor is locked in her chambers, those gathered for the victory party are told that she is sick that evening, the courtiers exchange knowing glances as they are told this news.

Why not use this whole rebellion as a learning opportunity for the boys, wonders The Old King? Why not indeed. Young Henry and Geoffrey will continue in the same capacity they served in before the rebellion, there would be no impairment to their allowances or spheres of influence, it was extremely merciful of The Old King. He stands to raise a glass and make a toast, "All things are as it were, as it should be and as it always shall." He drains his glass, but he can't shake the feeling that he has forgotten something, it is extremely disconcerting.

A letter arrives, The Old King rips it open and reads aloud, "Your son Richard continues to wreak havoc, ambushing our supply chains as we travel across central France. You hear the twang of his crossbow before you see him and then his men are upon you. They come out of the forests where they have been hidden, invisible just seconds before but suddenly upon you! Please send help." That was it, that was what I had forgotten thinks The Old King, Richard.

"Richard continues to fight?" asks the chastised Young Henry.

"Apparently so," begins The Old King, "He is alone, without an ally and with a small force compared to what he faces. What does Richard know? What is his ace in the hole? I know my son, he will have some kind of expert strategy, some kind of secret weapon, but what, what is it Richard?"

"Excuse me Sire," somehow the giant William Marshal manages to look small, he is not used to speaking in front of The Old King, "Perhaps nobody has told him that everybody else has surrendered?"

The Old King frowns, his head tilts, he addresses the room, "Has anybody told Richard that everybody else has surrendered?"

Feet are scuffed and the room is filled with general muttering, nobody will look The Old King in the eye.

"Right, let's send Richard a letter and tell him the war is over" concludes The Old King.

When Richard receives the letter, he immediately surrenders and declares himself at peace with his father. With Eleanor out of action, somebody needed to rule Aquitaine. Call me crazy, thinks The Old King, but I'm going to give the job to Richard.

"Richard, arise Duchy of Aquitaine."

Richard makes eye contact with his father and bows, "Thank you Father for this honour, I am sorry for my actions, I pledge myself to be yours forever." What Richard is thinking though is somewhat different to his words. You have imprisoned my mother, everything good in my heart has died, I will see you dead old man, make no mistake about that.

"You are my son Richard, forgiveness is natural," The Old King smiles benevolently and motions for him to arise.

Chapter 8: The Young King Henry enjoys a training montage

The Old King was certainly merciful to Young Henry, but there were limits. To think Young Henry would get away scot-free would be naïve. The Old King declares that his eldest son must complete a tour of redemption. This would take the form of a kingdom wide parade, where his eldest son would be, quite literally, in the shadow of his father. He would be expected to carry The Old King's bags, attend inconsequential, pointless meetings and pretend not to notice the smirks from courtiers when they addressed him as, *King*.

This too will pass, Young Henry tells himself, and it shall. The Old King is nothing if not concerned with efficiency, travelling with his son was a travesty of wasted exertion. Twice as many subjects could feel touched, inspired and intimidated by the father and son duo were they to walk different roads. The Old King had watched, day by day his son's resolve bend further and further, before eventually witnessing it break entirely. It seemed highly unlikely his son would rebel against him again, Young Henry was a shell of the man he had once been.

It is time for The Old King to talk with Young Henry about his future. When he walks into Young Henry's room, it is to find him staring vacantly at a blank, stone wall. His son keeps his vision fixed on the masonry, he doesn't dare to make eye contact with his Father. "Good evening Father," he says deadpan.

The Old King tries smiling reassuringly, although this looks more like a snarl, "It is time for you to consider what you would like to do, what kind of man you want to be?" The Old King understands the power of an open question.

"Well, I have been crowned King, I thought I might do that," Young Henry is confused.

"Of course, of course, there is no doubt in anybody's mind whatsoever that you are King," what The Old King means by that, is that everybody, including himself, has serious doubts at his eldest son's disposition for Kingship. Old Henry believes he has been building bridges with Richard and that there is something of himself in the lad, one day, not yet of course, he believes Richard could be a great King. Not that he needed to worry about that yet, 'I am young, succession is a concern for Old Kings,' thinks The Old King. He repeats his question to his son, "But how are you going to spend your time? What's your five year plan?"

Young Henry fears this is some kind of trap, "I would like to continue following you Father," he says in a deadpan voice.

The Old King laughs, "No you don't, be honest with me son, what do you want to do? Where do you see your future?"

There is yet another long silence, "I would like to be a hero of the great chivalric tournaments of France."

The Old King exhales a whoosh of breath. As usual, his son was not considering the bigger picture. Fighting in tournaments in France could result in him making a fool of himself in front of home subjects and on the international stage. He could lose money, resources, he could even die. The Old King is about to point these shortcomings out to his son before he stops himself. If Old Henry does want his son Richard to succeed him one day, well, tournaments were starting to sound like an excellent idea.

"It's a wonderful suggestion son."

Young Henry has found a new lease of life and is excited beyond belief. He goes to the armoury declaring he needs the finest armour, swords and warhorses for he is going on the tourney circuit. He is told, rather abruptly, he can have only what he can afford and that will have to suffice. Young Henry's eyebrows knit together in concern, his allowance had always been a pittance and tournaments were not cheap, he would also need to pay a retinue of knights.

With this in mind, Young Henry approaches Sir William Marshal. Young Henry is in full salesman mode and launches straight into his pitch, "Mightiest of Marshals, what would you say if I told you there was a way for us to double our income, increase our standing with the people and most importantly, regain our self-esteem?" rhetorically asks Young Henry. "Not so fast, put your cash away Marshal, for let me tell you how…"

"Young Henry, stop it, I swore to follow you, didn't I?" Marshal replies, "I did not swear to follow you for the pittance that you pay me, I did not swear to follow you as a lowly servant of your father as you are but… I did swear to follow you. I did bend my knee and I did take the vow, just tell me what is required and I will do it." Marshal means it too. He does not take the oath he has sworn to the Young King lightly, for Marshal, it is blood in and blood out.

Before describing the adventures of Young Henry and Sir William Marshal on the tournament circuit, we must first take a moment to forget everything we think that we know about knightly competitions. The twelfth century world of tournaments we are going to find ourselves in the midst of, are not defined by two parallel tracks in the dirt and a mighty smash of colliding jousters. We will be sat in the bleachers not for a display such as this, but instead, for a mighty war game played over many acres. This is a team sport whereby the objective for our participants is simply to capture other enemy knights.

Capturing not only scores a "point" in the game, it also awards the knight who has captured their opponent the opportunity to enter into a fun side game. The side games are, in fact, far more lucrative and appealing for the contestants than the main game. This side game essentially allows for the knight to take their captured hostages' armour, weaponry, war horses and anything else of value they may have on them. They are even allowed to imprison them until one of their followers pays a ransom. If these measures seem unsporting, the game has been designed this way. Kings of the period were keen for the experience to as closely resemble real combat as possible, they had a generation of knights they needed to forge and temper in the fires of these games.

The pageantry is majestic. Should you be so lucky as to be present when the teams arrive, banded together under different flags and atop mighty warhorses, scuffing their feet and snorting, you would have a story to tell your grandchildren. Flags would be fluttering in the wind, you would be able to spy celebrities of the day and say that you were there. Whilst this is indeed the birthplace of chivalry, it is by no means an embedded principle at this stage. We will see throughout these great events participants behaving in a manner seemingly unbecoming of this dawning age of heroes.

Take for example Philip of Flanders, one tournament saw him arrive with his full retinue in tow, the crowd cheer and shout his name, his attendance had not been expected. The journalists descend upon him like a pack of wolves, "Quick comment Philip for the *Knights Nightly News?*"

The crowd are inspired to be in the presence of one of the medieval heavyweights and wagers begin flying in supporting Philip of Flanders in the upcoming tournament, alas, the crowd are to be disappointed. Philip holds up a hand to silence those gathered, he calmly advises that he is only there to watch, "I'm still recovering from the last tournament," he jokes, clutching his side with a mock grimace. The crowd laugh good naturedly although they are a little disappointed, it would have been good to see him in action.

They aren't too sad though, they had seen the legend

in the flesh and what's more, he had joked with them. The participating teams charged off into the distance followed by the runners who would report back to the spectators on results, an announcement is made, "Team 1 has almost completely decimated Team 2 and 3, there are only a handful of knights left, the end will soon come."

Upon hearing this news, Philip of Flanders decides that actually, he would quite like to participate and charges his men in. Philip of Flanders wins the day hands down, for he has not endured the attrition the others have had to face from the initial conflict. Strangely, he isn't admonished for his underhand or unsportsmanlike strategy he has employed, instead, the people love it, they think it's great.

"Philip of Flanders, the ultimate strategist" the crowd cheer and shout.

This is the world that Young Henry, Sir William Marshal and his team of knights are about to enter. It is both fake and real, it is chivalric and dastardly, Young Henry and Marshal are going to love it.

With the tournaments such as they are and played over such great distances, to explore Young Henry's experience in them by sitting in the stands and observing would be impossible. All we would see is the kicking up of dust at the beginning and an announcement at the end. The strokes of this would be far too broad for what will prove an extremely formative period for The Young King Henry.

Instead, to tell this story we must embrace the abstract, for what Young Henry is about to enter is a training montage. Cue "Eye of the Tiger" by Survivor…

#RISING UP, BACK ON THE STREET, DID MY TIME, TOOK MY CHANCES#

It is raining heavily.
Mid-Shot of a path through a forest in Normandy

France.

Two men ride through the lashing, sideways rain, it is Young Henry and William Marshal. Their horses look bedraggled, their hair is plastered down by the relentless downpour. The camera zooms out, a trail of men become visible following in single file behind the two knights.

The party is clearly down on their luck.

#WENT THE DISTANCE NOW I'M BACK ON MY FEET, JUST A MAN AND HIS WILL TO SURVIVE#

The party file into an encampment full of knights. The knights Young Henry and William Marshal must ride past are dressed in splendour. Their mood is high, the whites of their clothing is somehow dazzling, despite the mud and rain.

There are shocked faces from the crowd at Young Henry and William Marshal's shabbiness. Someone from the crowd throws mud; it hits Young Henry in the face. The crowd erupt into laughter.

#SO MANY TIMES, IT HAPPENS TOO FAST, YOU TRADE YOUR PASSION FOR GLORY#

The Young King Henry and William Marshal's party charge into a tourney: they are disorganised, it is chaos, Young Henry is captured almost immediately. William Marshal fights three men alone, for a moment it looks as though he might prevail but he is pulled from his horse.

DON'T LOSE YOUR GRIP ON THE DREAMS OF THE PAST, YOU MUST FIGHT, JUST TO KEEP THEM ALIVE

The Young King Henry is furiously swinging at a training post: his slashes are clumsy but forceful, sweat pours down his face and he is growling.
William Marshal watches on.
The final swing from The Young King splinters the post.
Marshal nods, the ghost of a smile tickles the corners of his mouth.

IT'S THE EYE OF THE TIGER, IT'S THE THRILL OF THE FIGHT
RISIN' UP TO THE CHALLENGE OF OUR RIVAL #

It is Christmas Time. Young Henry and Sir William Marshal are at one of the Plantagenet family gatherings.
Camera notes: Point of view perspective from Young Henry, he is watching his Father, The Old King. Old Henry rises from the throne and walks out of shot. Young Henry's gaze remains on the throne, his eyes narrow and his teeth clench.

AND THE LAST KNOWN SURVIVOR STALKS HIS PREY IN THE NIGHT, AND HE'S WATCHING US ALL WITH THE EYE OF THE TIGER

Young Henry is panting: he is crossing blades with William Marshal in a training yard. Henry swings left, he is parried. Marshal pivots on his heel and smacks Young Henry with the flat of his blade across the shoulders. Young Henry falls to the dirt.

#FACE TO FACE, OUT IN THE HEAT,

HANGING TOUGH, STAYING HUNGRY#

Young Henry's party are at a tournament, it is about to start, Young Henry is Grinding his teeth, William Marshal is smiling maniacally.

THEY STACK THE ODDS TILL WE TAKE TO THE STREET, FOR THE KILL WITH THE SKILL TO SURVIVE

The teams charge. Aside from the grinding teeth, Young Henry could not look calmer. Marshal is still smiling although this now looks terrifying. There is an opposing team of twelve knights one hundred metres away from them.

IT'S THE EYE OF THE TIGER, IT'S THE THRILL OF THE FIGHT, RISING UP TO THE CHALLENGE OF OUR RIVAL, AND THE LAST KNOWN SURVIVOR STALKS HIS PREY IN THE NIGHT, AND HE'S WATCHING US ALL WITH THE EYE OF THE TIGER

The two teams clash. CAMERA NOTE: Quick edits, it is unclear who is winning.

RISING UP, STRAIGHT TO THE TOP, HAD THE GUTS GOT THE GLORY#

Young Henry and his party are celebrating. They have clearly just won a prestigious tournament and they are partying. Young Henry is led off screen by a topless and buxom mademoiselle.

WENT THE DISTANCE NOW I'M NOT GONNA STOP, JUST A MAN AND HIS WILL

TO SURVIVE #

Young Henry and William Marshal are riding hard
uphill into the face of an upcoming charge, sleet and
harsh rain batters their faces, their gauntleted fists
pump together before the two teams clash in an
explosion of steel and cacophony.

IT'S THE EYE OF THE TIGER, RISING UP
TO THE CHALLENGE OF OUR RIVALS #

William Marshal is leading a captured knight's horse
by the reigns. Young Henry follows behind. They
pass under a tree, the captured Knight leaps up and
holds on to a branch, escaping. Young Henry sees
this, Marshal does not, Henry smirks.

AND THE LAST KNOWN SURVIVOR
STALKS HIS PREY IN THE NIGHT AND
THEY'RE WATCHING US ALL WITH THE
EYE OF THE TIGER #

Marshal tows the empty horse into the festival area.
Young Henry can no longer contain his laughter, he
is openly laughing by this point.
Marshal turns around, he is shocked, flabbergasted,
he puts his hand to his cheeks, where is his captor?
Young Henry whoops with laughter slapping his
thigh. Marshal cracks a smile, Marshal and Young
Henry hug.

THE EYE OF THE TIGER

Young Henry stands atop a podium, a wreath is
hung over his shoulders. The crowd cheer him
wildly.

THE EYE OF THE TIGER

Young Henry raises his arms to the crowd. He kisses his Queen Marguerite, Marshal is watching the Queen.

THE EYE OF THE TIGER

Young Henry charges downhill in full regalia atop a mighty war horse. He looks majestic. His horse's hooves barely seem to touch the ground.

THE EYE OF THE TIGER
An opponent falls from his horse. Marshal and Young Henry embrace one another's wrists in a knightly handshake.

Camera fades to black.

And just like that, Young Henry was an overnight success ten years in the making. He and Marshal became celebrities, their names were known far and wide. They were sports star celebrities of their day. Children across the land would play sword fights with sticks, "I'm The Young King Henry," one would shout whilst his friend would retort, "Well I am the great knight Sir William Marshal."

Young Henry's position in life has changed and he is fully aware of this. Whilst the adoration of the masses is far more intangible than a castle, or a battalion of men, it is certainly an asset of significant worth. The Old King knows this too. Young Henry is no longer prepared to play second fiddle, he is soon to make another play for his father's throne.

Before we explore what form this will take, we will use the next chapter to check in with Richard. It is worth noting, the Richard we are soon to observe is not the Richard of previous chapters. He is not fun, nor is he light-hearted or chivalrous, for Richard is angry. He is angry because he has been given the sink or swim responsibility of ruling Aquitaine, a notoriously independent and outspoken region. He is angry because he must swear fealty and feign loyalty to his father, a man who has molested his fiancée. Most of all though, Richard is angry because he misses his mother, who remains imprisoned at The Old King's command.

Chapter 9: Richard rules Aquitaine with all the subtlety of a Sledge Hammer

Had a normal man endured the ten years that Richard just had, by now they would be dead, or, rocking back and forth in a padded cell gibbering incoherently. Richard though is no normal man, not by any stretch of the imagination. Although he would hate the comparison, he is his Father's son. He possesses the ruthless determination of The Old King, an ox-like constitution and a brutal, murderous temper. What of the grace, poise and charm of his mother? Despite her heavy influence during his childhood years, these traits do not seem to have been inherited by Richard.

Aquitaine had proven to be both a prestigious and challenging assignment. The area was a hotbed of political tension at the best of times, with Eleanor imprisoned it was downright rebellious. Barons saw this unsettlement as an opportunity to test their new ruler and carve out additional power for themselves.

Richard found himself be in a state of constant warfare from the moment he accepted the title. Whilst his mother had charmed her adversaries with her sparkling wit and personality, Richard is just not of this disposition. Instead, he travels tirelessly across his lands to fight skirmishes, impose sanctions and bully any who even consider undermining his authority. He is largely successful at this. He firefights across his region with the same ruthless efficiency we saw from his Father during the first rebellion.

These are not trifling affairs either. Richard almost loses his Dukedom at one point to a cartel of his own barons that conspired against him. So outmanoeuvred and outgunned was he, that he was forced to call in reinforcements. In a moment of forced humility Richard has to write to his Father, Young King Henry and Geoffrey begging for help. The rebellion was quashed. The tournament superstar, Young Henry, took the time whilst in the region, to meet with some of the key barons outside Bordeaux and bask in their adoration.

During his time wining and dining the Aquitaine dignitaries, Young Henry hears tales of the iron fist his brother Richard rules with and the draconian measures he enforces on his own people. Even though Young Henry is only in Aquitaine for a short time, the networks and alliances he is forming are deeper than those Richard has nurtured and will come into play later.

Richard is also learning. Few figures in History can boast exposure to the amount of campaigns fought or miles travelled as Richard; with the notable exception perhaps of The Old King. If Young Henry's time between the two rebellions can be described as a training montage, then Richard's is a baptism of fire. If it can be said that Young Henry lives in a chivalric fantasy world that is the tournament circuit it is equally true that Richard has both feet firmly in the real world and for Richard, this is an abattoir.

Richard sits at his writing desk, the hour is late and yet he cannot sleep for there is a lot on his mind. Richard has found himself stuck in an endless cycle that for the life of him, he cannot see a way to break. Richard's problem was this; The Barons complained about heavy taxation and rebelled, quashing said rebellion required a show of force, a show of force entailed soldiers, provisions and weaponry, all of which cost money that required yet further taxation. The circle was complete, like a dog eating its own tail to a bloody stump, Richard was driving himself to despair with this inescapable, ruinous cycle. Richard may be a great military strategist, but he is no politician and this problem is beyond him.

A servant enters Richard's chamber. He whispers into his ear and leaves. Richard sits completely still, suddenly, with cat-like speed, he snatches up the metal goblet full of wine beside him and hurls it across the room. He lets out a guttural roar. Calm returns to his face, "Enter," he shouts.

A well-dressed man sidles into the room, he looks nervously at the goblet on the floor in the corner. He tries not to think how much the red wine seeping into the cow-skin rug looks like blood. He swallows deeply.

"Three weeks Richard, three weeks my wife and I have been in your court. The first round of taxes raised, we understood. There are certain administrative costs associated with government. The Barons and I got it. The second round of taxation, which was more, I might add, was pretty steep, but again, we stood by you. The third round made me think, what on earth is he spending his money on?"

Richard looks completely calm, bored even, although if you look closely, you can see a vein deeply throbbing on his forehead. The Baron continues, "So I thought to myself, my beautiful wife Lady Angeine and I will come down to this Richard's court, we will understand the inner workings of this Plantagenet Lord."

"And what do I think of this great Lord?" The Baron continued, "Not a fat lot to be honest... Since I have been here, you have had four men blinded and nine executed. There is no noble lord in you, bearing the weight of leadership like Atlas did the world, reluctantly doing what is best for the nation, you seem to enjoy cruelty. You carried out three of the blindings personally for Christ's sake! You are a monster Richard, a bully and a psychopath, but just know this, I am not afraid of you. You cannot execute me like you have the others who have spoken out." The well-dressed man's face was bright red, steam poured from his ears like a locomotive thundering down a mountain out of control.

"Can I not?" Richard speaks softly, quietly, calmly.

The vein in his temple continues to throb, his left eye is now spasming.

The well-dressed man does not notice these tell-tale signs that Richard is about to explode, if anything he shovels more coal into the engine. The Baron is out of control travelling at a preposterous speed and little does he know, he is heading for a hairpin bend, he is disastrously close to being derailed.

"You need me," bellowed The Baron, "you need me to shore up the Eastern provinces. All of my lords and important decision makers within my region will look to me for leadership. One word from me, one word Richard, I could have all your Eastern Baron's calling for your blood. You cannot kill me like the others and you cannot stop me from leaving."

There is a long pause, the silence is deafening. Eventually Richard shrugs, his palms turned upwards, "Alas, you are right," he says quietly, "I do need you to make the Barons toe the line. I cannot stop you from leaving. Nothing you have said is incorrect."

The well-dressed man is unnerved. It all seemed too easy. He was used to getting his own way, he was a man of formidable force, but no resistance from Richard? That didn't make sense. He looks to confirm his victory, "So yes, you cannot stop me, or my wife Angeine, from leaving your court."

Richard's head tilts to the side, his face is a picture of mock confusion. His brow furrows, "I cannot stop, *you* from leaving, your wife on the other hand, now she is an entirely different story." Richard stands up and fills a fresh goblet of wine, "Shortly before you rapped upon my chamber door, my men arrived at your lovely private quarters." Richard takes a large swig from his chalice before continuing, "They did not knock, they had a key. They let themselves in. Your wife, no doubt, wasn't scared at the beginning, how could she know what was coming? Of course she couldn't. She thought this was something routine, or a misunderstanding perhaps?"

"Can I help you, she probably asked? Or maybe she was more forceful, yes she's a spirited one actually, no doubt she shouted at my men immediately." Richard draws himself up pushing out his chest and pompously imitating The Baron's wife, "Yes that's right, she launched straight into a lecture, wagging her finger in the knights' faces telling them that *these are private quarters and what the hell was their business here at this hour*?" Richard chuckles good naturedly. "My men will not have spoken with her, they will not engage, they have been ordered not to. They will have been fully armoured, anonymous, they are not people they are just an extension of my iron will."

The Baron is beginning to shake, his lip is trembling, Richard gestures for him to take a seat. Richard continues his dark narrative, "Silently they will have marched towards her. Now she is scared, I mean she must be by now, right? Her eyes widen. She screams. She runs into the back room slamming the door behind her, she fumbles with the key. Her shaking hands are desperately trying to secure the entrance but she can't get it to lock!" Richard's eyes widen in horror and he clasps his hands to his face, "Desperate now, she presses her back against the thin door in an attempt to barricade it. My men's silence is somehow made louder by the drivel pouring from her mouth. She will have shouted anything at this point to get this nightmare to end. She screams about you a lot, about your position mainly, she references your prestige, your importance. She threatens my men's careers, their livelihoods, they don't like that. *You won't ever work again, when my husband returns from his meeting with Prince Richard, your heads will be forever on spikes outside the castle*, that kind of thing." Richard offers The Baron a drink but he declines.

"It will only take one kick for the door to splinter and your wife to be thrown across the room. Her supple frame, her delicate proportions are no match against a two hundred and fifty pound, fully armoured knight booting the wooden frame."

Richard looks thoughtful for a moment, "Now I do hope that she didn't try to fight once they got into the room, I sincerely hope that. It could have gotten very nasty if she did. I hope a gauntleted hand did not backhand her defined, perfect, cheekbones shattering them, I hope her legs were not kicked out from under her, I pray that a razor-sharp knife was not held to her pretty little throat as she gasped for air, hyperventilating from the terror of it all."

"I just hope that she went quietly, for the love of God I hope she went quietly. She will have been taken straight to the dungeons. By now she will either be wailing like a banshee, tears, mucus and sweat pouring down her face, or, maybe she's silent, actually yes, she's a tough cookie your wife. White as a sheet. In such a state of shock that numbness has descended over her, to even consider the position she is in is too much for her, her breathing would be shallow. She will have been stripped naked of course."

The well-dressed man wretches at this. Richard pats his shoulder in a conciliatory fashion. Richard continues, his voice mockingly soft, "Oh no, no, no, no, don't worry. She won't have been raped. My men wouldn't do that. They know that I am the first person that will get a bite of that cherry. After I have had my way with her, then yes, some of my loyal lieutenants will have a turn, then some of their key personnel… a beauty like your wife will be highly desired across the court. So yes, I do need you to make the barons toe the line, yes, you will leave my court tonight, but no, your wife will not be leaving with you. She will stay here. She will make sure you further Plantagenet interests at every opportunity. She will be the angel on your shoulder and I will be the devil in your ear and make no mistake, I will not hesitate, I will not flinch, if you wrong me, if you do not support your lord, I will kill the bitch personally and make it slow."

This isn't artistic licence. A genuine complaint a number of the Aquitaine Barons raised was Richard seizing their wives and adding them to his harem of concubines.

Richard's brutality has both terrified and alienated the Barons. They will not take this forever. During a recent rebellion, they met the glittering Young King Henry, they have been wowed by his tournament celebrity and chivalry. There is no seem about it, the grass is greener on the other side, the barons want a change of leadership, the barons want Young Henry.

An Intermission with Exposition

The rebellion we have just witnessed is commonly referred to as, "The First Rebellion," this implies of course that we are hurtling inexorably towards a Second. As our main protagonists prepare to once more do battle between themselves, we have arrived at a suitable juncture for a slight respite. It's time for us to depart from our usual cast of characters and learn how it was that The Old King came to sit upon his throne.

Do you recall that cinematic moment during Chapter Seven, when both The Old King and Young Henry were contemplating a Channel Crossing from France to England? As they growled at white devils kicked up in the foamy spray, what was on their mind? Though we can never know for certain, we can make a very good guess.

The White Ship disaster (1120) had occurred just fifty-three years prior to that very moment, the high-profile tragedy was still in living memory for members of the court. The White Ship, or *Blanche Nef*, had been recently refurbished and was in perfect sailing condition. Popular belief was that the vessel was not only the fastest in the admiralty, it was also unsinkable. If that wasn't enough, the captain FitzStephen was of strong seafaring stock, his father had sailed William the Conqueror himself during the 1066 invasion of England.

King Henry I (Grandfather to the unborn Old King), declined to sail on The White Ship, instead favouring his usual chartered Royal Vessel, there's something to be said for a familiar pillow after all. His son on the other hand, Prince William, wanted to experience this lightning ship and colourful captain for himself.

King Henry I smiled ruefully as his royal yacht departed for France and shook his head. He looked across at The White Ship, no preparations had been made for the ship to mobilise and set sail. In fact, from his vantage point on deck, he could see yet more casks of wine being rolled across to where Prince William was delivering some kind of speech about a "Fuzzy Duck". King Henry waved as his ship departed and he lost sight of his son.

Meanwhile on The White Ship, the drinking continued, harder and harder. More wine was brought out, there was singing. Prince William was sick over the starboard bow. Somebody, we will never know who, decided that the boat should set sail and try to catch up with the long since departed Henry I. As ropes were cast off, a number of Monks decided this adventure was not for them, as did a nobleman by the name of Stephen. It was without doubt the best decision that they ever made.

The Monks and Stephen watched from the shore as the ship lurched ominously into the swell of the sea, teetering dangerously atop a wave before crashing down again. The bow dived dangerously below the water level before re-emerging like a drowning man, those aboard cheered raucously. The ship was certainly the fastest in the admiralty, it was away into the night before Stephen and the monks could recover from their initial gasp. It was not, however, unsinkable.

The heir apparent, Prince William, will die in the inky black swell that night, as will 298 other souls, there will be only one survivor. The captain FitzStephen will bob up for the briefest of moments only to hear that the Prince has died and decides the best course of action was to go back beneath the waves and never resurface. The heir to the throne and a significant proportion of the crown's leadership died overnight. The wreckage of The White Ship has never been found, in some form, it still sits at the bottom of The English Channel.

If you are feeling that comparisons could be drawn between The White Ship disaster and The Titanic, you wouldn't be the first. The calamity is sometimes referred to as "The Medieval Titanic". The similarities are clear, both were ships technically specified to the highest possible level for the period, both were completely avoidable calamities and both are alleged to feature boozed-up Captains. The name of the company that owned The Titanic even sounds similar, White Star Line, The White Ship. The fallout from this maritime tragedy should not be underestimated, the heir to the throne, Prince William, has just died.

Fifteen years after The White Ship Disaster, King Henry I himself will pass away without a son. He will die from eating an undercooked lamprey. Strangely, he is potentially not the only monarch one of these jawless, bastard-fish will take down over the course of this book - more on lampreys later though.

Tempting though it is to focus in on the lampreys, instead, perhaps, we should be acknowledging that King Henry I has just died without a male heir. In an ambitious bid of modernity from King Henry I, on his deathbed he decreed that his daughter Matilda should continue the bloodline and it was she that should sit upon the throne.

The courtiers gathered around King Henry I's body as the priest closed his eyes.

"He made it very clear he would like his daughter Matilda to take the throne," reverently whispers one courtier to another.

"Indeed, it was the dying King's final wish," mournfully replies the other.

"To hell with that though," concludes the first, "a woman on the throne, has the old man gone mad?"

Matilda was side lined and every noble courtier chucked their hat into the ring. Powerful men with a hundred different agendas all pulled in different directions. England looked as though it was to be torn apart at the seams by a bloody civil war. This is when the people of London spoke, they voted for who the next King should be. In reality very few would have been eligible to vote, so it would be more accurate to say that some person(s) of London voted, anyhow, a gentleman by the name of Stephen is voted in.

You have met Stephen already, he was the sensible passenger aboard The White Ship that decided the crew were too drunk to set sail and duly disembarked. You have also met Stephen in your modern day life, he's a nice bloke, he's a hell of a nice bloke actually. When you're running for a lift, he's that kindly smiling feller who pops out at the last moment to hold the door. When you go to call a taxi at the end of an evening and with a sinking heart realise your phone battery is flat, Stephen appears out of the darkness smiling generously and offers to help. He's "that guy."

King Stephen, the eternal nice guy, steps into the maelstrom and manages to calm things down. He has a tenuous claim to the throne as King Henry I's nephew and enough political clout to stave off some of the other rivals, the country is pacified and the nation is saved.

Except it isn't, Matilda is not happy, which is understandable. Matilda should have inherited her legacy and sat upon the throne. Whilst there had not been a queen regent in England for a long time, it was not unprecedented across other European countries so there wasn't a concrete reason that she couldn't rule. The (young) Old King, Matilda's son, was also furious. At this point in our tale though he is formidable, he has not yet perfected the psychology of fear he will later command, nor can he travel a week's journey in two short days. Matilda declares war with King Stephen and with this announcement, the civil war is well and truly back on.

Meet the deceased King Henry I's Master of Horses, a man by the name of John Fitzgerald. With this ever-changing landscape, he knows he must have his wits about him for things are about to get bloody. Fitzgerald will prove himself to be a slippery fish in this tale, flip-flopping like a grounded salmon between sides wherever he perceives opportunity lies best. He should automatically have supported Matilda really, as that was his master's daughter, he doesn't though.

Initially, he follows King Stephen and enjoys great reward for this, being granted Marlborough, Ludgershall and Hamstead castles. Fitzgerald is growing in influence but he is a mercenary and ideally, you do not want to place mercenaries in positions of such power.

As the tide turns against King Stephen, so too does Fitzgerald's allegiance, he switches to support Matilda. Fitzgerald's go-to tavern story from this period was defending Matilda who had been sheltering in Wherwell Abbey, pursued by Stephen's men. Fitzgerald had been a part of her royal guard. When Matilda managed to steal out the back of the church, Fitzgerald courageously remained within to delay the attackers. He and his men fought with such courage and ferocity that Stephen's soldiers were forced to retreat. As they panted outside, cursing the tenacity of the defenders within, they looked at the wooden abbey. The wooden abbey. Wooden. How could they have been so stupid? Light fire to the bloody thing! Smoke the bastards out.

John Fitzgerald remained fighting there for as long as he could. He even lost an eye from dripping molten hot lead. Cool story. Nasty scar. Very poor future depth perception for our Master of Horses.

Fitzgerald was eventually captured by King Stephen. Fitzgerald apologised, bent the knee, made various promises. Did Stephen execute the traitor? No of course not, Stephen isn't into executing people. Stephen wasn't going to trust the little weasel though, so he insisted on taking his son, Will, as a hostage.

Hostage is a harsh word. Will would be given all of the luxuries of the court. He would be trained as a noble and brought up with Princes. He would have a glittering career and walk a path few could ever dream of. Providing that his Father, Fitzgerald, did not betray King Stephen, "mess with me Fitzgerald, and I will brutally murder your son," summarises the nice guy Stephen, not really meaning a word of it.

Almost immediately, Fitzgerald betrays the King. Reuniting with Matilda he began harrying King Stephen's flanks and being generally rebellious.

Stephen hounded Fitzgerald down, laying siege to him at Newbury castle. As Fitzgerald continued to defy his former master, he pulled out his ace card. He sent message to the castle that he would slit Will's throat.

No reply was sent…now this was awkward.

A day passed and still nothing, perhaps the message got lost? Another is sent, saying the boy would be loaded into a siege engine and splashed against the castle walls.

Still nothing…

A final letter is sent advising Will would be blinded, castrated and pulled limb from limb by wild horses and at last, a reply is received. King Stephen opened it eagerly, expecting a full and unconditional surrender to save his son.

John Fitzgerald wrote back, "I can have other sons, splash, slash and castrate away. It's no skin off my nuts."

King Stephen is breathless as he reads this, he looks down at the wide eyed Will, it seemed a bit mean to do all of the things he'd written about in his letter, but still, he was a King and he was supposed to commit the odd atrocity. King Stephen doesn't want to though. He quite likes the quippy little lad and he decides he's not going to kill him. Thank goodness he doesn't. The boy Will, will one day grow up to be the great Sir William Marshal, he will save Eleanor of Aquitaine's life and loyally serve the Plantagenet family.

King Stephen will re-establish his reign but will die with no obvious heir. Without establishing a dynasty, the crown will once more be up for grabs and this is how the grandson of Henry I, son of Matilda, was able to enter this royal rumble and win. This contender was of course Henry II, The Old King.

Enough backstory, the main players are ready to

return to action. The situation we are returning to is a three-card trick, keep your eyes on the deck and don't be fooled by any misdirection or bluster, there's going to be a lot of that over the next few pages.

The first card in the deck to be turned over is the Jack of Diamonds, it is Richard, he is furious at his mother's imprisonment and wants to kill his Father. He also has, to some degree, resource backing him. He is the acknowledged and anointed Duke of Aquitaine, however, he stands on thin ice. The nobles that are forced to support his office both hate and fear him, they would happily see him dead or overthrown.

The next card to be flipped is the Jack of Hearts, it is The Young King Henry. In contrast to his brother Richard, Young Henry has no real influence or fixed power base despite his impressive title of, "King". What Young Henry does have though, in some ways, is worth more than any chain of office arbitrarily dished out for he has the love of the people. They think he's awesome. If you thought he was well connected before, well, you should see him now. His years on the tournament circuit have taken this to a whole new level. Young Henry has every influential knight, prince and lord in Europe in his phonebook eager to take his call.

The final card to jump to the forefront, is the King of Spades, it is of course, The Old King. In the first rebellion, we saw him firefight across multiple frontiers both persevering and succeeding, we saw him achieve the impossible, we saw him shout down a tempest for Christ's sake. The Old King is a nigh on invincible opponent to cross and almost impossible to beat.

We should also remember though, that The Old King's development curve has flattened somewhat in the last ten years, whereas both Richard and Young Henry have learned new skills, embraced fresh experiences and are very different men to those we started this story with.

We were also calling the Old King, "The Old King,"

ten years ago. By now he must be at least, "The Old-er King". Though he is only forty-nine years of age, decades of sitting in the saddle has left him a little bow-legged and bent, on occasion, after a particularly cold night, he must be helped on to his horse. A ride he would easily complete in three days now takes the "Old-er King" four. He is still quicker than many others though and his mind is sharp as a dagger. He will not be an easy target to take down.

Chapter 10: Perhaps The Old King should accept he isn't terribly good at hosting Peace Conferences.

There are striking similarities between the sprouting of the First and Second Rebellion. They both begin at a Plantagenet Peace conference and they both have, at first glance, the same cast of characters. The Old King is there, as are his sons Young Henry, Geoffrey, Richard and John, even Eleanor of Aquitaine has been released from house arrest to attend.

If you look closer though you will see it is not the same cast of characters at all. When Young Henry enters the church this time, he does not do so furtively, hooded or ignored. He throws open the church doors in full tournament regalia of gold infused white armour, the hall falls silent for only a reverent second before erupting into hysterical cheers. Young Henry is immediately swallowed by his adoring fans, the crowd are desperate to be close to him, to shake his hand, to touch the pommel of his sword. Young Henry diligently does his celebrity duties, he somehow makes everyone present feel that they have had a unique connection with him.

Eleanor of Aquitaine looks different too. She is still beautiful but worry lines crease her forehead and crows' feet cradle her eyes. The most notable difference though, is the silence that surrounds her. Previously, she had resembled a runway at a busy airport, courtiers had buzzed in and out bringing titbits of information, asking her opinion on things, there is none of this now though. Eleanor of Aquitaine is a no-fly zone, she is Chernobyl. Nobody approaches her, nobody even looks at her. If Eleanor of Aquitaine finds this solitude in public disconcerting, she does not show it.

Eleanor is comforted for she is not in complete isolation, one man braves the toxic radiation oozing from her every pore. Sat beside her, holding her hand, is Richard. He too looks different, if he was somewhat surly before he could now be described as downright feral. When Young Henry smiles at Richard in a good-natured fashion and goes to hug him, Richard just snarls at him.

Richard has spent far too long living on his nerves in a hostile environment, he is a creature of the wild and truly isn't comfortable in this sort of setting. Young Henry looks worriedly for a moment at his brother, before shrugging and turning back to his adoring fans.

As much as Richard is hating every moment of this public event, his youngest brother John is loving it. At sixteen years of age, he is fascinated watching the wheels within wheels of the Plantagenet governmental machine spin and orbit about the chamber, faster and faster. Lords would speak to Generals, who would stride across the room to consult with lawyers, who in turn whisper with advisors before nodding and passing signed letters to servants. This dance of information, communication and miscommunication never ends, the performers pirouette and twirl, faster and faster around one another and somehow, somehow, all of these messages flow to the hive mind of the organism, it flows to The Old King. How he possibly deciphers this constant chatter, rumours, lies and platinum-plated truths is beyond anybody's guess, but he is a master at it.

The Old King nods at a servant who has scurried over and whispered something in his ear, at forty-nine years old, it is fair to say he has aged well. He has a lean, wiry frame like a grey fox or a vindictive badger. There are signs though, if you look closely enough, that the last decade has not been easy for him. His once red hair is now grey and thinning, years of sitting in a saddle have shaken and shocked every joint. When he moves it is stiffly, he winces when he stands. Despite all of this, even dressed as he is in simple brown trousers and a plain black tunic, your eyes gravitate to the man. He is the ringmaster of this circus.

Somebody is missing though, someone who has become so familiar in the background he is almost taken for granted these days, Sir William Marshal is not here. Normally, he would be standing behind Young Henry, ominously flexing his muscles and smiling menacingly, he would always be on hand ready to give advice to his master or intimidate adversaries. Young Henry misses his reassuring presence like an amputee feels phantom pains in their absent limb. Marshal is many miles away though, he is currently fighting in a tournament in France with Philip of Flanders. How could Marshal fight in a tournament for one of the Plantagenets' rivals, well, it's complicated, or it isn't. Young Henry and Marshal have had a falling out over a woman, or not over a woman, like I said it's complicated. The story of Marshal and Young Henry's falling out is certainly a story, but it isn't one for now. Worry not, it's a story that we will be revisiting.

The Old King stands up to address the peace conference, "Thank you all for joining us. Clarity is key for the successful running of any organisation," begins The Old King hurriedly, "If a goat herder did not understand that their primary duty was to tend to goats, how would said goat herd ever prosper?"

The Old King really isn't great at speeches. Nobody, and I mean nobody, has any idea why he is discussing goats.

The Old King paused, he had watched Philip of Flanders deliver a speech recently and he had used pauses rather effectively, "Or if a fisherman did not understand his primary responsibility was to catch fish, would you say he was a good fisherman? Highly," The Old King paused again, "Unlikely. Today, we are going to clearly define all of the positions of power within the Plantagenet regime and what responsibilities each of my sons' shoulders shall bear."

The crowd leaned forward, now this sounded interesting.

The Old King watched the crowd lean forward. His pauses had...worked.

The peace conference was going rather well, thought the Old King. The rebellion of ten years past is behind us. What could be more natural than for a family to have the odd cross word? The occasional fight? An irregular civil war? Perfectly natural. Character building, in fact. It has all worked out for the best, he thought, as he watched first Geoffrey and then Richard bend the knee to Young Henry. The plan was that Richard and Geoffrey would remain formally rulers of their own kingdoms, whilst also being answerable to their elder brother, Young Henry. Naturally, Young Henry had to be answerable to somebody so he would report to The Old King of whom would sit happily atop his feudal pyramid scheme controlling everything.

Whilst on the face of this it seems like a promotion for Young Henry, it really isn't. How could Young Henry's brothers rule their lands autonomously, whilst also answering to him? It made no sense. Also, Young Henry still did not have lands or income streams of his own. Geoffrey had Brittany, Richard had Aquitaine, Young Henry needed his own powerbase to build up his entourage and household, he couldn't rely on the allowance his Father paid him or his tournament winnings forever if he was to hold such an office.

Young Henry decides, not for the first time in this book that if his father won't give him his birthright, he will take it. Just as The Old King is preparing to wrap up the event and thank everybody for attending, Young Henry steps forward centre stage.

The Old King's right eye begins to twitch. What is the point of rehearsing the event to the last second, outlining every bit of miniature from who would speak at what point, to when each family member would be permitted to take a bathroom break, if people weren't going to have the decency to stick to the schedule? I mean really! What was so hard about following the plan?

Breathe in, out, in, out, The Old King tells himself. What could possibly be the harm in Young Henry saying a few unrehearsed, undiscussed and unsanctioned words to the gathered masses?

"What a wonderful day. There could not be better people to spend it with," shouts Young Henry pumping his fist into the air. The assembled crowd cheer and scream his name.

"You are all great men and yet you must answer to somebody. I am a King, yet even I must answer to somebody," Young Henry's palms are turned upwards in a comedic shrug, "My Father will remain forever the *overlord of all overlords, the leader of leaders, the King of Kings*," Young Henry is making quote marks in the air.

The crowd laugh at Young Henry's jest, they are hanging on his every word, a chant begins from the crowd, "Young King Henry, Young King Henry," they are banging on the pews.

Young Henry kneels at the Old King's feet. The Old King shoots Young Henry a look as if to say, *I do not know where you are going with this, but if you cause me any problems or embarrassment, I was the one who gave you your life and I will happily, painfully take it away from you again.*

Young Henry holds up a hand to silence the crowd, "Geoffrey will remain Duke of Brittany."

"As for Aquitaine," Young Henry continues, "I have heard tales of how my brother Richard rules his land and I have sworn to support the barons of that region in their quest for freedom from this tyrant."

Remember when Young Henry was called in to help Richard during a rebellion from his abused leadership team? Do you recall how Young Henry took the time to meet with the leading barons from Aquitaine? It turns out that Young

Henry did more than just meet with them, he also forged alliances and joined a plot to overthrow Richard.

Not only has Young Henry just publicly declared war on his murdering, psychotic brother Richard, he has also just forced his Father's hand. The Old King will have to choose between his sons, Young Henry or Richard, Richard or Young Henry? It's a dangerous game of chicken Young Henry has embarked upon, for he is playing against two of the most formidable medieval war lords who have ever lived. Let's hope he knows what he's doing.

Initially, The Old King tried to parlay for peace and broker a deal between his sons, but it wasn't forthcoming. Upon realising that neither Young Henry or Richard could afford to lose face by backing down, The Old King took a course of action nobody could ever have predicted, he did nothing, it was inconceivable.

Please note, he was probably not doing, "nothing". He was readying men, lobbying key Lords and ensuring his own position was secure. What he was not doing though was weighing in on the argument between his sons. This served to infuriate both Young Henry and the ferocious Richard.

"How could the Old King not see [*insert other brother's name here*] was wrong?" said Young Henry / Richard.

What could explain this uncharacteristic behaviour? The Old King could have been battle weary. Waging any form of warfare is both physically and mentally exhausting, to do so against your own offspring, well, that would not be an exercise you would wish to repeat in a hurry.

Equally though, The Old King would be the first to confess he wasn't sure which of his sons should inherit the crown, had you asked him ten years ago he would have said Richard in a heartbeat, but, things had changed, for Young Henry's fame and popularity had muddied the waters. The Old King may have been applying Darwinism to his unruly children, survival of the fittest, whoever wins deserves the crown.

Richard accepted quickly that help would not be forthcoming from his Father. First Richard marched for Poitiers, where his brother was assembling an army of mercenaries. Richard and his men routed the small army but managed to take hundreds of prisoners. All were executed or blinded, none were spared or ransomed. It was a clear message to Young Henry, *you are not in a tournament or war game now big brother, this is real life, this is real war, let's find out if you have the stomach for it.*

Richard did not halt to take stock of his victory or to celebrate. He rode eighty miles in a forced march to Limognes. Here, he routed yet another of Young Henry's mercenary forces. The prisoners from this conflict were not blinded or put to the sword, instead, they were drowned in the river Vienne. Richard held the final prisoner's head under water as he watched with a professional curiosity. The body struggled, went into violent convulsions and finally, still. He released the cadaver and watched it float away.

The hundreds of bodies decayed in the water as they drifted lazily southwards. The fast flowing fresh water did little to stave off the putrefaction of the corpses, if anything, it catalysed the rotting process. The bodies congealed together into one big fleshy mass that could be smelt for miles around. It morbidly drifted through the French wine growing regions bringing with it a plague of flies.

Does Young Henry realise what he has done yet? Is he scared now? It's difficult to imagine he isn't.

The Old King can take it no longer, he sends a letter to Young Henry, he wants a meeting with his eldest son at the Castle of Limognes.

There are a number of different intentions the Old King may have had in arranging this meeting. He may have been riding to meet with Young Henry to formally ally with him to bring down Richard. The Old King may even have been prepared to give up some of England to Young Henry, or a part of Normandy, unlikely, but possible.

Equally though, it could have been nothing so positive, perhaps he was riding hard for Castle Limognes to backhand his eldest son hard across the face, shake him violently and demand what the hell he was thinking fighting with the clearly superior Richard?

We will never know what the Old King intended to discuss, for the meeting never happened.

As The Old King and his men rode hard through the fields outside Limognes, night was falling. The moon was full and the sky was clear. This put a chill in the air and the breath of the horses and the men steamed in front of them, creating a comet trail that can barely keep pace with the king's column.

Although it is pitch black they ride at full speed, The Old King knows no other way. It is dangerous, of course it is, a rabbit hole or felled tree has killed more than one night time rider. This never seems to happen to the Old King though, some whisper he doesn't actually ride, he flies by some sorcery, how else could he possibly travel such distances so quickly?

The Old King is certainly making good time on his journey tonight. The Castle of Limognes, where the Young Henry is residing, looms in front of him blacker than the surrounding night sky. There is not a single light on in the keep. If The Old King thinks it looks ominous, he gives no call to his men nor does he pull on his reigns.

The Old King is already riding at full speed and yet somehow, at the sight of the Keep, he spurs his horse faster. He pulls ahead of his men. His light tunic flows in the breeze behind him. The thud of the Old King's horse's iron clad shoes thundering on the soil is a familiar and comforting sound, it is fast and rhythmic, steady and consistent, it is his heartbeat.

The Old King hears and feels a displacement of air fly past his face, his men behind him shout in panic. The Old King pulls up his horse sharply. The hooves skid on the wet grass and for a heart stopping moment, it looks as though The Old King will be thrown from his saddle, of course he is not though. The Old King was born in the saddle and expertly shifts his weight to remain astride his mare. Three more whistles fly past his ear, a man behind him screams in pain.

"The bastards are shooting at us?" The Old King mutters quietly, it is a question. Three more bolts whizz just inches above The Old King's head, *"THE BASTARDS ARE SHOOTING AT US!"* this time it is no question.

The crossbow was a medieval weapon of some controversy. A crossbow shoots an arrow, or bolt, as arbalests call it, at 300 feet per second. This speed is certainly fast enough to kill a man, it is fast enough to pierce plate armour. This is why the crossbow was a weapon of dispute. Plated Armour usually denoted landed gentry who were prepared to be captured by others of their class who would be similarly armoured, equally though, they expected to be fairly safe.

A crossbow was cheap and allowed a commoner to not capture a High Born, but kill them, from a distance no less. It was an absolute equaliser. Those who wielded it in highborn circles were considered scum.

The free markets tell a different story though, crossbow mercenaries were valued significantly higher than their Longbow Counterparts. We digress, the talk of armour piercing crossbow bolts is somewhat redundant, for The Old King is not actually wearing any armour on this Winter evening as he rides hard for Limognes.

The moon emerges from behind a cloud. The scene is lit up in mercurial silver. The Old King can see, without a doubt, the arrow that is going to kill him. It is flying straight towards his face at 300 feet per second. Time slows down, but not enough for all of The Old King's life to flash before his eyes, all he can think is, *I can't believe the bastards are shooting at us…*

A split second before the bolt destined to kill the King

reaches its mark, unexplainably his horse rears. She stands tall on her back legs, kicking wildly into the black void. The Old King is thrown, unceremoniously, from the saddle. The barbed projectile intended for the King strikes his horse in the throat. Crimson blood spurts from her neck, she screams, her legs splay out and she lies thrashing on the floor.

By foot, The Old King runs off into the night. He has to say it once more, he can believe it now but he is furious, *"The bastard shot at us."*

Frantic diplomacy began on the part of Young Henry. Messages were sent to his Father explaining the near-murder from his men was just an accident, it was one of those things. Hell, they'd probably all laugh about it later…

Besides, what kind of nutter rides full tilt at an armoured garrison during wartime, unannounced and under cover of night fall? It didn't cut it for the Old King who would have preferred the still warm entrails of those responsible, but his son was not forthcoming with this, in fact, no punitive action at all was taken against those who had shot The Old King's horse from under him. Whatever The Old King's intentions were for his meeting with Young Henry will remain a mystery, for The Old King now rides for Richard to join the war against Young Henry.

We are less than four months in to the second rebellion and although this time Young Henry still has his luggage, on every other front it is not going well for him. Two of his mercenary armies have been put to the sword or drowned and he has alienated his Father, the only man alive residing in Europe who had the potential to beat Richard.

Chapter 11: Young Henry might actually pull this off

It is an unseasonably cold Spring in Limognes. The fields surrounding the castle are solid with ice, frozen mist perpetually hangs low over the undulating grass plains. Sleet, snow, slush and rain lash down relentlessly, it is miserable. Young Henry stands on the ramparts of the Castle. Now, Young Henry is not the greatest of military strategists, but even he can see that his situation is dire. His father and brother's men surrounding the walls calling for his blood confirms this suspicion.

Young Henry does know though, how to radiate confidence to his men in a way that few can replicate. The way he stands, how he walks, the cadence he carries his speeches with, in fact, were you to look at him now, standing atop the battlements the wind whipping through his hair and a slight smile playing across his lips, you'd be forgiven for thinking he has not a care in the world. You'd be completely wrong though, Young Henry is very worried. He suspects his father and brother will make their assault soon and believes he will be absolutely defeated. Even if they didn't make a move soon, there were serious problems within the castle itself and his men might just walk any day now.

The cold wind scythed through gaps in the stone masonry and the limited firewood they had left was being heavily rationed, this made it unpleasant during daytime for the defenders and unbearable at night. Fresh supplies of firewood could not be brought in and they were literally burning through what little they had.

Candles, now there was another issue. The evenings, as evenings tend to be, were dark, however, there was still work to be done and yet their supply of wax was at crisis point.

Young Henry commands such reverence from his years as a celebrity on the tournament circuit, that there is not yet talk of desertion, how long this loyalty would last was anyone's guess.

What Young Henry fails to comprehend though, is that although it is bad within the castle walls, it's far worse for the sieging army. Camped out in an exposed field during one of the worst Springs that Limognes has ever seen, The Old King and Richard were spending less cognitive thought on considering an assault, than they were trying to stop their own men deserting.

Richard watches disapprovingly at his father as he shouts down another council meeting who wish to retreat. His father has overexerted himself. Richard watches The Old King shake his fist at the sky and command Spring to arrive sooner, Richard swears to himself that once he is in charge, he will not make the mistakes of his father.

Young Henry though is blinkered, he can see only his own perspective, he has no insight into quite how close to winning he actually is. Under the cover of nightfall, he slips away from the siege. Young Henry leaves behind his men to fight for him in a battle he no longer believes they can win. In some ways, this is prudent, after all, if he is captured the game is up, however, he may have just set a course for a self-fulfilling prophecy of defeat.

Before he leaves though, he does something clever. He sends a letter that is not easy for Young Henry to pen, he sends a letter to his old friend and ally Sir William Marshal, he wants the big man back at his side for the months to come.

We will explore the schism that developed between best friends Marshal and Young Henry at a later juncture, however, one thing you should remember, is that William Marshal and Young Henry *were* best friends. Whatever happens between true best friends, whatever goes down, there is always a certainty of reconciliation. When Young Henry and William Marshal first met again in the countryside of France, initially, there was some awkwardness, a little shyness from both parties. They make eye contact infrequently and only communicate in monosyllabic grunts.

"You K?" asked one.

"Aye," replied t'other.

"Fine," concluded the first.

"Good," settled the second.

"Excellent," agreed the first.

A smile begins at the corners of Marshal's mouth, a grin explodes across the Young King's. The two men rush across the room to embrace one another. They speak well into the night, they speak of past glories and triumphs. They speak of the insanity of fame and the tournament circuit, the maidens they had met and the sights they had seen. Not until they are both well and truly drunk, do they dare to talk of the future.

"What *hiccough* are we going to do then, about your Klazomaniac of a Father?" asks Marshal.

Young Henry would prefer not to admit he doesn't know what Klazomaniac means, so his answer is intentionally vague, "A father is like a son and a son like a Father…" Young Henry slurs. Marshal waits for him to continue but he doesn't.

"Riiiiight," began Marshal, "Your control freak Father and psycho brother are over exposed, their men are vulnerable on the siege of Limognes and if we relieve the citadel right now, we could sweep through the region like a warm knife through a knob of butter."

"Exactly, that's what I was saying." Young Henry claimed.

"From there, we could stir up the barons in Aquitaine where you already have allies. That would pull Richard's gaze from central France and shift his attention back South."

Marshal knew his stuff, but he is also not the King, "at least, you know, that's how I'd play it if it were me" he qualifies.

To be fair to Marshal, he delivers on everything he has promised. The two-pronged attack across Limognes whilst simultaneously exciting the barons of Aquitaine into rebellion proves devastating for The Old King and Richard. Young Henry has found himself firmly on the front foot and what's more, this time he knows it.

The bookies were furious, they were set to lose millions. Everyone had bet on an Old King and Richard victory, home in time for Christmas and a thorough spanking for Young Henry in front of all the courtiers. Five months into the conflict and with plenty of campaign season left, it is all a very different story, Young Henry is actually winning. He stands to do what nobody else has ever come close to, he stands to overthrow The Old King.

The people see celebrity Young Henry's prodigal comeback with Sir William Marshal as biblical. He represents a glimmer of hope, a change in the old guard. The Young King is strong without being cruel, he is prepared to fight but not hungry for it and he is representative of a new era of the Plantagenet dynasty. He is the dawning of a new golden age.

Young Henry continued to power deeper into enemy territory, seizing castles across his father's lands. Just as Marshal predicted, the Aquitaine barons were well and truly holding Richard's attention. Young Henry seemed to have an endless stream of mercenaries raiding areas in Normandy, although if he was completely honest, Young Henry was getting a little concerned about the state of his bank account. He has been funding this war though his tournament winnings which whilst substantial, are in no way significant enough to support the amount of mercenaries on his payroll. Young Henry is seriously in debt and if he does not win this war soon will be in serious trouble.

If love of the people were shillings and pence, than

Young Henry would be a rich man, people cheer him as he rides through the town of Uzerche. The Young King, at just twenty-seven years of age, could not be more of a man right now. Marshal is next to him, his eyes scan the crowd searching for any potential threat, ever the professional soldier.

"Lighten up Marshal," smiles the Young King as he waves out to the crowds, "they aren't going to try and kill us, they love us."

Marshal scowled for a moment before relenting, he raised a clenched fist aloft in the air, "The Old King is Dead, long live the Young King," Marshal declares. The roar from the crowd is deafening. Young Henry kicks his horse into a gallop up the hill towards the citadel.

That night, Young Henry does not come down from his chambers for dinner, he is tired. It is hardly surprising. Young Henry has youth on his side, but the last nine months had been gruelling. Marshal smiles ruefully, knowing without doubt they would both come out of this war with a few more lines, scars and wrinkles, they were getting older. Although Marshal would never admit it, his heart had exploded with pride for his friend and master as they had ridden through Uzerche earlier that day. Young Henry was no longer the petulant child Marshal had first met, he was not the inexperienced rookie playing at rebellion as he had a decade before, Young Henry was a King to follow.

In the early hours of the following morning, there is a commotion in the citadel, servants rushing through the stone passages wake Marshal from his slumber.

"What is this rumpus?" grumpily demands the giant, "Are we under attack?"

"The King, his sheets are sodden," breathlessly explains one of the Young King's servants as he rushes off with fresh linen.

Marshal chuckles wheezily, too weary for dinner but not too weary to drink some wine in your chambers Young

Henry and wet the bed like a child? It was a lesson every man must learn, if Marshal was totally honest, he was not entirely sure he had himself completely learned this lesson himself regarding wine.

It wasn't something to worry over, Young Henry had been under a lot of stress recently, who could begrudge the monarch enjoying a tipple or two, or five for that matter? If it helped him drift off to sleep then what was the bother?

As Marshal enters the Young King's chambers though, he realises with a cold, chilling certainty that his friend's ailment is neither alcohol related nor minor. A heavy stench of foul excrement and sickness dominates the King's bedchamber. Marshal approaches his friend, he is emanating heat and sweating heavily, his sheets have just been changed but are already growing dark and damp with perspiration.

Marshal is no doctor, but he knows that when an illness strikes this quickly, it isn't good. Still though, he is young, he will shake off this ailment, Marshal tells himself. He tries not to let the horror on his face show as he approaches Young Henry's cot.

"What are you doing waking up the whole castle for some minor head cold Kingling, I was trying to get some sleep? I've worked hard the last few months trying to make you look good," banters Marshal bravely for internally, he is recoiling.

Young Henry's eyes struggle to focus on the big knight, as his pupils narrow he seems to recognise Marshal and smiles. Young Henry tries to sit up but stops suddenly, his face contorts with pain and his stomach cramps, he coils into a foetal position and rocks for a time. He soils his britches. Young Henry recovers himself and fixes his stare on Marshal, he smiles weakly, "Do I look like the noble King of England and half of France?" Young Henry asks.

"Well, not so much right now no, although, if I'm being honest, not sure you ever did…" teases Marshal.

"We almost did it though, didn't we? We almost won.

Did you hear the people cheer today?" the Young King is staring off into the middle distance.

"Aye, I did," Marshal's heart is breaking, Young Henry's lip is quivering.

"We nearly beat them. We redefined chivalry, we did so much, I wish there was more time, I'm scared Marshal. How do you think I'll be remembered? Do you think I will be remembered?" Young Henry's brow furrows. He is begging Marshal for an answer that he doesn't have.

"Enough of this. You have a minor fever Kingling, you are going to recover, we are going to beat your bastard of a father and psycho of a brother. You need to stop talking like this and get some rest."

"I'll be fine?" asked Young Henry tearfully of his friend, clinging on desperately to this golden thread of hope.

"Aye, I am certain of it," Marshal has never been less certain of anything in his life. He leaves the chamber to give his friend time to rest, Marshal will spend the night in prayer.

Marshal is a formidable warrior but even his sword cannot cross the scythe of the Grim Reaper. He watches the Young King's condition steadily worsen, his days are spent in vigil beside his friend's sickbed.

The Young King had contracted dysentery. Dysentery is responsible for killing almost a million people per year even today, in the twelfth century it was rampant. Dysentery is an infection of the intestine that causes severe or even bloody diarrhoea, dehydration, fever and eventually death. The infection itself can be picked up through all kinds of means, Young Henry would have been at risk from a number of these; infected water, a chef that did not wash their hands, swimming in a dirty lake, take your pick.

In modern times, a confirmed diagnosis of dysentery would not require immediate attention. If after four days the infection had not subsided, antibiotics would be tried. If antibiotics were not effective, an immediate release drug called metronidazole, part of the nitroimidazoles family, routinely would be administered. This is a serious treatment and not one to be given lightly. It will essentially napalm all infections in the gut.

This talk is a little irrelevant though, Young Henry is living eight hundred years before Alexander Fleming will accidentally manufacture the first antibiotic on an unintended culture plate, it is even longer than this before researchers in Tokyo will discover the nitroimidazole family of drugs. Young Henry will have to fight this infection himself. Marshal watches with growing worry as the clock ticks past four days of symptomatic infection.

Young Henry's bouts of diarrhoea became more and more frequent and less and less controllable. It is explosive, a foul smelling black, viscous tar speckled with blood. All of the water in his body has been purged out of him, he is as dehydrated as a prune. His voice is cracked, his throat is bone dry, not that he has the energy to speak often.

His fever continues to spike and the infection reaches his brain. The elevated internal temperatures are interfering with his usual cognitive processes and he is mostly delirious, he shouts out for people who are not there and does not recognise those that are.

He talks of his father, often. His hallucinations are vivid and brightly coloured with strange, psychedelic imagery. Young Henry dreams that he is trapped within a tree, his father is an ivy creeper crawling around him, choking him, strangling his very soul, pulling him down towards the earth.

Young Henry awakens with a gasp, a number of men he does not know surround his sickbed, "Who are you?" he screams trying to get out of bed, he collapses on the floor. William Marshal holds back a sob as he helps his friend back into his cot, he tries not to think how devastatingly light Young Henry feels in his arms.

At some point, the prognosis shifts from treating his mortal coil to salvaging his eternal soul. Blessings are made and last rites are read. His eternal salvation in heaven though cannot be guaranteed for Young Henry has betrayed his mortal father which is a sin, it doesn't help that his mortal father is the closest thing on Earth to God. For Young Henry to rest peacefully, it is paramount he receives a blessing of forgiveness before he dies from his Father. All senior members of the church agreed that as things stood, Young Henry's soul was destined for eternal damnation.

Word is sent to The Old King explaining both his son's condition and the disastrous balance his son's soul rests in. The message explains in no uncertain terms, that his son was dying and there is not a lot of time. The Old King must attend swiftly and pardon Young Henry to ensure him a favourable position in the afterlife. To be fair to The Old King, he wants to go, his advisors are less convinced this is wise though.

"It stinks of a trap sire, last time you rode to him he tried to shoot you. It is clearly the kind of skulduggery he will resort to for victory, it means we are winning, think nowt of it."

The Old King's brow furrows, he can see the logic. Were he advising somebody else, he would probably tell them the same. This is his son though and The Old King really feels that he should attend.

The Old King's advisors chattered excitedly about how whether it was a trap, or if indeed Young Henry was actually dying, either way, it signified victory. The Old King was transported to almost three decades earlier when he had first seen his son and heir suckling at his wife Eleanor's bosom. He tried to recall how he had felt that day but couldn't, in reality, he hadn't actually been present for the birth of his eldest son.

"Richard, was I a good Father?" The Old King asks his son.

Richard is startled by the question, "No."

Though it pains him, The Old King will not travel to

visit his firstborn son on his deathbed. Instead, he will make the small gesture of removing a sapphire ring and blessing it with forgiveness, this will be sent in his stead. The Old King feels numb, surely his son was not really dying?

On the 11th June 1183, Young Henry dies. He is naked and shivering on the cold stone floor in front of the crucifix. His closest men, including Sir William Marshal, will hear his final repentance. He apologies for his crimes against his Father, he begs forgiveness, he seems to lose his lucidity and shouts for his Father to come closer, he is reminded he has not attended though it is unclear whether Young Henry comprehends this. He gives his cloak to Sir William Marshal and begs him to take it to Jerusalem, to join the Crusades in his name and then finally, Young Henry is done. He clutches the ring of forgiveness to his heart before falling forward to the floor.

Chapter 12: What happened between Young Henry and Sir William Marshal?

If today the world feels a shade darker, or last night you thought that there was one less star twinkling in the sky, that's because it is and there was. The nation feel the loss of Young Henry like parted lovers feel an ache in their hearts. He was to be the great Plantagenet hope for the people, how could they not mourn his loss? Through his fame on the tournament circuit and prolific presence in public, he ascended to an unprecedented level of legendary status. Whether this status is deserved is debateable, but it is hardly one we need to engage with now. Should we be dwelling on the fact that Young Henry only *almost* beat his Father and brother Richard due to an unseasonably cold March? Do we need to concern ourselves that the battle plans were drawn up almost entirely by his House Knight, Sir William Marshal? No, let's just jump on the we-love-Young-Henry bandwagon.

People even suggested Young Henry should be made a Saint. The flames that burned oh so brightly for the 'Cult of Young Henry' though, are quickly pissed out by The Old King and Richard. The people are scared to oppose these two snarling wolves. There is no one for the movement to rally behind, Sir William Marshal has wisely left the continent fulfilling Young Henry's deathbed wish of joining the Crusades in his name. From a self-preservation point of view, this was undoubtedly a shrewd move from Marshal.

Upon his death, Young Henry proves himself to be a central jenga block. He is easily removed and causes no real damage to the overall structure of the Plantagenet tower. After all, Young Henry did not actually command many responsibilities or landed interests. His legacy is such, that he is neither Henry II (his father) nor Henry III (his future nephew), he is a relative unknown in the History books.

Young Henry did not completely pass away unnoticed though, he did leave behind one very tangible thing, an absolute mountain of debt. With no financial engine behind him, Young Henry had ran out of his tournament money almost immediately upon embarking on The Second Rebellion. He learned the golden lesson of Wall Street quickly though, a firm handshake and a dazzling smile will normally outweigh a sound credit rating on a balance sheet, he had mercenaries begging to sign up on tick, and why not? The boy was a natural salesman, he was also a King. They could see the common folk screaming his name, The Old King was old news! Young Henry's potential was on a par with early Apple stock, until it wasn't, and The Young Henry Ponzi scheme collapsed in on itself.

Overnight, the French countryside was filled with angry roving bands of mercenaries who were owed money by the deceased Young Henry. They were furious and there was very little they could actually do about it. They could ask The Old King I suppose, but he was very unlikely to pay it, after all, it was him they had been fighting against. One band of mercenaries decided, rather unsavourily, to descend upon Young Henry's funeral procession and demand the money they were owed.

The mercenary captain made it clear that his beef was not with Young Henry's ethereal spirit, but rather with the very real mortal debts he had left behind. He demanded payment from the funeral procession. Little did he know, he was speaking to the wrong people, the funeral procession has been relying on charity as they travel through the French villages even to be able to proceed with their procession. The crowds who had once cheered Young Henry's name uncontrollably and thrown chastity belts at him are more than a little conspicuous by their absence. The mercenary captain continued to demand his money but as he shook each procession member down, all he found was empty pockets. The Young King had died a pauper.

Although Young Henry wished to be laid to rest in Rouen, the bishop of Le Mans thought it prudent to stop the funeral procession and lay the body to rest in consecrated ground in their cathedral, lest the party be attacked on the road. Some have criticised the bishop for trying to create a pilgrim site, but the reality was that public mood was getting uglier, whilst the relic market was increasingly buoyant, growing double digits year on year. A metacarpal here from The Young King or a femur there, would have gone some way towards paying off the debts he owed. A swift burial in consecrated soil may well have been the safest option.

Young Henry's body was later moved and can be found at his stated preferred resting place, The Cathedral of Rouen. There he sleeps alongside his future nephew Arthur, John of Lancaster who presided over the trial of Joan of Arc and grimly, the heart of his brother, Richard.

Before we finally say goodbye to Young Henry, I did say that we would explore the schism that developed between Young Henry and Sir William Marshal and give you the reason for their feuding, well dear reader, I can do better than that, I will give you two reasons.

Story One

Sir William Marshal sits alone in his quarters. His chambers are sparsely furnished and the wine he drinks is cheap, the kind that if you indulged in more than a bottle, you may temporarily lose your eyesight. No candles are lit, Marshal's quarters smell faintly of stale alcohol and body odour. If you expected Marshal to be living in more luxurious accommodation considering his tournament success, so did I. Marshal earned a celebrity wage, which whilst substantial, was not the same as a landowner.

Marshal's master was poor though and unlike other nobles unable to parcel out land packages to his loyal followers as a reward, for he has none himself to give. Young Henry and Sir William Marshal's operation is a nicely decorated, but largely hollow, Easter Egg.

Marshal is drinking quickly tonight. He is furious, he is upset, he is embarrassingly drunk and righteously ambivalent. A single tear rolls down the giant's cheek.

Can you blame him? For Sir William Marshal is in love. His body yearns, nay screams, for the lady of his desire. Why is he crying I hear you ask? That's a fair question. Normally, love is a cause for celebration, those afflicted with this condition will usually shout it far and wide, from the roof tops no less. I AM IN LOVE. Those in love, see the world through such a vivid spectrum of colours, they see in such high definition, that the mundane is transformed into the sublime. Food tastes better, sex is more electrifying and life has a purpose, they have found the other half of their soul, they are complete.

Right now, William Marshal is seeing not in high definition, he is seeing through blurred drunken eyes, he has not bothered to eat supper that evening and his life certainly doesn't have a purpose. He is a freely spinning compass, he is completely and utterly lost. For Sir William Marshal's love is a forbidden fruit. He is in love with his master's wife, he is in love with Marguerite.

Marshal is being torn apart by the loyalty he feels for his Master and the love he has for the beautiful, Marguerite. His stomach is in knots, he is screaming with the inner turmoil of it all. Marshal, the very paragon of honour and chivalry, is having sex with his master's wife.

Word was taken to Young Henry by one of his subjects in November of 1182. Young Henry could not believe it. He had handpicked Marshal for greatness, elevated him way beyond anything he could have expected from his humble beginnings and this was how he repaid him? The Old King would have stormed into Marshal's chambers personally and slashed him to pieces in his bed, Young Henry is not the Old King though. Richard would have had him arrested, he would have taken Marshal's wife and defiled her in front of Marshal before slitting her throat, he would have kept Marshal indefinitely on the cusp of life to prolong his suffering, Young Henry is not his brother Richard either though.

Young Henry also needed William Marshal. They had an upcoming tournament in Northern France for one thing and he was a big part of their team, Young Henry literally, could not afford to lose this event, he needed the tournament winnings. Young Henry was also planning to take on Richard for the lands of Aquitaine, if he was to succeed in this, he would need loyal men beside him, he would need Marshal.

It is possible to be rational on paper. It is easy to write down the pros and cons of a situation and calmly decide the best course of action. It's not quite so simple to shut out all emotion and walk the road you have elected to. Young Henry and Marshal will fight in the tournament of late 1182. They will win, they will collect the tournament revenue, but it is evident to the spectators that a coldness exists between them that was not present before. The Young King cannot shed the image of the giant Marshal ravaging his beautiful Marguerite. The searing scene was burned into his retinas so that even when he shut his eyes to sleep, he could still see the offending scene.

Marshal left the King's party following the tournament. He rides off with a heavy heart alone on a dusty road, sad violin music plays. He is a knight without a lord, a galley without direction and a hero without a quest. In February 1183, Marguerite will also be sent away to Paris. The Young King has never felt so alone as he prepares to do battle against his brother Richard.

Sir William Marshal is the hero of a thousand tournaments, at just thirty-six years of age, he is considered to be one of the most experienced veterans alive, it doesn't hurt that he's a celebrity too. It's hard to picture Marshal as naïve, but in playing politics and courtroom manoeuvring, he may as well be a schoolboy.

It is not hard to see that Marshal would be a catalyst for jealousy in Young Henry's court. Marshal had unprecedented access to Young Henry and a relationship that would be impossible for any other to emulate. Think back to our montage of Young Henry and Marshal from the tournament circuit, remember their adventures, their comradery? They would embrace, they would laugh, their relationship went way beyond lord and knight, they were best friends, perhaps even brothers?

Late at night, under the ghostly galleon of a smugglers' moon, five of Young Henry's men sit in a clearing deep in Fontainebleau Forest. They have left the main encampment as they do not wish to be overheard for what they discuss is controversial, they are discussing the problem of Sir William Marshal. A dark night for dark deeds, a wolf howls far off in the trees, a low fog hangs about the branches. The men agree that Marshal has ideas far above his status, they also agree the Young King should cultivate relationships with men of superior breeding and vision than Sir William Marshal, namely them. Going to the Young King with this argument was an impossibility for he wouldn't listen. Marshal had somehow cast a spell on Young Henry so as to have him in his pocket, the men in the clearing discuss how they will break this enchantment.

The men agreed Marshal's name needed to be discredited, besmirched even. They would drive a wedge so far between the Young King and Marshal that their relationship could never be salvaged. The men talk with the wide brush strokes of strategic chess players who have long since ceased considering the humanity behind the pawns they sacrifice.

Sir Thomas of Coulonces, the leader of the five men, does not go straight to Young Henry for that would have been too obvious. He begins what can only be described as a campaign of whispers.

"Sir Thomas, do you know where Sir William Marshal is?" asked the court clerk, requiring Marshal's signature for an order.

"No I do not. I saw him leaving the Lady Marguerite's quarters earlier today, I haven't seen him since then," Sir Thomas pivots on his heel and walks away.

"Did Lady Marguerite seem angry to you today?" squeaked the Young King's horse master as he scrubs the sweat off a stallion's flanks.

"Relax, don't worry, I'm sure she was not angry at you, she was just tired," Sir Thomas winks at the young lad, "She said she had been up late into the night with Sir William Marshal, if you catch my drift."

"I have never seen a lady ride a horse as well as Lady Marguerite," states a shrew-like elderly matron of the court.

"That is not the only thing she is said to ride well…" Sir Thomas' eyebrows are raised suggestively.

After almost a month of this, local drunk and general loudmouth Ralph Farci takes the rumours to Young Henry who listened to Farci slur, with more detail than he cared to hear, about how his best friend on planet Earth had betrayed him with the woman that he loved. To his credit, Young Henry does not believe the rumours. He dismisses Farci, the man is deep in his cups and hardly a reliable witness, it just can't be true.

But a man cannot unlearn something, he cannot forget a story such as this. He cannot un-think the plethora of positions he was advised Marshal and Marguerite's limbs intertwined in. Even though it isn't true and Young Henry knows it isn't true, I mean it can't be…can it? A small shadow of a doubt chips away at him like a trickle of water will eventually cut stone. Young Henry's attitude to Marshal changes, at first it is unperceivable until it isn't.

Marshal is effectively frozen out. He protests his innocence, of course he does, but it is too late. The seeds have been sewn and the damage is done. It was breaking the big man's heart. It came to a climax at the Plantagenet Christmas party of 1182. William Marshal had kept his distance for a couple of weeks but he returns amidst a backdrop of whispers and accusations, to once and for all prove his innocence.

He declares to Young Henry he will fight three men, one after another in single combat. If he loses he would be hanged happily as guilty, if he won though, he wanted to be reinstated and absolved of these insubstantial accusations. Young Henry is interested but nobody is prepared to fight the big man.

Marshal offers to have a finger removed from his right hand to prove his innocence – how exactly this would prove it, I don't know, but Young Henry declines. He just wants Marshal to leave.

Marshal will spend a tournament season fighting for Philip of Flanders, he will win titles, money and prestige, but his heart is not in it. When he receives a letter saying his master is in trouble and needs his help, he wastes no time in riding in for his side, a true friend always will. The pair will have one last hurrah together before Young Henry is plucked from this Earth by a cruel and violent affliction.

Though Young Henry will die penniless, failed and forgotten, we should not focus on his mortal remains, instead, we should consider the actions of Sir William Marshal immediately following his master's death. Ever the faithful vassal, he will travel to Jerusalem in the name of Young Henry. He will lay his master's cloak reverently upon the steps of The Holy Sepulchre, he will join the Crusade and fight in his name. Hopefully with this, Young Henry is able to find some peace.

Chapter 13: King Louis VII of France, it's a boy!

It's important to have an arch enemy, it gives the mind something to focus on and a reason to better oneself. For The Old King, his archenemy is the Capetian King, Louis VII of Eastern France. It is a mismatched fight though for The Old King always seems to win, but we do not get to choose who we fall into rivalry with.

Their vendetta ran deeper than what would have been typical of two medieval Kings whose lands border one another, for their rivalry was personal. Both of these Kings had been married to Eleanor of Aquitaine. Although it may sound silly, how could The Old King not wonder how he measured up in certain departments against his enemy, Louis?

Although there were certain things The Old King would never know for sure, he did know this. He was a lot richer than Eleanor's ex-husband, I mean a lot. The Old King's empire was a wonder of efficiency, highly profitable and insanely well organised. Louis didn't run a bad ship either, but he couldn't compete in size, nor girth of territory.

There was also the matter of dynasty that put The Old King way out in front again. For a King, heirs are the name of the game, specifically male ones. Louis may have annulled his marriage with Eleanor due to them being related in some shape or form, but in reality, it was because she had not given him a male heir. He blamed her entirely for this, setting out his stall that the sperm swimming in his loins couldn't be any more manly, they shaved with bare razor blades and cut down trees with hand axes.

His theory was completely undermined, making him

look more than a little foolish, when over the next fourteen years Eleanor of Aquitaine gave The Old King not one, not two, but four healthy boys.

Louis finally got the son he so desired from his third wife.

"King Louis sir, it's a boy!" gushed the midwife. His son was perfect, sure, all parents say that, but Louis means it. There has never been such a perfect son in all of Christendom. Louis watches on with paternal pride as his son grows up and commits like none ever before have to their schooling. He is fast becoming a master in book learning, debate and weaponry.

"King Louis, I'm here to talk to you about your son Philip," said the Royal Doctor.

"Isn't he perfect? Isn't he the absolute prime example of physical health and athleticism?" Louis booms good naturedly.

"He's dying, Sire."

It was true, at age fourteen, Louis' son Prince Philip Augustus was struck down with what began as a cold, evolved into a fever and congealed on the lungs in the form of deadly pneumonia. Louis would do anything to save him but he knows that he needs some kind of miracle greater than even he is able to orchestrate.

The last time we saw a miracle, it came in the form of The Old King winning a war on all fronts. He did this completely unaided and without help…although, did he really do it without help? Didn't The Old King's fortunes transform the moment he took the time to make a pilgrimage to the tomb of Archbishop Becket in Canterbury? Had the Lord not looked upon him favourably for his act of devotion at the shrine to God's own agent on Earth? Louis knows what must be done, he will sail to England and visit the Tomb of Thomas Becket. There, he will pray for the life of his only son, he will pray for Philip Augustus.

Arrangements were made. The fifty-nine year old

Capetian King would set sail with just a handful of men, incognito, across the channel to Southampton. He would travel unannounced from the Hampshire city to Kent's own Canterbury. There, he would bow low before the shrine to Thomas Becket, he would beg God that he himself should be taken instead of his son.

Technically speaking, if Louis was to be really technical, he should have given The Old King a heads up. After all, he was a foreign King about to make landfall on another's sovereign soil. The Old King was something of a worry-wart though and would be bound to complicate things. Were he to hear about this mission of mercy, he would no doubt shout and bluster for a time and even if he did eventually agree to Louis' request, he'd probably want paying for it.

"No," thought Louis, there was no need to bother The Old King about this. It would just be a quick pilgrimage, in and out, *Ave Maria*, save my son, here's some Myrrh, Amen. As Louis' boat approached Southampton though, his heart grew heavy. Stood on the dock, smiling a wicked and wide grin, was The Old King with a gang of fully armoured men.

How had the snake heard tell of his journey? The Old King would no doubt try to use this to his advantage. He might tax Louis heavily, or, if he was feeling particularly sly this campaign season, imprison him and claim a heavy ransom from the Capetian barons. The man had an insatiable appetite for power and this was an opportunity on a silver platter. The Old King continues to smile his snakelike grin as the boat approaches. Louis would have downed anchors and turned about right now, but his pilgrim is incomplete, he truly believes this might save his son and he will not stop until he has reached Canterbury.

Do you know what? The Old King didn't tax or arrest him. The Old King even went so far as to personally escort Louis from Southampton to Canterbury Cathedral. The two men rode together each day at the front of their respective columns and by all accounts, they seem to have both quite enjoyed the other's company. As to exactly what they talked of, this, unfortunately, we will never know. Did they discuss matters of state and business? Almost certainly, at least at first. Did conversation move beyond this sphere of professionalism to discuss family matters, parenthood, hobbies and the mental pressures being a king took upon a man? We'll never know.

Louis will pray at Thomas Becket's tomb, his prayer will be that God takes him instead of his son. He will make a gift of one hundred barrels of fancy, Capetian wine per annum for the monks who govern the cathedral. Louis will return safely to Eastern France with no skulduggery from The Old King. The fatally ill, fourteen year old Philip Augustus will recover from his pneumonia, however, Louis will become sick himself upon returning from his pilgrimage and will die within the year peacefully in his bed.

An Old King dies, a young Prince lives. The Capetian King is Dead, long live The King.

Chapter 14: Pogonophobia; a fear or discriminatory disposition towards beards

Little Johnny Lack-land who had once kicked his legs, left and right, to and fro, as we opened this very book, is no longer now so little. It is 1185, John is nineteen years old and whilst in many ways he is now an adult, in others, he is doomed to be the eternal younger brother. He has watched his siblings plotting and pivoting, jousting and jostling, rioting and raping whilst all the time he has been shut at home in his room, bored.

John's inaction in the rebellions has not gone unnoticed by his father though, he owns The Old King's heart in a way none of his brothers can say that they do. Whilst this love is in itself a currency, John is unsure what it is worth, he can feel tectonic plates shifting away from his father, he senses that his time is soon up. John has done what any sensible Prince would do in these circumstances and has begun taking steps to widen his political sphere of influence. He has written letters here and sent messages there. The narrative of what he writes is generally the same, "I am wasted, I can do more than I do currently, I am open for a job."

As if by magic, shortly after John makes it aware to the wider market he is open for business, he hears a knock upon his chamber door.

"John," The Old King knocked carefully, he had barged into John's room once before and…well… it would be best not to repeat such an experience.

"Yes Father," a breathless voice called from within.

The Old King slowly opens up the door, "John?" John

smiles docilely at him from his bed.

The Old King is keen to keep his favourite son on side, engaged and onboard, "John, I want you to govern Ireland." The Old King whispers dramatically.

"You want me to govern Ireland? That windswept and rain drenched rock with one hundred goats per square kilometre?"

"Yes, Ireland, I was made King of Kings there some time ago, I've not really done much with it since. What do you think?" Asks The Old King with a salesman's wink.

"Ireland?" John sounds dubious.

The Old King's eyes begin to narrow and his tone is curt, he does not enjoy being questioned, even by his favourite son, "Yes, you are a competent diplomat, a trained strategic mind and of my blood. Ireland will be your making."

"Ireland," John sighs it, this time in acceptance.

Meanwhile in Ireland, it is raining. Heavily.

The wind is blowing a gale and howls about the mountain tops. It has been like this for the last three weeks, the storm was probably just getting started and the worst was yet to come. A solitary goat picks her way up the rocky mountainside.

If the goat is phased by the foul weather, she gives no indication of this. Her kind have lived in Ireland for four thousand years by this point, she can imagine nowhere else, if anything, thinks the goat, this is fine weather, a clement day for late July, she wished that all were this mild. She lets out a long and happy, "bleeeeeaaaaaaaaaaaaat" that reverberates across the mountainside.

John hears the stray bleat of a goat carry across to him on the wind as he steps off his ship, further down the jetty, he can just about spy his welcome party through eyes that are squinted against the lashing rain. God he hates this place. He is sodden, shivering and his lips are blue. He doesn't look much like the prince he is as he shuffles off the ship, treading carefully on the rotten planks of the jetty praying none give way beneath him.

The goat on the mountainside can see the royal landing party arrive and she isn't impressed with this, "*prince*". She's seen it all before after all. Across Ireland, there were in fact nine different kings, some would say ten, who knew how many princes? The goat was patriotically proud to have met eight of the kings herself, one had even fondled her ears and called her beautiful, although of course… a lady never tells what had truly occurred between them.

The goat had even met, a decade earlier, this little princeling's father. The Old King, to be fair to him, had been a man of presence. He had arrived in all his grandeur, declaring himself to be the King of Kings in Ireland, no less! Nobody could really find either the reason or the motivation to argue with him. Best to have a party, celebrate this Old King, after all, Ireland had embraced King of King's before, why not this one? He had travelled a long way to be fair to him and did seem very keen.

Prince John rubs rainwater from his eyes as he walks down the jetty, the blurred welcoming party shift into focus and John is immediately disappointed. Eight big-bearded men stand on the pier, a large Irish setter hound sleeps next to their feet. John is livid.

"Considering my father is King of Kings in Ireland, you would think a larger welcome party would have assembled," John hisses this through gritted teeth to his hand servant, eyeing up the eight elderly bearded men and their sleeping dog.

Of course, King of Kings in Ireland is a purely symbolic title, thinks the goat. It holds no administrative power, it's a completely hollow accolade. The Old King from across the water had been so insistent about it though and demanded it with such intensity that the kings of Ireland had handed it over. After all, it's not like he could start sending them letters from across the water demanding they send men to fight in some far-off war!

John drew his hood close as he addressed the eight Kings before him, "My father, King of Kings in Ireland, has been sending letters from across the water demanding your men fight in some far-off war."

His delivery is marred by both his chattering teeth and his sodden mop of hair, which is plastered to his forehead.

John looks expectantly at the eight bearded men as they smile benignly, the Irish Setter eyeballs John, his upper lip lifts baring his teeth for a moment before he yawns and rolls over. John is getting frustrated.

It was a case of misunderstanding due to the diversity of cultures, even across a relatively small geographical range the populous can vary as infinitely as the snowflakes that fall across the same soil, reasoned the goat. John had assumed his Father's status as, 'king of kings' would mean he wielded executive power and this just wasn't the case. That one of the eight Irish King's Dogs had found time in his busy schedule to attend, was actually something of an honour.

John, the competent diplomat, in what can only be described as a fit of delirium, begins to tug on the assembled Irish kings' beards, mocking what at the time was considered to be unfashionable facial hair. Suffice to say, this is a faux-pas in diplomatic circles and not one I believe has ever been ever repeated before or since, by anyone, ever. The rest of his tour isn't much better.

John will return to the Plantagenet homeland within the year, having made no real inroads with the locals.

Chapter 15: This is not a joke, Jerusalem has Fallen

The Old King, as always, is carrying burdens upon his shoulders that would cripple a mere mortal. Relative to recent times though, The Old King is actually feeling fairly foot loose and fancy free. His rival, King Louis was dead, he has been replaced by his son King Philip who although has potential, was still in the scheme of things a pup. The Old King did not believe he came even close to being a match for him.

Three years earlier though, things hadn't looked so rosy for The Old King, in fact, rebellion had seemed all but inevitable. The Old King's second eldest surviving son, Geoffrey, had cosied up with Philip. Cosied up was an understatement, he had basically moved into the Capetian Court, even landing a job as chief of staff for Philip's household.

Whispers hissed on dark castle ramparts between shrouded men in cloaks as the diplomacy round began anew, both The Old King and Geoffrey lobbied hard for support for the upcoming war. These whispers were prematurely silenced before they could progress to battle cries when Geoffrey met an untimely death following an injury from a jousting accident. Whether The Old King felt relief at the death of this political rival, or sorrow at burying yet another of his sons, is not something we will ever know for certain. Either way, there's no denying that it was convenient for The Old King. From a dynastical point of view The Old King was still safe, he still had two other sons left after all.

Speaking of his other sons, Richard was being a pain and moaning about things, but when wasn't he? He wanted more power, as per usual. John is older now though and so whenever Richard becomes too bolshie, The Old King just gives a bit more of his inheritance to John. It was winding Richard up something rotten, The Old King found it all rather funny.

Richard has not survived two wars with his own family to not become King of the empire, that being said, Richard does not have many options open to him. Yes, Richard commands and rules Aquitaine with an iron fist, but it is still The Old King who holds the balance of power, resources and soldiers between the two. Richard will just have to lump it.

The Old King can feel these tensions bubbling up and bafflingly, he decides to hold another peace conference. I mean God knows why, pretty much every peace conference or party The Old King has ever organised seems to have resulted in a war or the murder of an Archbishop and of course, this one is no different. Richard storms out of the event with Philip in tow behind him. Now this *was* a concerning development for The Old King. Richard had the expertise but not the resources to fight him, whereas Philip had the resources but not the expertise. The Old King would really prefer not to fight both of them at the same time.

Cue a lot of back peddling from The Old King, who quickly reaffirms Richard as his primary heir. A public reconciliation is staged between Father and Son but onlookers notice how frosty things still seem between them. The Old King has managed to avert the disaster of fighting a war with Philip and Richard on two fronts, for now. Although he has reacted swiftly and decisively, it has been uncharacteristic to see The Old King so completely blindsided and exposed. Do we take this as a sign of The Old King getting sloppy in his twilight years, or, is he facing far superior opponents in Richard and Philip than he ever did in Young Henry?

The leaves begin to brown, it is October 1187 and

everybody's gaze is about to be diverted East. Events transpiring almost three thousand miles away are going to dictate the future of both the Plantagenet and Capetian empires in Europe. The King of Jerusalem is about to drop the ball, he's going to lose control of the Holy City. Jerusalem will fall to an Arabic Sultan by the name of An-Nasir Salah ad-Din Yusuf ibn Ayyub. History books will remember him more commonly as, The Sultan Saladin.

The King of Jerusalem, Guy Lusignan, was captured but spared by the Arabic Sultan who does not wish to kill the Christian King. If the name of Guy Lusignan sounds familiar, it should do. He was responsible nineteen years earlier for the ill-fated raid on Eleanor of Aquitaine, whom Guy intended to kidnap and ransom for much needed funds. The kidnapping went wrong though and turned bloody when Earl Salisbury was accidentally killed. Sir William Marshal had flown into a berserker fury and although fought well, was ultimately captured himself after being stabbed in the leg through a hedge.

People were horrified by the death of the Earl. Nobles such as the Earl of Salisbury were not randomly killed on the road in The Old King's lands, it just didn't happen. Lawlessness was relatively rare, but if it did occur, anyone with a title would be captured and ransomed, not killed. The Old King was furious. As a knight of Aquitaine though, Guy Lusignan does not have to answer to The Old King, instead, his trial was presided over by Eleanor and Richard. They wished to hit their monthly crusader targets the Pope kept pushing onto them, so they decided not to kill Guy, instead, they sent him off on The Crusades.

Lusignan began as a general in the crusader armies, but the next few years saw him grow both in stature and prestige. He eventually married Sibylla, sister to Baldwin IV, The Leper King of Jerusalem. Baldwin died young; leprosy will do that to you in the Middle Ages.

Although typically thrones did not pass to sisters, the

people loved Sibylla. It helped that she was also supported by Rome. Sibylla was the hands down favourite to inherit the regency of Jerusalem, except for one problem, nobody liked her husband Guy. It was agreed that she could be crowned Queen of Jerusalem, on the condition she nullified her marriage to Guy. It was a difficult decision for Sibylla, I mean what's a woman to do? She truly loved her husband but come on, the chance to be the Queen of Jerusalem doesn't exactly come along every day.

Sibylla reluctantly agreed to the deal, she did have her own return condition though. Once she divorced Guy Lusignan, she wanted to be allowed to marry whomever she saw fit, wherever she saw fit, however she saw fit. Sibylla wanted to be permitted to marry for love.

Fair enough, thought the old beards that ran her council. Surely no one could be worse than the Earl-Murdering, Hedge-Stabbing villain, Guy Lusignan? The council agree to Sibylla's condition.

Once permission was granted, Sibylla chucked Guy in the bin like last night's takeaway and was crowned, Queen of Jerusalem. She then immediately invoked her right to marry for love, she chose Guy Lusignan.

The elders of the court were very annoyed, "surely somebody put in the small print that she couldn't just re-marry Guy Lusignan?" apparently no one had though. Sibylla handed over her crown to her husband, making Guy Lusignan King of Jerusalem.

Guy had made it, I mean he's a King for Christ's sake, he's one step below God presiding over the Holiest City on Earth. Guy planned on spending the majority of his time being fed grapes and fanned by giant palm leaves, he quickly learned though that the realities of being King of Jerusalem, were not quite the same as his expectations. In fact, he'd go so far as to say the job was a nightmare. The problem with Jerusalem, is that it just meant too much to way too many people.

A single city where a messiah for one major world religion had been crucified and a prophet from another had been schooled, was bound to cause problems. You just don't get these issues with small market-based towns in the Midlands. No one has ever done a pilgrimage to Penkridge, nor a Crusade for Nuneaton, it just doesn't happen, how Guy Lusignan wishes he was King of Stoke-on-Trent.

During a good season, Guy's job would have been tough, everybody wanted a piece of Jerusalem, at the time period Guy was operating though, it was especially impossible. Every generation will see a great warrior born of such immeasurable prowess, fortitude and guile, that they will redefine life's parameters and burn down the establishment. Guy was unfortunate enough that in his generation, two had been born.

Guy had already met one, Richard, and he was about to meet the other. A Sultan by the name of Saladin. Saladin had united the Muslim Saracens under his Eagle Flag. The Sultan was also less than three miles from Jerusalem and had his eyes firmly set on the city.

Saladin won his siege, of course he did. You have heard of Saladin and you have not heard of Guy Lusignan. This caused ripples across Europe. Our Plantagenet Protagonists are answerable to Rome, particularly since the death of Thomas Becket and The Old King's oath that he, or one of his children, will go on crusade to make amends.

The Old King doesn't want to go to Jerusalem though. He feels he is busy enough managing his own empire and so far, he has managed to put off making the trip by sending coin in his stead. The thermostat has just turned up considerably though. The Pope has declared a state of spiritual emergency.

"Jerusalem has fallen, may I repeat that, Jerusalem has fallen," The Pope addresses Philip Augustus, Richard and The Old King about where their priorities should lie. The Pope makes it perfectly clear: WE ARE NO LONGER

ASKING ANYMORE, WE ARE TELLING. PUT ASIDE YOUR PUNY, INSIGNIFICANT, SCHOOLCHILD LITTLE FIGHTS, WE MUST UNITE AGAINST SULTAN SALADIN. WE MUST UNITE. WE ARE ONE.

"We just aren't one, at least I don't think so," drawls Philip as he drinks lazily from his goblet of Chateau Red Wine. Philip is of the school of leadership that says management will always be stressful, what's the point of getting het up about things? He works hard to keep his chakras neutral and his chee positive. Philip reclines back in his chair, his feet are crossed on the long trestle table which is surrounded by his privy council. Philip addresses them now, "Old man Henry won't see it that way either, the second I leave my Kingdom to go and fight for some city halfway across the continent, he'll have his feet in my loafers and his tackle in my codpiece." Philip shrugs to indicate he has made his point, but also, that he wasn't going to get stressed about it.

The Old King is furious. He reads and re-reads the letter from the Pope, an involuntary snarl starts in his throat and his upper lip curls back. There were *always* problems in Jerusalem, in fact, the city seemed to be nothing but problems. Why exactly that was The Old King's problem, he wasn't quite sure? Okay, he had made an oath, but that was when the accursed Pope, God bless his soul and may he reside over Christendom forever, had excommunicated him! What the hell was a man to do? The Old King involuntarily crosses himself for his blasphemy. What the Pope didn't seem capable of understanding, was that it was not easy for a man of The Old King's stature and sheer quantity of enemies to leave his Kingdom.

Philip's advisors tried to offer counsel, "Sire, it is strictly forbidden for any Monarchs to attack another Kingdom whilst they are on crusade, the Pope has made this very clear."

"That they have, but it's one thing to make rules,

another entirely to enforce them," calmly quips Philip, "Write to the Pope, tell him I'm on my way."

"But Sire, you just said…"

"I know what I just said. I have no intention of actually going, just send the letter," Philip smiled good naturedly at his scribe.

The Old King paces up and down his chamber like a caged animal. The red plush carpet, with a lifetime springyness guarantee, had a threadbare path that followed the restless monarchs endless, incessant, back and forth, forth and back. Occasionally, The Old King stops his pacing to clutch at his stomach.

"Sire, it is strictly forbidden for any Monarchs to attack another Kingdom whilst they are on crusade, the Pope has made this very clear…" nervously stammers The Old King's advisor.

"Fool," The Old King turns upon his heel to stare bugeyed at his assistant, "What do you think will happen the second I leave my land? It's too risky. Within a week Philip would be drinking my Bordeaux and befouling the honour of my wife."

"The wife you have locked up and kept imprisoned for the last fifteen years…?" The advisor said, well he didn't actually say that, he just thought it and wished that he was bold enough to say it.

The Old King, Philip and the Pope were at an impasse. We were seeing a live experiment of what happens when an unstoppable force encounters an immovable object. Not a lot, it turns out. It certainly doesn't result in either The Old King or Philip setting off for Jerusalem.

The Pope was going mad. How could they not understand that Jerusalem was lost? Various intermediaries were sent between the two. The Pope seemed to think it was a matter of timing, if they synchronised watches and arranged to meet on the way, how could either be concerned?

158

This, in turn though, opened up a new can of worms. What Knights do you take with you? A Monarch with no ulterior motives would take his best men to ensure a quick victory and safekeeping of their own skin. Submitting a B-Team of Knights suggested skulduggery, after all, why would you leave them behind unless you planned warring on another front?

It was getting ridiculous. Every day that Sultan Saladin was allowed to rule in the Holy City, his position was becoming ever more entrenched.

The Pope no longer had Sir William Marshal in The Holy Land to rely upon either, Marshal has returned from his crusade to Jerusalem on behalf of the deceased Young Henry. He had reconciled with The Old King and been accepted into his service. Whilst The Old King was a little cheesed off Marshal had fought against him in prior conflicts, he was wise enough to know that men of Marshal's experience and skillset are not easy to find.

Not so fast, I hear you say, what adventures did Sir William Marshal get up to on his crusade to The Holy City of Jerusalem? Frustratingly, we just don't know. Marshal's time in Jerusalem remains a mystery.

This wouldn't be unusual for almost anyone else from the period. Record keeping was sketchy at best during Medieval times and non-reliable notes on knights of non-royal birth, was absolutely the norm, for Sir William Marshal though, this omission is baffling. Marshal is the most documented Knight of this period, he had a biographer for goodness' sake. A crusade should have been the pinnacle of his career, the lack of detail in this when almost every other area of his life is so fastidiously recorded, is in itself fascinating. How could we know nothing about the big man's time in The Holy City?

We do know a little more than nothing. We know that upon arrival in Jerusalem, Marshal presented his former master Young Henry's cloak at the Church of the Holy

Sepulchre, as he promised he would. We also know Marshal got ripped off for rolls of silk that he thought beautiful, but others were less convinced and... that's pretty much it. It's not a lot to go on for a knight with a biographer during his own Crusade. Why would Marshal spotlight every other area of his life but then force us to view these key, two years, through an opaque lens?

Knowing what we know about Marshal, it is unlikely he was quiet over this period. The Knights Templar were frenetically active in Jerusalem during the two years Marshal was in the city. It isn't impossible that he was even present in Jerusalem when extensive excavation work began under Solomon's Temple (formerly Al Aqsa mosque) and some great treasure was found. Even today we do not know what, if anything, the Knight Templars discovered under there, but speculations have been made that their efforts succeeded in unearthing either The Holy Grail or the Ark of the Covenant. The Knights certainly dug down to hidden tunnels under Solomon's Temple and what looked like some kind of secret bunker that pre-dated them, surely something of importance had been buried down there?

The Order of the Knights Templar no longer exist, at least not officially. Conspiracy theorists would disagree and claim that the order have disguised themselves as the Freemasons, the New World Order, The Bilderberg Group, or some other equally nefarious outfit. The Knights Templars considered themselves to be the men at the back of the room. They made difficult decisions for the greater good and did what needed to be done. They were defenders of the peace, they were Kingmakers.

The final piece of the puzzle to share when discussing Marshal's time in Jerusalem, is where the big man will eventually be buried. Marshal will not die in this book, but when he eventually does, he will be laid to rest in a gothic revival, domed church with a defensive turret sat atop it, in the centre of London. The architecture does not match the uniform town houses of nearby Fleet Street, for it was never intended to, it has been built to bear resemblance to the churches of the Middle East. Sir William Marshal has been buried in the English Head Quarters of The Order of the Knights Templar, to be buried here, Marshal must have been in incredibly good standing with the order. Why Marshal's time in Jerusalem is a mystery, is perhaps not a mystery at all.

The pressures the Pope is putting on The Old King to join the crusades are only exacerbated by rumours that Richard and Philip Augustus are once more meeting regularly, by all accounts, they seemed to be getting along like a house on fire. The men were both of similar ages, highly competitive and born into very visible, scrutinised Royal Families.

Whilst they were undoubtedly friends, everything Philip did actually wound the hell up out of Richard. Philip was eight years Richard's junior, yet he had already sat on his throne for a full nine. This was something that Philip wasted no opportunity to jab Richard on, "One day Richard, when you are a King, you will understand the pressures of leadership, just enjoy your time as Prince, it will be some of the best years of your life."

Richard wants to fight his Father and claim the throne for himself. This is no doubt the intention of Philip's barbed tongue.

Have you ever planned a party? You send out the invites, prepare the Hors d'oeuvres, take the time to painstakingly select wine and delight in creating the perfect playlist. At a quarter to start time though, butterflies somersault in your stomach. What if nobody attends? What if the crisps are left to stale and the sandwiches to sweat? What if your friends do not actually like you and have no intention of spending the evening with you? This was The Old King's Plantagenet Christmas party of 1188.

The invitation that would previously have had horses'

hooves kicking up dust across the empire was largely ignored. The Old King's camp was now a dangerous place to reside. Two stalwart allies remain at his side, the giant Sir William Marshal and his youngest legitimate son, Prince John.

Anticipating another European war that will distract from Jerusalem, The Pope jumps on it and organises a peace conference to get Richard, Philip and The Old King pulling in the same direction, namely East. As per usual, the peace conference isn't great.

The leaders met on the banks of the River Maine near Le Mans. You know it isn't going to be the most peaceful of peace conferences when all participants arrive in full armour and hands remain on hilts. That things didn't kick off then and there is something of a miracle, the Conference descends into petty squabbling quickly though. Custom dictated both sides should withdraw peacefully before any form of attack was made, Richard and Philip are done with custom though. They want The Old King out the way. Their troops do not withdraw at all, instead, they flow straight into the heartland of The Old King's territory in Western France. It's a cheap shot from the younger generation.

The Old King can do nothing but ride hard for the sanctuary of the nearby town of Le Mans. He does not ride with the speed we are accustomed to, his eyes are cloudy and have lost their fire. His right hand remains clutched not on his saddle, but to his stomach.

Richard and Philip begin seizing The Old King's territories across Normandy and France with reckless abandon.

Did The Old King know that right now, his back was against the wall and the danger was all too real? Of course he did, The Old King was an astute politician and military commander, he was under no illusion that things were serious. Did The Old King honestly think that there was a possibility he would lose against his son Richard and Philip Augustus? Probably not. It had become normal for The Old

King to achieve the impossible, why would this time be any different?

Sir William Marshal didn't feel quite the same. Unlike The Old King, Marshal had been on the losing side on more than a few occasions, he knew when the end-game was afoot and what defeat smelled like. The battlements of Le Mans reeked of it.

Chapter 16: Are you going to kill me Sir William Marshal?

The Old King and Sir William Marshal stand on the battlements of Le Mans. They watch Richard and Philip's armies arrive. Marshal's lips are pursed and his brow is creased, their number is far greater than had been expected. The Old King looks horrified for the fleetest of moments, before he tuts derisively, rolls his eyes and spits over the walls. The soldiers cheer The Old King's defiance.

"Come Marshal, let's take a ride down do the river side and view the sport, show them we are not afraid," The Old King is already walking away. Marshal has to hurry to catch him.

"Sire, is that wise? I am happy to scout for you and report back, why risk yourself?" Marshal urges caution to his commander.

"There is no risk Marshal, it is important the men understand this. The River Huisne is impossible to cross by foot, everybody knows that."

To be fair to The Old King, thought Marshal, he was right, everybody did know that.

"This is a marathon, not a sprint Marshal, that armour will slow you down. We are days from combat yet. They will need to travel many miles downstream to find a suitable crossing point." The Old King's light tunic fluttered in the wind as he rode, high up in his saddle, he always looked the most alive when atop a horse.

Marshal was not one to disagree with the Old King and so he remains silent, in no world though was he about to take off his armour. Marshal has a bad feeling about this.

The Old King tries again, "Marshal I say, that armour

will slow you down, we are on a mission of reconnaissance, nothing more. All of you men," The Old King gestures vaguely about the party, "remove your armour, you will need your strength later." The Knights begin to unburden their cumbersome loads. They arch their shoulders and stretch their necks with satisfying cracks.

Though the Old King would never admit it, just the thought of bearing the weight of full armour for an entire day, exhausted him to his core and he felt self-conscious being the only not wearing it. It is interesting to note, not all of The Old King's men obey him, some instead choose to follow the example of Sir William Marshal, he has become a role model to many of the younger knights and many decide to keep their armour on; thank goodness they do.

Richard and Philip's army is camped alongside the fast-flowing deep river. There were divisions of knights, infantry men and crossbow wielders in great numbers. Marshal surveyed them and tried to estimate their number. The enemy would need to travel downstream to find a suitable crossing place, this would take a day, maybe a day and a half, they would then be forced to approach the heavily guarded city of Le Mans. They had enough men to attack the walls, maybe even breach the outer curtain but their losses would be heavy and it was difficult to see how they would manage to overcome the inner citadel.

A detachment of Capetian Knights rode over to the river, they see Marshal observing them and deliver a mocking salute. Marshal looked worriedly at the crossbowmen and his King, he was surprised they had not jumped into action and tried their luck at cutting the head from the Plantagenet snake. Marshal realised with some sadness, that they probably didn't recognise him. The Old King's once tight curls of red hair were largely gone, what hair he did have was shocked white and exploded in random tufts from his liver spotted scalp, he wore a basic tunic and faded breeches. He had always been wiry, now he was stick thin and angular, he looks like a beggar, Marshal thinks sadly.

The unit of knights ride to the water's edge. One detached his lance, he probed the fast flowing river. Marshal watched with what amounted to abject horror as the lance barely submerged beneath the water. Though not discernible by eye, this river bend was not at all deep, nor was it even particularly fast flowing, Richard and Philip had stumbled upon a perfect crossing point. The enemy knights wasted no time, they charged towards Marshal and the unarmoured King and Knights.

Marshal and the small number of men who had ignored the King's order to go unarmoured, charge forward to meet the Capetian Knights. Arrows begin to whistle in as the crossbowmen seize the opportunity this newly found crossing point represented. The arrows soon cease though as the knights clash together with the roar of thunder, they do not want to shoot their own men after all.

Marshal can only see through two thin slits in his helmet and it is a world of flashing blades, blood and wild fury. He looks for his King and is relieved to see him riding, full tilt, back towards the castle with the other unarmoured men. This battlefield was no place to be effectively naked to the attackers. Marshal is shocked back into the fray, as he senses more than sees, a whirl of movement from his left. Instinctively, he jerks his head back whilst leaning heavily to the right, his opponent's blade misses him by the thinnest of margins. Letting out a roar, Marshal delivers a sideswipe reply with his broadsword, it is a clumsy swing, connecting only with his opponent's shield, but it is enough. Marshal is a man of Herculean strength, the noise explodes out across the melee and his rival is knocked from his saddle. Marshal searches for his next opponent growling gutturally.

The fighting is pitch and confusion reigns, Marshal witnesses one of his men being dragged along the floor, his foot caught in his own horse's stirrups dash his brains out on the rocks by the river. Just as Marshal watches this, he himself is pulled from his horse by a lightly armoured infantryman who draws back a short sword in preparation to deliver a deadly strike.

Marshal is lucky, for he lands atop his would be killer and hears something snap. Marshal is winded but manages to push himself to his feet swiftly, to stay on the ground is certain death. Marshal bellows, "To me, God is with Marshal and for The Old King," the vastly outnumbered Plantagenet knights bunch closely together.

Marshal knows from his tournament days that a unit of men is far stronger than the sum of its parts. Standing shoulder to shoulder with his knights, Marshal and his men cut, hack and stab with a grim determination. They look like bloodthirsty butchers silhouetted against the morning sun, cleaving in wide scything cuts that spray up red mists of crimson.

The weight of the Capetian numbers begins to take its toll though and even Marshal and his men cannot contain them, they are forced to retreat. Retreat is one of the hardest commands for a general to master, if the men panic they will turn and rout, which is literally the worst thing they can do. This will be when the real killing begins, they will be sitting ducks for their attackers.

Marshal orders his men like the experienced veteran that he is and to their credit, they do not break and run, they maintain their composure, dignity and courage. Step by step, metre by metre, they retreat calmly towards the castle always remaining tightly regimented, shoulder to shoulder with their comrades. It is difficult going, they must fight for every metre of retreat won and to not let any of their opponents encircle them or gain access to the walled city.

The first of Marshal's men begin to enter the partially raised portcullis and the relative sanctuary of the city. Only Marshal and his squire, John Earley, remain exposed and holding off the Capetian Knights, "Now!" bellows Marshal and they both turn, darting into the castle. The portcullis drops behind them with a resounding clang.

The Capetian army curse that their entry has been barred. Their grumbles turn to shouts of alarm though as arrows and rocks rain down upon them from the battlements above. Reluctantly, the Capetian knights retreat and begin to spread out around the exterior of the Le Mans castle walls.

This will not be a long or drawn-out siege. Richard and King Philip's fortuitous river crossing has meant they have not been required to run the gauntlet of defences set up along the main approach to the city. They therefore have both the numbers and the means to turn over the final rock The Old King is hiding under. Once the order to attack is given, the battle is pitched and hellish immediately. Marshal heroically holds the Southern gate against wave after wave of Philip's men, but it is not enough. The Old King brings word to Marshal that two of the other gates have fallen, Richard and Philip's men are in the town itself. Reluctantly, The Old King and Marshal retreat into the inner citadel, for the city itself is lost.

The Old King orders the town to be torched, to slow the unstoppable tsunami of Capetian troops. It is a dark order and it is one that leaves the defenders fighting in narrow alleys and ginnels, blinded by smoke they lash out at figures looming suddenly out of the ember filled haze. The fighting is beyond strategy, chivalry or sanity at this point, most of the time it is difficult to even say with any certainty who was actually on who's side. Marshal smiles grimly, hadn't that been the case though all the way through this goddamn family conflict?

Marshal watches, saddened, as a young and beautiful peasant girl stands alone in the street, her face is still though her lip trembles. She is looking back at her small stone home, her little thatched roof is ablaze. Surrounding her are a scattering of meagre possessions that she has been able to save, a wooden cup, a plate, a bowl, a singed feather blanket.

She is too shocked to cry. Soot is smeared across her forehead.

"Sire, it is time we take our leave," Sir William Marshal says to his master.

The Old King nods numbly, he is still waiting for an eleventh-hour reprieve to deliver him from hell. Whether it is the cursed smoke or something else, Marshal cannot say for sure, but he notices The Old King's eyes are streaming.

It is a rout. As the town burns, Richard and Philip ride into the city of Le Mans and claim it. They have already decimated most of the Old King's seats of power and he is running out of places to hide. A strong Easterly wind blows across the city and parts the smoke for a few seconds, the sun beats down, spotlighting The Old King and his closest men riding impossibly fast away from the conflict. The remaining defenders do not continue to fight for long.

"Care for a hunt, friend?" casually asks Philip.

"Aye," growls Richard, snapping his visor closed.

Marshal, ever the paragon of chivalry in these tales, insists on covering The Old King's retreat with a small band of men. He waits atop a hillside. He can see dust rising in the distance and knows that their pursuers will reach them within the hour. He breathes deeply as the cloud of dirt grows ever closer.

Finally, after what feels an eternity, the Capetian men come into focus on the horizon.

Now that was interesting, thought Marshal, that was seriously interesting. Fluttering in the warm evening air, was the regimental standard bearing three golden lions rearing against a regal crimson background, it was the royal standard and it meant that Richard was in the valley below. Richard has only a small unit of bodyguards with him, all of whom were already weary from the days fighting. Richard appears to have made the rookie mistake of overextending himself, he is now extremely vulnerable. On a silver platter before Marshal, is a chance to win this war for his master.

The trick to being a good war-time Medieval Monarch, is to give the appearance of being in the centre of every battle without actually endangering yourself too much. That's probably why The Old King wanted to be at the riverside earlier, the perception of danger. As a medieval monarch you absolutely needed to be there, but being at the centre of every charge, in the aorta of every bloodbath? That would be madness. Because of this, it is fairly unusual to hear about Monarchs actually crossing blades personally with leaders, or significant lieutenants, of their rivals. Taking all of that into consideration though, that is exactly what we are about to see here.

Richard and his men dismount in the valley, stripping down their armour and drinking deeply from their water canteens. Marshal cannot believe his luck, he also yearns to end this insufferable waiting. He thunders down into the valley, his riders at his side, his focus is unwavering and his objective is clear, he is going to kill Richard.

Richard, who has been so sure of every step he has made during this rebellion, suddenly feels the ice cracking under him, the world is moving in slow motion. Richard grabs the pommel of his horse and pulls himself into the saddle. The attacking knights are in a flying V-Formation pounding down the slopes of the valley, at the head of the wedge is Sir William Marshal who is smiling demonically.

Richard is unarmoured, his white tunic blows in the wind, he draws his sword in defiance and stands up in the saddle roaring. Richard's display is characteristically brave, but pointless, Richard's sword and unarmoured form will be a poor defence against the veteran Marshal and his three metre, razor sharp lance. Richard's bodyguards spring into action hurling themselves into Marshal's path but they are scattered aside, unable to land even a single blow on the experienced soldier.

Marshal is close enough now to see the whites of Richard's eyes. Marshal is not a vindictive killer, but he is a soldier, he will do what he is ordered to. The only problem is, nobody has ordered him to kill Richard, Marshal can say with no real certainty that The Old King would want him to kill his oldest surviving son. Whilst Marshal and Richard are not best of friends, they are certainly familiar. After all, Marshal has spent pretty much his entire professional career in servitude to the Plantagenet family, firstly Eleanor, then Young Henry and now The Old King. Marshal has attended meetings with Richard, they have fought alongside one another, Marshal has got drunk with him and laughed at his jokes. Something passes between the two men

At the last moment, Marshal lowers his lance, instead of killing Richard, he skewers his War Horse killing it instantly and smashes into the side of the Prince. Richard is thrown fifteen feet from his horse and his breath is slammed out of his chest as he hits the floor. Marshal wrenches his lance upwards, it explodes out of Richard's horse in an arc of red mist. The sound of the equine's back snapping as the lance cuts through it carries across the battlefield, Marshal roars.

He circles back around, ready to capture Richard, but the moment is gone, it is too late for now Richard's men are organised. They have formed up around him and their superior numbers are telling across the battlefield, their probing spears are driving the chancer attackers back. Marshal and his men retreat and join The Old King at the Palace of Chinon.

In years to come, Richard will tell the tale of how armed with just a sword, he stood high in his spurs and deftly parried Marshal's lance at the final moment and heroically sprung clear of his saddle, so as to avoid certain death. You and I know this isn't true, so does Marshal, Richard does deep down too although he will never admit it.

Chapter 17: My legitimate children were the real bastards

At the Palace in Chinon, The Old King is dazed. His stomach aches, burns and stabs with anger. His days are spent relentlessly writing letters to key Barons he wishes to win back to his side, it is rare they return his correspondence. As before, the reality of his situation is somewhat marred with his impeccable record of achieving the impossible, surely he'll do it again, I mean he just has to…doesn't he?

The Old King clenched his fist in defiance. His leathery skin stretched over his knuckles so thinly it may as well be paper, his hand starts shaking. The Old King's stomach hurts and his limbs ache, he sinks to his knees, sobbing and screaming at the unfairness of it all.

"Why can I have no peace? Why? That is all that I want. Why must I forever be plagued by my children?" The Old King has dedicated his life to his nation and yet rest will not be his reward. The Old King has spent his life achieving the impossible, carrying the burden of leadership and even now, when his joints are rusted shut and his stomach burns with a thousand piercing daggers, even now, even now, he can get no sleep. The Old King bites hard on the straw mattress of his bed and unleashes a muffled scream with an internal agony.

He could not tell you whether or not he slept, or just lay there, in pain, he could not tell you how much time passed although some must have, for the candle burned down to the wick. He could not tell you when he stopped hyperventilating, it seemed like he had been trying to calm himself for days, months, maybe even years. His eyes are streaming and he whimpers sadly. Most concerning for The Old King though was that it felt like something inside of him had burst, the ache within his stomach now screams with red-hot fire, as poisoned pus permeates his guts.

The Old King feels like he is going to die, even if destined to pass alone in his chamber, The Old King wishes his final moments to be with a sword in his hand. He draws it smoothly from its sheath. The tonal ring as the sword comes free causes a flicker in The Old King's loins he has not felt for many years. He does a few practice passes in the air. Suddenly, as if from nowhere, a spectral vision of his deceased eldest son, Young Henry, appears before him.

"Come on Father, you're too old for this, you need to give in, it's time for the younger generation to take their turn," Young Henry stated this in the calm, soft and melodic voice he had always been blessed with.

"What? No. You're not meant to be here. I'm as fit as I've ever been. I beat you didn't I? I can destroy Richard and this upstart Philip." The Old King gnaws at his fingernails. He furtively glances around the room as if at any moment, every corner of the chamber might populate itself suddenly with spectres of his dead rivals.

Young Henry sighs, "You were fifteen years younger when you beat me the first time. The second time, let's be honest, you got lucky."

"I'm stronger than I've ever been," The Old King mutters distractedly.

Young Henry looks annoyed. He swings his blade in a slow sideways arc towards the Old King's midsection. Clutching his sword in a two-handed shaking grip, The Old King barely manages to raise it and parry in time. A dull ring sounds across the chamber. Young Henry laughs, although it is with sympathy.

"Stop," stuttered the Old King, "Please stop, I am not well, please stop."

"What do you think Richard is going to do to you Father? You've been lucky this far, it's time to give in. Richard is an animal." Young Henry lowered his blade and shrugged apologetically.

Young Henry had made an unfair comment. The Old King had not been lucky at any point in his career. He had fought tooth and nail for every inch of his kingdom against outside vultures and his own flesh and blood. The Old King's upper lip bared and he launched forward, swinging a clumsy strike at the ghost of his deceased son.

"Oh! What's this? There's life in the old dog yet hey!" Young Henry parries easily and smiles at his hunched-over and panting father, he spanks him lightly on the arse with the flat of his blade, "Come on Old Man, let's dance!"

The Old King may be doubled over, but in some ways he has not stood this tall for some time, he barks and snarls and spits nails. He lunges at the ghost of his deceased son. Their blades flash and cross. At first Young Henry is clearly humouring his elderly Father. Each block is punctuated by a patronising comment, Young Henry attacks at half power, at a fraction of the speed he is capable of commanding, the whole dance has the feel of a training game.

Which each swing, parry or half-butterfly arc, the elderly King is loosening up though and with each step, he becomes stronger. His shoulders no longer creak, his stomach does not hurt and he is smiling. He is enjoying himself. With each blow he becomes faster, deadlier. What had started as absolute confidence on the face of Young Henry, is slowly turning to terror, once again he is being beaten by his father.

The Old King watches the overhead swing from his ghost of a son cut towards his head, at the last moment he twists, grabbing his son's wrist he uses his own momentum against him and hurls him over his shoulder. As the ethereal form of Young Henry flies across the chamber before hitting the stone floor, he explodes into a thousand shards of light.

The Old King stands, alone, in the middle of the master chamber, he is panting heavily and holds his sword aloft in victory. Sweat drips freely from him and his muscles tremble from the exertion. The Old King feels…fantastic. He hasn't felt so alive in years, his gut no longer burns and his path ahead is clear. How an earth could I have felt a slave to circumstances when I am a master of my own destiny, The Old King wonders with a grim smile?

Now he could see clearly, The Old King could see a thousand political manoeuvres that would put Richard and Philip on the backfoot. Beating Richard, that was simple. He had a massive weakness. The barons of Aquitaine, how could he have been so stupid? The Old King giggled at the simplicity of it all. Providing he had Sir William Marshal with him, who was stood outside his chamber, and his son Count John of course, who was managing issues on the Southern Borders, the plan would work, it couldn't fail.

The Old King felt a wave of love for those two key people who had remained loyal to him, in particular his son John. Family love should be a given, but that wasn't the case for The Old King so yes, he cherishes John's love and loyalty above any other.

Three booming knocks sound upon the chamber door, "Sire?"

"Enter," The Old King is pacing with a restless energy his servants have not seen for some time. His synapses were firing wildly, there were so many moves he could make against these usurpers. The Old King was actually looking forward to the fight, he relished it, he needed it. He would retain his kingdom, he would imprison Richard and Philip, he would impart his legacy to his youngest son, John.

"Sire, as requested, the list of traitors who have defected over to the ruinous Richard."

The Old King snatched the parchment from the servant. Their eastern frontier, that was the way to smash Richard and Philip. Crossbowmen on the ravine, shoot down, cause a landslide, retreat to the river, burn the bridge, excite the Aquitaine barons, it was all so obvious. The Old King unrolled the list of traitors, at the top of the list was a name he did not expect to see.

It was John, his favourite son. The Old King sits back on the floor. The searing pain in his stomach returns with vengeance.

The Old King is spent. The bottomless reservoir of energy he has drank from throughout his entire life has ran dry. The news that his youngest and favourite son has betrayed him has, metaphorically at least, killed him. Preparations are made for The Old King's complete and unequivocal surrender. A meeting is arranged in a neutral field outside the town of Chinon.

A life of constant tremor shocks from his horse's hooves hitting the dirt at full speed, has left The Old King's joints shot, he can barely walk. For a moment, he looks at his equine standing a full half metre taller than his own hunched stature and he hangs his head. Wordlessly, Marshal steps forward and lifts the Old King into his saddle. If Marshal is horrified by how little The Old King weighs, his face does not show it.

The Old King rides out to the centre of the field alone, for this was one of the conditions. His baggy plain tunic is drenched in sweat and clings to The Old King's sides, his ribs are visible. He meets Richard and Philip in the middle of the field. A stabbing pain curses his stomach and he clutches it once more, doubling over, he sobs loudly but manages to turn it into what could passably be interpreted as a roar. The Old King will not raise his head for this entire meeting.

Philip, to be fair to him, is shocked. He can't believe this little old man, broken and bent and not long for this world, has been the arch nemesis that he and Richard have expended so much energy overthrowing. Philip motions for The Old King to sit if he would be more comfortable, this suggestion invokes a snort of derision from the senior monarch.

Looking at the shadow that had once been his Father,

Richard feels no sorrow or regret. The Old King had imprisoned Eleanor of Aquitaine for sixteen years, that was time Richard would never get back, "I swore I would make you pay for what you did to my mother and today is the day I deliver on that promise," snarls Richard.

The Old King will hand over the entire empire to Richard, what else could he do? He didn't really have another move open to him. In the final moments of the meeting, The Old King hugs Richard closely and whispers in his ear, "God grant that I may not die until I have had my revenge on you." The Old King will not get his wish.

Henry II of England a.k.a. The Old King, died 1189 July 6th. Modern doctors who have assessed records that described the symptoms he suffered from in his final days and the chronic stomach pain he endured for a long time prior, have declared it likely he died from a perforated stomach ulcer. There are a range of causes for a stomach ulcer, but the one that should jump out to us, is stress. When wasn't The Old King stressed? If it wasn't Young Henry, it was Richard, when it was finally no longer Richard, it was John. At least now, with any hope, the old man can get some rest.

Richard visits his father's body and kneels by his deathbed. Richard would rather be taking a long piss on the old man's corpse, but still, one must honour tradition and so Richard does his best to look respectful. A blood clot suddenly became dislodged and haemorrhaged from The Old King's nose. Those who witnessed it took this to be a sign that from beyond the grave, The Old King was pointing his finger at the man responsible for his death, Richard.

King Richard, the first of his name, was crowned in 1189. He will come to be known as the infamous, Richard the Lionheart. He frees his mother, Eleanor of Aquitaine, she is sixty-seven years of age by this point but still sharp as a razor. She returns to Aquitaine to assist with ruling the province, the barons cheer her return.

As for The Lionheart, he can hear bells in his future.

Not wedding bells, although he is under pressure to get on and do that.

"Richard, yours has been the longest engagement in the history of the world, I just don't understand why you don't want to marry my sister?" pouted Philip Augustus.

What Philip doesn't know, is that since Richard's bride to be was defiled by his own father, he has no intention of marrying her. Richard just isn't sure how to get out of the engagement.

No, the bells The Lionheart hears in his future are not the bells of marriage, they are the bells of Jerusalem. Like his mother before him, Richard wants to go on crusade. The Pope would also very much like him to. Since losing Jerusalem, The Pope has been pleading with all of the European Kings to sail East immediately.

Chapter 18: Let's get married in Greece

The Lionheart assembles his forces in Northern Italy. The docks are crawling with men and the King has enough soldiers to fill one hundred and fifty warships. This Crusade is not a token gesture from Richard to appease the Pope, he is deadly serious, he fully intends to win back Jerusalem on behalf of Christendom. The scale of invasion force that Richard is taking with him is staggering, regimented men, as far as the eye can see, great war ships, flat packed siege engines. The people love him for it. If this does not guarantee every man, woman and child in the Plantagenet empire a favourable judgement when they reach the pearly gates, what possibly could? Those that grumble and ask how much this was all costing and foretold of an increase in future taxes are scolded as naysayers, "how can you not feel pride? Stop being such a miserable old sod!"

As the Lionheart walks across the boarding plank onto his ship, his crimson cloak billows in his wake. Once he has boarded, he turns towards the gathered, cheering crowds and raises a fist high towards the sun in salute. The spectators roar their approval. Richard tilts his head, he is used to bullying and abusing the people, not being cheered by them, this was new territory for The Lionheart.

"With a goodly wind and fair fortune, we will be near the Holy Land in just a few days." declares Richard.

"We are nowhere near the Holy Land," mused Richard just a few days later, "and this wind seems to be getting worse!"

The Lionheart is right, the wind was indeed getting worse.

The fleet of ships is caught in a tempest and the driving gales batter the vessels into buffering waves. The tumultuous swell of the ocean raises the sorrowful sailors high into the clouds before smashing them back down again into the depths of hell. The trick was, to hit each wave before it broke at exactly a forty five degree angle, even for an experienced sailor though this was a fiendishly difficult task.

"Hold steady!" the Captain screams as he is smashed with salty sea spray. Frantically, he searches for assistance to wrestle the sluggish wheel that is in danger of breaking his hold. Simultaneously, he is crying out for a brave soul to climb the mast and cut the sails.

Seamen beg to jettison cargo and gain a modicum of control over the bucking triremes across the fleet, "Please Captain, before it is too late!" the order is not given. In reality, it is probably already too late to hurl the cargo overboard, the lashing, relentless rain has no doubt rendered the cargo water sodden and impossible to lift. Besides, who wanted to explain to The Lionheart they had thrown his favourite trebuchet overboard? In many ways, dying at sea seemed preferable to facing the wrath of Richard.

The fleet is scattered across the pitch black waters. The majority of Richard's ships manage to safely make landfall at the island of Crete. If the Lionheart was frustrated with the lack of progress they had made, he didn't show it. If anything he seemed delighted at the turn of events, he thought the whole thing a tremendous adventure. He had been previously concerned about the boredom of a long sea voyage and yet here he was, not two days in and already barking out orders in the midst of a genuine crisis. It wasn't quite as good as an out and out military campaign, but it was pretty damn close.

The Lionheart was concerned though, three of his larger ships were missing and he would like them back. Word arrived that they had sunk in sight of the port of Cyprus. Troublingly, word was also brought to him that the wreckages had been pilfered and his surviving men arrested into slavery by the Emperor of Cyprus, that wouldn't do at all. These ships carried both important men and valuable treasures. The Lionheart still wants to do battle in the Holy Land and do a bit of a Crusade and all that, but in Cyprus, he has a rival ruler who was really close that he can fight right now.

When the Lionheart arrives at the island, it is to find great sea chains are raised and the port is closed. Interestingly enough, a ship carrying the Queen of Sicily and her maidens bobbed around in the open waters outside the island, trying to survive the hangovers of the great storm. The Lionheart wastes no time in paying a visit to the Queen of Sicily adrift at sea, to charmingly reassure her and her maidens that he was there to save them, everything was under control, they should not worry about a thing. Whilst the Queen of Sicily makes eyes at the Lionheart, Richard cannot tear his gaze away from the daughter of the King of Navarre, Berengaria, who is also aboard the vessel. Of course Richard likes this maiden, her name literally translates as "Bear Spear."

After peacocking in front of his damsels in distress, Richard sends a messenger to land demanding the port is opened. The letter is ignored, rude, thought the King. A second letter is sent and also ignored, double rude, the Lionheart is now snarling involuntarily.

The fourth letter finally does receive a response and it is one The Lionheart is delighted to read, "The Emperor of Cyprus advises that he will not be freeing any of the Lionheart's men and he does not fear the Plantagenet King," mutters Richard. The Lionheart smiles, "Attack, we attack Cyprus immediately!"

The Lionheart and his bodyguards are the first onto the beach. Supported by an endless rain of arrows from the archers upon the decks, they soon rout the vastly outnumbered defenders. The men still aboard the ships cheer as the great sea chain is lowered and the port is clear once more. The Queen of Sicily signals her approval with the whisper of a smile and the slightest nod of her regal head.

The Emperor of Cyprus flees from the port to the countryside, with his men loading Richard's stolen loot into the wagons. They disappear into the mountains, The Lionheart does not give chase, he doesn't know these lands and to pursue them blindly would be foolish. Also, he wants to get drunk with the Queen of Sicily and her entourage.

That evening, whilst the King is busy wining and dining the Queen of Sicily and her ladies, he receives word from the Emperor of Cyprus. The Emperor advises Richard that he will do battle with the Plantagenet King and even gives directions where his camp can be found. Richard furrows his brow, the man was clearly hoping to draw the Lionheart away from the walls of the captured port.

Richard stays up well into the early hours of the morning, talking and drinking with the Queen of Sicily, the daughter of the King of Navarre and their maidens. Despite this he is still up a long time before first light. The man has an iron constitution, he is as strong as an ox and a night of drinking is not going to stop him rising in time for a battle.

Silently, the Lionheart and his men advance upon the position the Emperor has outlined in his directions. They are nervous, the whole think reeks of an ambush, but still, they have the numbers and Richard wants to impress. He also doesn't really believe that The Emperor of Cyprus will have given the true co-ordinates to his camp. Turns out he had though, not only that, they'd all also decided to have a lie in. The Lionheart and his men arrive to find the majority of their opponents asleep.

Richard and his men make short work of butchering the sentries, they then move on to the tents. They creep, by moonlight, silently from canvas to canvas, slitting the throats of the officers within. By the time the Emperor is awoken by one of his men's screams it is already far too late. The slaughter is largely complete. He runs, naked and without provisions into the night followed by a small band of men. The Lionheart, who was scratching his head, bemused at the easiness of it all, found the treasure in two wagons at the centre of the encampment.

Alone, scared and without even a sock to hide his tackle, the Emperor sent messages to the Lionheart to sue for peace. The terms offered were unbelievable, the Emperor would give up his daughter for marriage to Richard, surrender all of his lands, give the Plantagenet King his armies for use in the crusades and even personally accompany him to the Holy Land. This was sworn in front of an honourable band of witnesses.

When something seems too good to be true though, it usually is, that evening, the Emperor once again took flight, planning to escape the island. When The Lionheart was told, he found it all quite funny. They were on an island for Christ's sake, where could the Emperor possibly escape to?

Richard sent forth his armies and surrounded the waterways with his war ships. When the Emperor was eventually caught, he threw himself down at the feet of the Lionheart. He begged that he should be spared, he also pleaded to avoid the indignation and discomfort of being clasped in iron chains. The Lionheart listened patiently before agreeing to his request, there was no need for iron fetters, instead, he ordered chains of gold and silver were made for the Emperor. Yes, the Lionheart is sadistic and bloodthirsty, but he does possess a certain style and maybe even a dark sense of humour.

The Lionheart will marry a member of the Queen of Sicily's entourage, the daughter of the King of Navarre, on a ceremony right there on Cyprus. His ranks are swelled with the Emperor's men and the Lionheart will eventually flip the island of Cyprus to the Knight Templars for a tidy profit, before even later buying it back for less and selling it again. Richard's Crusader army felt invincible as they drummed the rhythm for the oar strokes and propelled themselves East.

The Lionheart stood on the prow of his ship and smiled, this was what adventuring was all about. He held his new bride close to him as the wind whips through his hair and he points his sword towards the Holy Land.

Philip is not going to like this, thinks Richard.

Chapter 19: The Siege of Acre

Philip is having a rough time. He is camped outside the mighty walled city of Acre in the Holy Land and he is doing everything he can to siege it. To say this was proving difficult, would be an understatement. It isn't even so much the Saracen defenders that are troubling him, instead, like a human that has developed antibodies, the very land was trying to expel the foreign invaders from their core.

Firstly, there was the heat, it was unrelenting and the Westerners fresh off the boat from cooler climates hated it. Dressed in full armour and marching around a desert should have been a guaranteed route to Heaven, quickly though, the men cooking in their tin can armour had been transported to Hell. Supply chain calculations and military manoeuvres were all warped from what Philip was used to.

By his best guesses, men seemed to be drinking almost three times as much water as they typically did when marching about in the temperate climates of France. The horses couldn't find sufficient plant life to remain energised and, well, alive. Philip was enduring an impossibly steep learning curve on desert warfare and men were dying daily as a result of his bad decisions. He had never felt the weight of leadership weigh so heavily as it does right now.

As the men pissed dehydrated black sludge and sweat their way through the days, they found comfort both in their faith and the certainty that things couldn't get any worse. After all, the desert wasn't about to get hotter, supply chains should soon normalise. This was as hard as it was going to get, thought Philip, of course, that was before the tarantulas turned up.

They arrived in plagues and droves, infinite in their number and murderous in their intent. They would scuttle out at night, rising from the sand in colonies and scurrying all over the men's naked, clammy flesh. Heroically, the Crusaders would arise to chivalrously do combat with these largely non-lethal arachnids. You could hardly see the experienced warriors' skin, so covered were they in the insects that weighed around 0.0005% of their own body mass. The men parried, they thrust, they screamed and they pranced, dancing their insane dance under the full moon and flickering camp fires of the desert.

Eventually, the heroic crusaders fight their way through the beasts to form a unit. Bravely, they nobly bang pots and pans together, this startles the eight-legged freaks who scurry off into the blackness. For God and Christendom, The Crusaders drive the insects back.

It almost certainly didn't happen like the records from the period suggest. Whilst there are certainly tarantulas in The Holy Land, it's difficult to find any zoological scholarly heavyweight who can corroborate any instance, ever, of tarantulas behaving in this manner. For one thing, Tarantulas don't really live in plagues or droves and like many sentiment beings, they try not to get beaten up. They will not typically attack an armed encampment of fully grown men of whom could easily kill them.

It's certainly possible a number of solitary spiders were disturbed from the burrows they resided in. They may well have scuttled into the dark desert night. They wouldn't have slowed as they ran over unfamiliar lumps and bumps in the desert, the sand was changing all the time after all. The spiders were scared so they ran faster as these bumps shifted and moved, but again, the nature of sand was quite shifty and movey and these particular insects had never encountered humans before. As the men began screaming, the vibrations would have travelled up the hairs on their eight legs and spooked them further, some may have bitten out in fear.

A tarantula bite is not dissimilar to a bee sting, absolutely it's unpleasant, but probably not lethal. To say that the tarantula's had any real impact on The Crusaders physically seems unlikely; it can't have been good for morale though. These men were many miles from home, they bedded down alone each night under unfamiliar stars and they did this all at the bequest of a Pope none of them had ever met. As they continued on their Holy mission, to find even the insects of this strange, scorching land were both terrifying and hostile, would have certainly darkened their mood.

More of a problem for Philip though than either the heat or the spiders, was the influenza epidemic that was ripping through his camp. The cramped, unsanitary conditions of the sieging army catalysed the sickness leaping from patient to patient at an alarming rate. Respiratory influenza diseases kill people today, this is with all of the wonders of modern medical science, the medieval crusaders camp was a petri dish of infection and death.

Philip walks through his army camp trying to both lift morale and not get sick himself. He hands out water to the thirsty. He gives pep talks to those healthy enough to engage in the upcoming attack and dodges the question that is constantly asked of him, "When will Richard the Lionheart be arriving?"

Philip had expected Richard almost a month ago, he brought with him both coin and a large proportion of their army. Philip thought his friend would show up, but he doesn't know this for sure. Reports had reached the Capetian monarch that fierce storms had ripped through the Mediterranean Sea and the Lionheart's fleet had fallen victim to the tempest. Philip deeply hoped his friend and future brother-in-law was okay, he also knew that without The Lionheart's soldiers, The Third Crusade was lost before it began.

Philip is broken, he is all but defeated and has never felt so alone. Upon the soft breeze drifting in from the sea, he begins to hear the unfamiliar sound of woodwind instruments, blaring out medieval dance music. What new devilry was this, Philip wondered, what fresh hell? Perhaps it was some kind of counter-attack from the Muslim defenders? Perhaps it was the Sultan Saladin riding down from the mountain tops to break the siege? Philip ran towards the sounds of music and what he saw bewildered him completely.

Sailing into view, was the Lionheart and his one hundred and fifty majestically rigged ships. Music was blaring from every vessel, men were dancing about the decks, great sails bore the Lionheart's three rampant lions. Horns began to sound as the fleet prepared for landfall announcing their arrival further. The Lionheart stood on the prow of the lead ship, he wears white flowing robes, in his right hand is held his sword that points at the city of Acre, in his left is his crossbow which is pointed towards the sky.

"Acre, the city is ours!" shouts the Lionheart, his soldiers cheer.

Philip and his men cannot flipping believe this. They have spent over a month with their skin burning under the fierce sun, battling with giant spiders, angry Saracens and being indiscriminately wiped out by a fever. When The Lionheart does finally bother to show up, he seems to be the commodore of a floating festival.

Philip shakes his head slowly as Richard makes landfall, "Good journey Richard?"

"I have done battle with storms sent from Hell," The Lionheart replies striding into camp.

"I did hear about the storms, I'm glad you're safe," says Philip.

"I invaded Cyprus," Richard marches towards the centre of the camp.

"Okay, why?"

Richard doesn't answer, "And I took the most beautiful bride in all of the world, you're going to love her."

There is a pregnant pause. "You're engaged to my sister Richard, or did you forget?" snarls Philip, he is furious.

"I didn't forget, I love her though and you can't stand in the way of true love Philip, come on," Richard speeds up his march stopping only to fill his water canteen from a communal trough.

"Richard, be careful, the camp is sick. I have fresh water behind the lines that the men have not drank from," even though Philip is furious, he needs Richard.

Richard winks at him, "Philip, I have been chosen by God to do his work, he will not strike me down with sickness, set up a meeting with this Sultan Saladin, I wish to take the measure of mine enemy."

A meeting is set up with Saladin immediately. Once it is time to parlay though, Richard is unable to attend, for he is burning a high fever and unable to stop vomiting. Richard has caught the sickness and despite the field doctors' best efforts, he is not getting any better. Philip also catches it about the same time but seemingly a more mild dose. Philip is back out and about two or three days later, whereas Richard seems to be steadily getting worse.

Saladin, for his part, proves that chivalry is not a reserved prerogative of the Wests. He sends a basket of iced dates, figs and pomegranates to his rival. Saladin wants to defeat Richard, but not like this.

In juxtaposition to the Lionheart's flat-packed siege engines, which have by now been unloaded from the ships and grow taller every day, Richard himself is shrinking in stature. His condition is worsening. Eventually, the trebuchets are ready. Each is individually named, the two largest are christened, "God's own Catapult" and "Bad Neighbour". Philip visits the Plantagenet King's sickbed to advise the Crusaders are ready to attack. Richard cries out no, he begs him to delay, to wait. The Lionheart cannot bear the thought of being left out of his moment of glory, it is he who should be leading this attack not Philip! Philip watches Richard drift in an out of lucidity before deciding no, he will go it alone, before the influenza has killed too many of his soldiers to make the attack even possible.

The attack starts well. "Bad Neighbour" rains destruction down, killing twelve men with its first missile. It even manages to pulverise part of the Cursed Tower that has guarded the North-East parapet of the city for decades. "God's own Catapult" holds her own too, smashing sections of wall and dropping rocks that reverberate across the city. Saladin attempts to break the crusaders' control of the coast by sending a small, innocent enough looking supply ship to the city.

Now that the decision had been made to attack, meagre food supplies would be unlikely to make much difference to the siege and the naval warships ignore this tiny cog, instead they continue their bombardment of the walls. Cunningly though, Saladin has actually laden the ship with over six hundred fighting men, it nearly gets through too, but at the last minute The Crusaders see this Trojan horse for what it really is and attack.

It does not all go the way of The Crusaders though, for they are fighting a war on two fronts. Not only do they face the defenders of Acre, but Saladin is countering every strike, every attack that they make. Saladin charges down from the mountains bellowing unfamiliar war cries and stinging The Crusaders' flanks like a scorpion.

Saladin has his own siege engines too, his golden child is named, "Evil Cousin" and it spits back at The Crusader's ballistic team with venom. A number of Western catapults were disabled and Greek fire was liberally poured down upon the attackers.

Remember Philip of Flanders? The great strategical genius who cheated in knightly tournaments against Young Henry? He dies during The Siege of Acre of the same pox The Lionheart currently battles with.

It is the ground tremors from the siege projectiles that shock Richard from his sick bed. He is drenched in sweat but he feels the vibrations on the ground and it feels good. His servants rush to him as he frantically turns his head left and right, trying desperately to take in his surroundings with feverishly blurred vision, "Carry me to the front lines, the battle has began without me!"

"Sire, you are sick, you are not well, what is best is for..." the field doctor is grabbed by The Lionheart, who repeats himself however this time screaming in the man's face.

As The Lionheart is carried through the disease, death, darkness and despair of the camp, he seems to perk up a little. He begins to chat to those who carry him, about his time in Aquitaine and his mother. Once he is just behind the front line, where those who have been wounded in the initial assault are screaming, limbs missing, horrific burns, The Lionheart is positively jovial, he is joking even. He keeps trying to high five people. Richard begins to frown, a defender on the wall sticks his head up, "shoot that one!" shouts Richard pointing wildly, "Quickly," the defender ducks, "Oh it's too late..." Another popped up like whack-a-mole, "Go for that one now!" once more Richard's men are too slow, "For goodness' sake hand me that crossbow..."

Richard lies on his sickbed before the walls of Acre, sipping orange juice through a straw with a cold flannel on his forehead and takes pot shots at defenders upon the ramparts. Even in his feverish state, most of the time his aim is true. As he props himself up on his fluffy pillows beneath the beating sun, killing random adversaries that dare to stick their heads above the parapet, Richard finds himself smiling, he is starting to feel better.

The Crusaders win and conquer the city of Acre, Saladin retreats with a guerrilla army into the nearby mountains. By the time the final defender has surrendered, Richard even feels well enough to walk into the conquered settlement himself. Climbing over the rubble, he blinks through the dust at the city walls, flying high fluttering cinematically, are Philip Augustus' Capetian flag and

Leopold of Austria's. The Lionheart is not happy, he sees red. He marches up the steps and storms his way across to the offensive protruding flag poles.

"No!" Richard screams, his courtiers draw back, they have seen his temper before and want no part of it, "Absolutely not! This crusade was mine and Philip's, but more mine. It certainly wasn't," Richard is reeling in the Austrian flag frantically, "Leopold of bloody Austria's!"

"Now see here," squeaks Leopold, "I was actually in the thick of the fighting whilst you were lying there in your sick bed."

Richard mimics Leopold in an offensively, effeminate high-pitched voice, "I was actually in the thick of the fighting whilst you were in your sick bed," Richard returns to his normal tone, "who brought the most men?"

"Well, I suppose you did Richard."

"That's King Richard the mother-flipping Lionheart to you," Richard rips the Austrian flag down, scrunches it into a ball and drop kicks it from the walls. King Leopold storms off chuntering angrily.

"Richard, can I have a word with you?" Philip asks.

"Of course" Richard replies.

"I need to leave Richard, I need to return home to Eastern France."

"Leave? Don't be ridiculous we've only just got here!" Richard throws his arms up in the air.

"No, you've only just got here Richard. Philip of Flanders, the great strategist, has died. He had substantial land holdings throughout Northern France and he dies without an heir. My country is in danger of being ripped apart by civil war fighting for his territories, I need to go home or I might not have one to return to." Philip shrugs to his friend.

Philip does need to return to France to preside over the arguments for the lands of Flanders, that isn't a lie, but he is also not being completely honest. Philip is furious with

The Lionheart, for he wants to be a good brother and he has no intention of riding side by side with the man who has just dumped his sister when they had been engaged for so long. Philip swears he will make Richard pay for spurning his sister for some Cyprus floozy.

Richard is concerned. Philip and he got on, to a degree, but their families didn't have the best track record of playing nice. He makes Philip swear on every available Holy relic present that he won't attack Richard whilst he is away in the Holy Land. When this isn't enough, he makes him swear the same in front of a band of honourable men. What else can Richard do? The Crusade isn't done for The Lionheart, he will not yield until he has won back Jerusalem, that's just his nature. As The Lionheart watches Philip swear on the final relic they have available to them, the Holy Jock Strap of the Messiah, a messenger scurries up to them.

"Hello Sire, um, a quick word, well, message really, more of a message," he laughs nervously, "King Leopold of Austria has departed, left, you know, that is to say he has officially set sail as it were," the messenger braced for a classic Richard blow up.

"Has he really…" Richard is stroking his chin, "Who's that then?"

The messenger is confused, "Well, he's the King of Austria…" Richard stares blankly so the messenger continues, "You know, he's the one who often wears a crown? You've definitely met him sire, on a number of occasions in fact."

"Of course, of course I have," Richard nods smiling but his vague expression makes it clear he doesn't remember him at all, "Why's he left then?"

"He's very upset about the flag incident Sire."

"Ah," realisation dawns on The Lionheart, "he's the flag guy! Of course, yes I know him. So why's he left then?" asks Richard once more.

The messenger just isn't sure where to go at this point,

"Well, mainly about the incident sire, with the flag, that one, he's extremely upset."

The Lionheart shrugs, he looks confused and he waves the messenger away. Like that, The Lionheart is now the solitary commander of the coalition crusader forces.

His first action is to visit the prisoners from the siege. Here, it is fair to say, he has won a staggering booty. Shackled in the courtyard, are over two thousand of Saladin's prize soldiers and non-combatant men, woman and children. Richard smiles evilly, it's always good to have some prisoners.

A deal is struck with Saladin. Richard will return the Muslim prisoners and pay one hundred thousand gold pieces and in return receive the *True Cross*, a shard of the original cross that Jesus himself was nailed to. The morning of the exchange however, a messenger is sent to Richard, "due to unforeseen circumstances the deal would have to be delayed."

This was frustrating for The Lionheart, who only possessed slightly more patience than his late father, but these were fast paced times and communication channels were poor, he sighed deeply, there was little he could do after all.

Richard busied himself with work in the city of Acre. He personally supervised the packing up of the great catapults, he was keen that as soon as the exchange was complete momentum should be maintained, they should get straight on the road for Jerusalem. "God's own Catapult" and "Bad Neighbour" are both flat packed and loaded on to carts. A new date is set for the exchange of the prisoners for the True Cross.

Once again, infuriatingly, the deal is delayed. At the last minute, Saladin demands all of the prisoners released before the True Cross handed over. This was unacceptable to The Lionheart who smelled foul play. Where was his security? How did he know Saladin would keep to his side of the bargain? Negotiations collapsed. Richard watched

Winter roll in and he ordered labourers to rebuild the walls, higher even than before. He knew that idle hands did the devil's work so he wanted to keep the men busy, he wasn't sure he was succeeding in this endeavour though.

The city was a den of vices; prostitution, gambling and drunkenness ravaged Acre, The Crusaders loved it. Even members of the clergy of the city were renting their rooms by the hour to ladies of the night and their clients, it was greasy and it was killing The Lionheart. This wasn't how he had envisioned a crusade.

Now Richard is no prude, he enjoys sex (not that he has ever paid for it before) but on a crusade all manners of fornication was forbidden. He was watching noble men, on a mission from God, catch the clap from whores, drink themselves into oblivion and lose pay they hadn't even earned. The longer this continued, the more entrenched the behaviour seemed to be. Providing the swop was soon completed, The Lionheart was confident he could realign The Crusaders' moral compass back towards righteousness and Jerusalem.

Spring blossoms, with it is yet another delay to the deal. Friction again sparks on the clarification of who would hand over their side of the deal first. It galled The Lionheart it was even a question, he had two thousand prisoners for Christ's sake? It also infuriated him that by now he had lost all momentum he had built up, by this point he had been stationary in Acre for almost a year. Whilst his chainmail rusted from the salty sea air, Saladin's men were travelling the land, reinforcing their position and preparing themselves for the inevitable assault on Jerusalem. The Lionheart's blood boils as he realises the constant spoiling of the deal was no coincidence, Saladin was doing it on purpose.

On the 20th of August 1191, Richard the Lionheart leads the two thousand prisoners and a number of Muslim non-combatants from the city of Acre to the top of the nearby hill of Ayyadieh. There, in full view of Saladin's field camp, the unarmed men, women and children are brutally hacked to pieces by The Crusaders, it will come to be known as The Massacre of Ayyadieh.

Saladin and his men are distraught as they hear the screams of their captured comrades butchered like cattle. They attempt a rescue attack but The Crusaders beat them back and the massacre continues in full view of all.

This was considered bloodthirsty, even for the time period, but kind of inevitable. Richard had a particularly nasty strand of the Plantagenet temper that we have seen explode before, he also has a track record for massacring prisoners. The Lionheart certainly knew how to send a message. He was also all about the logistics and practicalities of warfare. What the hell was he meant to do with two thousand prisoners? Once he left Acre and got back on the campaign trail he wouldn't be able to guard these men, he couldn't transport them and he didn't want to feed them anymore. Did Saladin really expect Richard to do anything else?

In retaliation, Saladin will execute the thirteen hundred Christian prisoners he is holding. He will also send a rider to Damascus with the one True Cross.

Chapter 20: Richard the Lionheart, King of the Wilderness and nothing more

The True Cross was not the only Holy Relic out there. There was the Holy Lance, the spear that pierced Jesus' side as he hung upon the cross, the Turin shroud, the cloth Jesus' body was swathed in when he was buried. Even the Virgin Mary's belt got the nod as divine.

The first crusade upturned and unearthed many of these treasures. The cynical amongst us would conclude they were deemed Holy simply to inflate their value and offset the mammoth costs from the campaign. After all, the authentication process was hardly diligent. Any Knight Crusader could confirm whether an item was divine or just a ladies' belt. The industry of divine artifacts has weathered the years rather well. On Ebay today, one can buy a *divine touched nail*, which is to say a nail that has been caressed by another nail that was actually used during the crucifixion of Christ. If you were wondering, The 'buy it now' price was £899 at the time of writing (2020).

We aren't here to talk about holy nails, lances or belts though. We also are not here to ascertain whether they are worth £899, or more, or less. We are here to talk about the True Cross. The True Cross was certainly worth far in excess of £899 to Richard the Lionheart and the Crusaders. Men who ride into battle with the True Cross in proximity are invincible, they are blessed and have been seen time and again able to achieve the impossible.

The True Cross had been held aloft before tens of thousands of brave young men, who will die far from home. It will punctuate hundreds of speeches from ambitious generals. The True Cross will guide Peter the Hermit and Alexios as they break the siege of Nicaea, using the unorthodox strategy of rolling their war ships inland across great logs to bear down upon the city. It will be present when Baldwin III turns tail from the formidable Altuntash's wife. In short, The True Cross was everywhere, until it wasn't.

The Battle of Tiberias saw to that. Guy Lusignan was the commander in the field. As Guy prostrates himself at Saladin's feet in surrender and hands over the True Cross, Guy is offered a goblet of water. Guy declines it and passes it to his brother. Just as Guy's brother goes to take a sip, Saladin kicks it out from his hands. What Guy was not aware of, is that offering a drink to a prisoner in the Islamic culture was a sign the recipient was not to be killed. Saladin is quite annoyed at Guy refusing the drink. He advises that although Kings do not kill Kings, Guy's brother would be beheaded immediately. Saladin carried this out personally himself.

Following the Massacre of Ayyadieh, Richard leads the majority of his forces South, leaving behind only a skeleton army to defend the city. He has not, after all, travelled half-way across the known world for Acre, he has come for Jerusalem. To get there though, Richard and his men will need to pass through the Port of Jaffa. The Port of Jaffa is a small coastal city, a mere eighty kilometres away from his target of Jerusalem. Richard marches south, whilst his fleet of ships hug the coast, crawling painfully slowly alongside him transporting cargo, food, water and the ever ready protection of a regiment of archers on deck.

Every step felt like ten for the Lionheart. His concern was not unfounded either, his men were constantly harried throughout the march by Saladin's raiders. They would fire crossbow bolts into The Crusader's flank that was not protected by the sea and then dart away into the desert. The Saracens were trying to get The Crusaders to break rank in anger and pursue them where they would be easy prey. The Lionheart did what he could, he took care to deploy Generals that would maintain order and instil calmness.

After almost a week of this, the attacks stopped. The Crusaders were permitted to travel in peace for a few days at least. The Lionheart both cursed and cheered when the only road reached the forest of Arsuf; a fifteen mile stretch of woodlands. Whilst the cool foliage offered a shelter from the beating sun, it was also the perfect place for an ambush.

Sure enough, shortly into the forest, The Crusaders begin to see flashes of enemy scouts. At every turn they see them, scuttling off into the denser undergrowth visible one second, invisible the next. The Crusaders steeled themselves and marched on, they assessed every tree for threat whilst struggling to hear anything above the pumping of blood in their own ears. The forest seemed populated with Saladin and his men, every shadow was an assassin.

The actual assaults followed by this psychological warfare, was taking its toll on The Crusaders. It was even starting to erode the Lionheart's concrete resolve. Richard requested a parlay with the Muslim troops, he wants to come to some kind of agreement. Saladin was unavailable so Richard met with his brother, Al-Adil. Richard calmly proposed the Muslims should retreat back to Egypt and return all of The Holy Land to the Crusaders, it was a big ask. Al-Adil laughs Richard out of the meeting.

When Saladin does finally decide to commit to a main attack upon The Crusaders, he chooses his theatre of war well. Whilst there was sufficient tree coverage to hide his attack, it was also sparse enough for cavalry charges. The Lionheart is not known as the greatest military leader in Europe over this period for nothing though. He has painstakingly organised the troops of his army from the Templar Knights, to the Bretons and auxiliary soldiers into closely ordered battalions. No detail was left to chance. The great organiser of men and champion of warriors, suspected an attack from the rear. He put infantrymen and arbalests here to defend the rump of the column. These protectors are in turn watched over themselves by his famous shock troops, the Knight Templars.

Saladin began the attack with darts and arrows from the darkness off the path. He had his men bang on percussion instruments and their shields. This had the effect of throwing terrifying thunder about the trees, assaulting not just the men on the ground physically, but also their senses. This harrying was exhausting and the Lionheart's rear guard were forced backwards steadily, cowering behind their shields.

After what felt like forever of this, with the rear guard travelling painfully slowly but somehow still, just attached to the column, Saladin began the cavalry attacks. He slams wave after wave against The Crusaders, smashing his horsemen into the infantry troops who braced for impact. The Crusader crossbowmen tried to pick off the riders, but it was a difficult task. The tree covering meant that the Muslim riders were upon the Crusaders before a clear line of sight presented itself. With the Lionheart's strongest Generals deployed about the different regiments, the column was just about holding it together. Saladin himself and his own brother rode into battle, shoulder to shoulder with their men who fought with a renewed fervour, invigorated by the presence of their leaders. This proved too much for a number of the Crusader crossbowmen, who cast aside their heavy weapons asunder so that they might be able to desert with greater speed.

Word was sent to The Lionheart by the Generals who begged, "Use the Knights Templars. We need to return with a cavalry charge of our own." The Lionheart refused though, he wanted to allow Saladin's forces to over exert themselves and when they had barely the energy to swing a weapon, that was the moment he wanted to unleash the cavalry. It was a sound strategy, a bold one, but it was also risky as Hell. Leave it too late and there would not be enough fight left in his men to rally.

Eventually, it became too much for the Holy order of

the Knight Templars. Two of their number ignored Richard's orders and broke rank, they charged at the Turkish troops. The rest of the regiment were not to be denied this glory and were hot on their heels. Battles were fluid affairs and it was difficult to maintain control during the heat of combat at the best of times, The Lionheart knew this and whilst he was angry they had not waited for his orders, how he felt was now irrelevant. The charge had been made and what's more, it wasn't actually badly timed. The Lionheart shouted encouragement to any of the men that still were waiting for orders to charge against the Saracen soldiers, it was now or never.

The Knight Templars break away from the column and pour into Saladin's men. They whoop war charges and almost immediately are blade to blade with the enemy. This is bloody and gruesome, skull shattering combat. The confusion is only exacerbated by the darkness of the foliage and the unfamiliar terrain. The Lionheart has seen enough pivotal moments of combat to recognise that this is one, he charges in with his own bodyguard unit and he deals terrible destruction. He lashes left and right with his razor sharp Danish axe and band of bodyguards, the screams of the Saracens he kills are audible to Saladin a mile up the column.

The Lionheart's cool, composed commands he bellows somehow cut through the raucous noise of the battlefield, the Knight Templars continue to advance but this time in a more organised fashion. The Turkish men are forced to retreat.

Saladin was found, weary and sheltering under the shade of a ragged cloak. He has given away his personal tent to be used as a field hospital, he has given away his horse to a man whose leg had been pierced by an arrow. Saladin lies under the ragged cloak hyperventilating, eventually, breathing raggedly he stands and commands himself to some degree.

Saladin actually recovers quickly from this loss and

rallies his surviving troops. They abandon Jaffa to the Lionheart and his men. Instead, they ride cross-country towards Ramla to fortify the road and set up ambush points. This next checkpoint would be a mere twelve miles from Jerusalem. An advantage the Saracens undoubtedly have in their arsenal, is knowing exactly where The Crusaders final intended destination is.

Richard and his men's relief at reaching Jaffa cannot be underestimated. Nobody thought the road to Jerusalem would be easy, but The Crusaders felt like they had been through Hell. They spent almost two months in the sanctuary of the city, licking their wounds, recovering, preparing themselves. Besides, the orchards of Jaffa made a pleasant change to the diet of dead horses and desert insects they had lived from on the road.

As todays stretched into tomorrows, which in turn passed into next week, there always seemed a good reason not to leave. Best to not rush preparations, best to double check things and take it slowly. Besides, it was too hot to stress and run around in circles kicking up dust devils. Some of the prostitutes from Acre had even managed to make the journey South to join the men, as if The Crusaders needed another reason to stay. Hadn't they already done their part in the siege of Acre and their efforts to secure the port of Jaffa? Didn't they deserve to enjoy the leisurely pace of life and the security the walls of the city afforded?

Only the Lionheart found it hard to relax. He, like his father, must remain in constant forward motion to stay alive. One day, whilst out hawking in the hostile countryside, The Lionheart is surprised by a party of Muslim Scouts. Outnumbered and outgunned, the Lionheart races back for the port city, hotly pursued by his enemy. The King is only saved by one of his hawking companions abruptly pulling up his horse and claiming that he is the *"Malik,"* or King. The Lionheart escapes to safety as the Turks incorrectly cheer, believing that they have caught Richard the Lionheart.

The Lionheart has had enough of this necessary, but frustrating holiday. Yes, he and his men had some achievements under their belt, but The Lionheart does not do things by half. This godforsaken Holy Land, with its spiders and its whores, its deserts and its forests, its sands and its Saladin, was not going to beat him. The Crusaders were forty miles away from the Holy City, he could almost see the spires. It was time to finish this.

Although the Crusaders were closer than they had ever been, nobody was under any illusion that this final forty miles would be the hardest to date. They would also be required to leave the coastline and travel inland. This meant the support they had enjoyed from the fleet of ships carrying the majority of their supplies could no longer help them. In truth, the men of the Third Crusade who had travelled across Europe with the most honourable of intentions, would have given anything to return to one of the dice pits or brothels of Acre. Even better, they'd like to be back home in Europe. It was with weary shoulders and heavy hearts the Crusaders set off along the final stretch of the rocky road to Jerusalem.

So close to his goal, somehow, The Lionheart's certainty fails him. The Crusaders travelled just eleven of the remaining forty miles away from Jaffa before once more setting up a base, this time in the ruined city of Ramla. Here, amongst the derelict stone buildings that afforded little protection against either the Winter nights or Saladin's guerrilla troops, The Lionheart and his men would live in a sickening purgatory for six long weeks.

Saladin, by this point, was ready for both The Crusaders and Winter. He had pulled almost all of his men behind Jerusalem's walls in preparation for the inevitable showdown for the Holy City. The final fight would not come this year though.

At one point, The Crusaders ventured forward from the ruins of Ramla and got within two miles of Jerusalem, *two miles*! The whole ride, The Lionheart kept his gaze averted away from the horizon, he did not wish to look upon the Holy City until he could say he had won it.

The Lionheart decides not to launch a siege on the Holy City. The fully garrisoned walls guarded by zealous defenders, would have been a tough battle at the best of times. With Winter drawing in and an army of Turks in the mountains, The Lionheart would have been facing a war on two fronts against a backdrop of freezing, sub-zero nights. Back in Europe, when fighting his elder brother, The Lionheart had already lost one siege to General Winter, it was not an experience he was in a hurry to repeat.

This is perhaps where we see the true pedigree and creed of the Lionheart as a military campaigner. It took every modicum, every iota of discipline and self-control that Richard possessed to not attack the city when he was so close. Even as he ordered his men to retreat to the ruins of Ramla once more, he heard the triumphant fanfare in his ears as he replayed the familiar fantasy he harbours of marching victorious into the Holy City.

Whilst Richard was displaying sound and mature leadership in his custodianship of the allied Crusader forces, at a casual glance from pretty much everyone in Christendom, he looked weak as Hell. The campaign seemed rudderless, adrift. In response, soldiers began to desert The Lionheart's forces at an alarming rate. Some returned to the relative paradise of Jaffa, others retreated as far North as the brothels of Acre whilst those most disillusioned, bartered passage home to Europe.

The Lionheart remains in his outpost base in the ruined city of Ramla for Winter, he is King of the wilderness and nothing more. Richard could have retreated to the relative comfort of Jaffa, for it is only eleven miles away, but continuing to man his outpost in the ruins makes him feel a little closer to The Holy City and until he has done what he came for he does not feel he deserves comfort.

Eventually, The Lionheart decides to channel his

pious energy in a more constructive direction than simply moping around derelict buildings in the middle of the desert. He announces a section of his army and knights would march to Ascalon.

This was a holy city (not The Holy City), that had been conquered during the First Crusade. The town had been all but demolished from Saracen raids and two of the great castles that once guarded the entrance to the city had been levelled. The Lionheart instructed that all men, regardless of rank or status, would commit themselves to the rebuilding of these fortifications to their former glory.

Initially, the project did not have a positive effect on morale in the camp. The Crusaders didn't want to march halfway across the country during the Winter months. The Lionheart though could not rest, he needed to be moving and doing something and this labour of love was perfect.

Having focus is important and eventually this project did begin to buoy the mood of the soldiers. The sight of The Lionheart in rough breeches and a tunic, sweating, shoulder to shoulder with his men hauling stones into place, reaffirmed his comradery with the troops. The great walls of the castle growing from the ground to the sky also stirred something in the chest of even the most cynical of soldiers. The bricks and mortar involved in the rebuilding of Ascalon, represented a tangible reflection of the Crusaders' efforts and sacrifices. It had not all been in vain, it hadn't been for nothing. The Lionheart and his men had conquered Acre, they had completed the long march down to Jaffa, their victories and progress was as real as the great fortresses taking shape before them. Their day would come to fight for Jerusalem but today, all that mattered, was building the Castle of Ascalon.

As he built, The Lionheart continued to contemplate his unsolvable problem. He didn't want to be bombarded with projectiles from the walls of Jerusalem, whilst simultaneously having to watch his back in case the Turks attacked from the rear. No matter what perspective he assessed the conundrum from though, he could not see an answer. It didn't help that his attention was also getting pulled in other directions. There was squabbling between Guy Lusignan and some of the other nobles regarding who should be King of Jerusalem. The Lionheart found this quite frustrating and had to point out that until they had actually conquered the city, there was not really a conversation to be had.

Conrad of Montferrat will eventually be elected as the King of Jerusalem. He is the cousin of the former Pope and strongly aligned with Rome, which produced a mixed response in The Crusader ranks. Some saw it as rather fitting that The King of Jerusalem was close to the Papacy, Richard and Guy are less sure though this is a good thing. Guy is more than just unsure about it, he publicly blows up over it, he can only be appeased when The Lionheart sells him the Kingship of Cyprus. Whilst this allows Guy to retain a title of King, it is a significant demotion. Although Richard has taken the time to appease Guy, The Lionheart himself is miffed at this turn of events. Here these elites were jockeying for the Kingship of Jerusalem, whilst The Lionheart was busy wrestling with the very real operational challenges of making this a reality, "Who could deserve the title more than me?" Richard asks of the starry desert sky.

A few days before Conrad was to be crowned, he was assassinated by members of the Hashshashin Guild, "The Order of Assassins". Conrad had gone for dinner with a local Bishop only to be advised that the Bishop had already eaten and therefore was not hungry. Conrad decided to return home. As he navigated the winding alleyways of Acre ignoring the propositions from ladies of the night, he was descended upon by two, fully shrouded killers for hire. Their attack was swift and deadly. Conrad was stabbed twice, once in the back and once in the side. The attack was bungled though, Conrad's guards leaped into action killing one of the assassins and wounding the other.

Some reports advise that Conrad died instantly on the spot, Richard's chroniclers state that he passed away at a nearby church hospital. The Lionheart's men even managed to record his final words. Predictably enough, these were that The Holy city of Jerusalem should be handed over to Richard. This death bed testimony witnessed only by Richard's close lieutenants causes a few furrowed brows, these turn into downright outrage though when under torture, the surviving assassin confesses it was The Lionheart who had hired them. Richard dismisses this as fake news, instead dragging Guy's name through the mud.

Rumours circulate that perhaps Saladin had ordered the murder although this seems unlikely. Saladin hated the Hashshashin Guild and had openly waged war against them previously, they would have been more likely to kill him than subcontract for him.

The murder remains unsolved even today. Richard will continue to maintain his innocence and demands that the Hashshashin Guild send a letter explicitly implicating him. If this was a bluff from Richard, it was a poor one for they duly send a letter confirming that yes, it was Richard that had indeed ordered the killing.

For the Kingship of Jerusalem, there will be a re-vote and concerns arise regarding the integrity of the ballot when Richard's nephew, Henry of Champagne, is announced as the winner. With the kingship decided, it was now time to get back to the business of actually winning the city of Jerusalem. Not for Richard though, The Lionheart was done, word was reaching him from home and it was troubling him. Both Eleanor of Aquitaine and Sir William Marshal had sent letters advising that Richard's brother John, was seizing control of castles in England and was even rumoured to be in conversations with Philip Augustus. The exact nature of these conversations was not known but it couldn't be anything good. It was time for Richard to go home.

Chapter 21: The Return of Jaffa

The Lionheart did not want to leave a power vacuum behind in The Holy Land, but he also needed to get home now or run the risk of not having one to return to. His war was over. Peace plans were drawn up between the Lionheart and El Adil, Saladin's brother. The terms were essentially that Jerusalem would remain under Saracen control, although Christian pilgrims would be permitted providing they were supervised and kept in fairly low numbers. The Crusaders would retain Acre and The True Cross would be returned to them. The Third Crusade could not be considered a success. Although Acre and Jaffa had been won by The Crusaders, the price they had paid for this was huge. The Plantagenet empire will be paying taxes for the Lionheart's failed efforts for decades to come.

At the final moment when The Lionheart was due to depart though, he postpones the deal. There were rumblings of dissent within Saladin's camp. Apparently, The Sultan was having difficulties with a rebellious nephew in Mesopotamia, there was even the possibility of a full civil war on the horizon for the Saracens. It was too good an opportunity for The Lionheart to miss. The fanfare was sounding in his ears and once more he gazes upon the spires of Jerusalem in his dreams. Richard decides that now was the time to go on the offensive.

The Crusaders sailed down the coast to the castle of Darum. After a fairly short siege of just four days, the Lionheart was victorious. Those who had remained on the battlements fighting until the cause was truly hopeless, were rounded up and cast from the walls to shatter upon the rocks below. Those that surrendered in the tower were spared, though their hands were bound so tightly with leather restraints that the prisoners were soon screaming in pain as extremities began to turn black.

With Winter done and momentum building for The Crusaders, The Lionheart decided to once more ride for the Holy City. Men who had spent Winter hunkering down in Jaffa and Acre flocked to return to his banner, he united Capetian and Plantagenet troops once more and he was ready to finish this. Richard's nephew The new King of Jerusalem (by name only!), Henry of Champagne, joined the Lionheart. Spirits were further bolstered by the capturing of a supply caravan travelling towards The Holy City. The wind was in the Crusaders sails, the anticipation and optimism was palpable and could be felt across the land, even by the Saracen defenders who huddled behind the battlements of Jerusalem.

Saladin sent riders out into the desert surrounding Jerusalem. Every well for miles was filled in with rocks. This move signed the death warrant for many of Saladin's own nomadic people who meticulously planned their routes across the desert based entirely on the formula of distance over available water. Saladin did it anyway though. Should The Lionheart march on the Holy City, he would be required to set up a supply chain of water carriers from Jaffa to the front line. This was more than just a logistical inconvenience for The Crusaders, it would present a devastatingly vulnerable target for Saladin to exploit.

The Lionheart and his armies rallied just outside the Holy City. They were so close that one day, whilst Richard was hunting a unit of Saracen scouts, he traversed a summit and actually cast eyes on the city that haunted his dreams; hazy in the distance with heat shimmer from the desert sands, were the spires of Jerusalem. Richard covered his eyes, he could not bear to look upon the city until he had delivered it from the enemies of Christendom.

The Lionheart and his wisest councillors meet in the desert. Once more, they were in spitting distance of the Holy

City and once more, there were reasons The Crusaders probably shouldn't advance. The issue proved more than a little divisive amongst The Lionheart's armies. The English thought it was madness, how do you conduct desert warfare without sufficient water supplies, surely only a fool would attempt it? The mainland Europeans had reached a different conclusion, why march a thousand miles through hell and back to not complete the final leg of the journey?

Once you took the emotion out of the equation, the question was basically, is it wise to conduct desert siege warfare without sufficient water supplies? The answer is of course, no. Definitely not. Absolutely, one hundred percent, no. Again though, Richard would have to lose face and give an order that looked incredibly weak. That it was probably the right call can have been little consolation as he instructs his men to begin the long journey North to Acre.

Saladin and his men, who had feared a full on conflict, could not believe that they had saved Jerusalem without spilling any blood on the sand. The Saracen army climbed the dunes near the Crusaders' camp. They watched them pack up the tents and cheered for hours as they watched them sorrowfully retreat away through the desert.

Over the next week, Saladin received two quite contradictory letters. The first was from, The King of Jerusalem, Henry Champagne. Saladin found Champagne's title a little laughable as he himself controlled the Holy City. Champagne was advising that providing Saladin gave up the Holy City, he would grant them the return of both Acre and Jaffa. Richard's nephew was keen to flex his non-existent political muscles, but now was not the time. The leader of the coalition Crusader forces, The Lionheart, had just ducked the battle turning tail and fleeing. Saladin was both annoyed and bewildered with the envoy that had brought him this letter, who the hell did these Westerners think they were?

The next letter to arrive was from The Lionheart. He proposed a treaty should be drawn up between the Christians and the Saracens involving a cessation of violence and visiting rights to Jerusalem for Western pilgrims, basically, the same deal that had been on the table before. It was Richard that had messed up the last deal though so this time he attempts to sweeten the deal by offering one of his nephews as a ward. Wards could either be married by their guardians, or traded off in marriage, whatever worked best for the guardian. Saladin liked this letter far more than the first one.

Saladin agreed Christians could have access to the Holy City, though it would remain under Saracen control. The True Cross would be returned to the Westerners and the invaders could keep the coastal cities they had conquered. As for Ascalon, the castle The Lionheart had laboured alongside his men to build, Saracen wanted this to be deconstructed. It had become a symbol of the Westerners' success and sacrifice, a tangible shrine to the hardships endured by the Christian invaders and a suggestion of hope for the future for them. This was a step too far for The Lionheart, negotiations collapsed again.

The Lionheart was done with this. Twice he had been within a few miles of the Holy City and each time had lost the battle before it had even begun. The Lionheart has learned a lesson that is still relevant today for military strategists, it is seriously difficult to defeat an impassioned and resourceful guerrilla force in hostile, unfamiliar terrain.

The headline would always be, Loser Lionheart fails to win Jerusalem, Richard was aware of that. The fact that the headline wasn't, Lionheart dies in unwinnable Battle, was of little comfort to a man of Richard's pride. There was time for one last hurrah though, one last chance to sail home on the winds of some kind of glory. Richard would march his entire armies up from Acre to, "Beyrut," (Beirut), three hundred and fifty miles North from Jerusalem in the country of Lebanon. The Lionheart planned to swiftly conquer the city and from there, with one final notch on his bedpost, he would return to Europe.

There was little strategic importance for this city in The Crusaders' overarching strategic objective to win Jerusalem. It was purely a vanity play from the Lionheart. It wasn't a stupid place to attack, after all, there was no way Saladin could be expecting it, except somehow he was…

To sacrifice Beyrut to the Crusaders and get the highly competent Lionheart off the chessboard in the Middle East, would have been a shrewd move for the leader of the Muslim forces, unfortunately though, his spies only brought him part of the story. Saladin only heard that The Lionheart intended to attack Beyrut, he missed the bit about this being on his way home. With The Lionheart consolidating Northern provinces, Saladin felt pressured to make a counterattack, he launched a strike on the city of Jaffa, The Crusaders' oasis.

Saladin marched with all of his armies upon the coastal city with its neatly lined orchards. The fighting was pitched and bloodied. The walls of Jaffa were defended by a smaller force than had previously been garrisoned there and the Saracen soldiers could see the gaps between them on the walls. Even so, the Christians fought with such ferocity and organisation, that the siege could have gone either way. All manner of projectiles were rained down upon Saladin and his men, even the infamous and deadly *Greek Fire*. Greek Fire is an interesting one, the recipe for this concoction of death is today lost to us, but contemporary sources advise it was a highly combustible solution that when combined with water would violently ignite. If poured onto a man with water he would be coated in sticky, inextinguishable flames. The exact composition of Greek Fire is up for debate but the savagery and horrors it inflicted upon the attackers is not.

Saladin himself was heavily involved in the combat, leading men forward to conduct feinting strikes against the walls and trying desperately to draw attention away from his units of sappers that were busy tunnelling under the walls. The sappers were digging frantically in an attempt to undermine the fortifications, as they dig, they are pummelled with missiles and death from the defenders above. Bodyguard units hold shields high above the engineers to defend them. As their picks and shovels hit the ground, they pray that none of the missiles from above or deadly fire will find a breach between the shields or a chink in the armour that they wear.

The battle hangs in the balance for three days, until finally, the Saracen Sappers compromise the structural integrity of the walls of Jaffa. With a deafening thunder, a section topples. The entire battle pauses to watch the collapse of the mighty fortifications and the wave of dust it kicks up. How many sections would crumble? Was this the end of the defence? Had the Saracens won? Once again the defenders' organisation is worthy of note. As the thrown up debris clears from the collapsing masonry, a new wall becomes apparent, this time it is not of stone but of men. A unit of armoured soldiers stand, shoulder to shoulder, shields firmly in hand. They bash their weapons against their shields to create a deafening din of defiance and bellow challenges to their attackers. The crossbow bolts from the remaining sections of wall begin to fly down on the attackers once again. The battle re-starts in earnest.

The Saracens will win the day. They will pour through the walls like water does through the crack of a dam, what begins as a small trickle swiftly turns into a torrent. Saladin is nervous though for the blood is up in his men and he cannot control them. He sends word to Christian non-combatants that they should not try to protect their homes or belongings and that they should flee into the night. Saladin was right to be worried. There was looting on a massive scale and a lot of innocents were put to the sword. As is fairly typical with this period, the writers from this time is neither lament nor demonise these actions. This kind of butchery isn't merciful or brutal, it just is what it is.

For Saladin though, this rampaging is a problem.

Whilst Jaffa has now formally surrendered, the defenders and refugees have barricaded themselves inside the citadel. Understandably, as the defenders watch the city burn and listen to the screams of their neighbours being executed in the streets, they are not in a rush to come out. The doors remain firmly locked.

Saladin knows that by now The Lionheart will have heard of what has transpired in Jaffa and will be prowling, panther-like South towards the city. The Lionheart can smell blood and would love nothing more than to catch the Saracens between two forces.

As the sun dips behind the horizon, Saladin is a lonely silhouette, lit only by the smouldering buildings of the city and blurred by acrid smoke. Saladin calls out to his men to listen, he implores that they needed to get organised and attack the citadel before it is too late. The looting has now mostly stopped, instead, the men are occupied in celebration. Saladin can hear his men singing raucously, did they not understand there was no time for this? He pleads one more time but is ignored again. Saladin drops to his knees in prayer before thinking, if you can't beat them, join them, he goes to eat.

The morning heralds the arrival of the Lionheart, trumpets are heard as a fleet of ships become visible, across the azure, glass-like ocean.

"Come on then little Lion cub," mutters Saladin, "let me cast my eyes upon you and see if you are all that the legends would have us believe."

Saladin sent word for his close adviser, a man of peace by the name of Baha-ed-din. Baha-ed-din will later become the biographer of Saladin, many a moonlight night will he spend peacefully recording bloody conflicts the Sultan commanded.

"I am an absolute pacifist and a man of peace Saladin," helpfully began Baha-ed-din, curious as to why he had been sent for in the middle of this particular mess.

"Yes, I know that. Time is short. We must act quickly if we are going to defeat the Westerners," breathlessly replies Saladin.

"Defeat yes. But perhaps we can defeat without bloodshed, with our words, with our minds and with our robust arguments?"

"Yes, yes very much so I certainly hope that is the case. That is why I have sent for you. You are to go to the citadel and convince the defenders to leave," Saladin is frantically strapping on armour.

"Peacefully," Baha-ed-din raises both eyebrows and smiles banally.

"Yes peacefully, please just go, time is of the essence," begs Saladin.

"It is only a fool who wastes time, for it is the most valuable commodity any of us mere mortals will ever trade in," Baha-ed-din stands there for almost ten full seconds before Saladin frowns at him and begins to shoo him from the tent. Baha-ed-din nods and waddles away towards the citadel.

Saladin then calls in his generals. Frustratingly, he does not have time to properly chastise them for the mess they have caused by not holding things together the previous evening. Instead, Saladin sends them directly to the shoreline to fight The Lionheart and his armies as they attempt to disembark, "Slow them down," he growls as they depart. With one hand, Saladin will offer peace to the men in the citadel, with the other, he will hammer a fist down upon The Crusaders at the beach.

Baha-ed-din's corpulent figure sits astride his mule as he ambles alongside old Jurdik. Jurdik had been old when he had fought next to Saladin thirty years ago in the Egyptian rebellion. These two senior gentlemen of great experience, lead a small column of men and discuss the finer points of spiritual enlightenment, places they had visited and how in general, older people were far better at most things than the younger generations.

A soldier runs up to Baha-ed-din, "Sir, The Lionheart has managed to secure a small area of beach and is using this as a landing point for the remainder of his army."

Baha-ed-din smiles calmly, a little bemused that he finds himself receiving military updates, what strange roads we walk, "Please young soldier, don't call me sir".

The soldier looks awkward, appalled even, "Well, what shall I call you?"

Baha-ed-din calmly reflects on the young man's question, "My name would be a good start don't you think? Look, as you get older and you consider things from different perspectives you will realise, that all of these ranks, all of this hierarchical nonsense is just that, nonsense. Under the eyes of God we are all equal. We are born the same under the blessings of the enlightened one and we will die the same. So I would ask you once more, what's the matter with just using my name?" Baha-ed-din winked at the soldier.

"Well, I don't know what your name is sir?" Baha-ed-din's companion Jurdik, howls with laughter at this.

Baha-ed-din and Jurdik arrive to find a crowd of Muslim local non-combatants surrounding the citadel doors. They spit at the walkway and throw stones although a cursory glance suggested the crowd was not armed. The men aren't worried for they have not travelled alone, they have soldiers accompanying them should anyone try to inflict any real harm on the prisoners against Sultan Saladin's wishes.

"Even with our men, I wouldn't fancy walking though that mob, would you?" Jurdik asks, surveying the angry crowd, Baha-ed-din nods thoughtfully. The soldiers were ordered to slowly move the crowd back, clear a walkway and allow the defenders to leave with some kind of dignity, some kind of honour.

"No, move them further back. Get that man out of here, he clearly has some kind of agenda or a concealed dagger…" The crowd management goes on as the sun continues to rise.

Finally, the first forty men and their wives are permitted to leave the citadel. They march out, their shoulders cowed, they are ready to be set upon at any moment. Every movement from their peripherals they anticipate as a missile, they flinch uncontrollably. The prisoners are pleasantly surprised. They walk a path through the crowds with all the dignity they can muster and announce to Baha-ed-din, "We surrender."

"Well, don't you worry. You will be treated with the honour you deserve. You will receive no brutality from this quarter I'll tell you that for free. I am Saladin's agent and you are under his protection. Now look, you must be thirsty, please, take some water".

As the men drink, one of their wives looks over towards the coastline, "Is that The Lionheart with thirty-five warships and his entire army fighting his way up the beaches towards this city?" she asks.

"Why…yes, I believe it is," Baha-ed-din nods, smiling in a kindly manner like a proud teacher addressing an especially bright pupil.

The group huddle together and hurriedly confer, a spokesperson emerges and advises Baha-ed-din that, "We've had a chat, we think we'd quite like to go back into the citadel."

"Back into the citadel?" Baha-ed-din's lips purse and he looks disappointed.

"Yes. We think so," the first group to exit the citadel all nod their assent.

Baha-ed-din sighs. He sighs the sigh of a parent who is letting their children make and hopefully learn, from their own mistakes. The group shuffle back into the citadel.

As The Lionheart approaches the city with his fleet of warships, it is with bated breath and a heavy heart. Winds had not been kind to Richard, it had taken him almost a day longer than he had anticipated to reach the city of Jaffa, he prayed that there was still something there to save. On the horizon, the city shifted into focus. The Lionheart could now make out the citadel and was pleased to note that no Saracen flag flew from the ramparts. Still, that didn't mean a lot, it could be a trap after all. For a bloodthirsty raging psychopath, The Lionheart really is a very careful military commander.

Richard takes in Saladin's men, lined up on the sand ready to bombard them as they disembark and the trenches that had been dug across the beach. Slowly, the Lionheart shakes his head, it would be madness to try and assault them. Yet again, The Lionheart turns away from the battle he so covets, he can hear Saladin's laughter in his ears.

"Look up there!" points one of the soldiers on deck. A dark shape becomes visible atop the citadel. Against the rising sun, it is no more than a shadow. Without warning, the amorphous shape hurls itself from atop the castle. It drops like a stone and cuts into the frothy, white swell below. Surely, nobody could have survived such a fall? The Lionheart waits one second, two seconds, nine full seconds before a head emerges, gasping from the water below. The men on the boat cheer. The fearless diver was a Christian priest and therefore one of The Lionheart's subjects. As the priest was pulled onto the boat, he was so thrilled to meet Richard he could hardly contain his excitement. He chattered to the King about how the men in the citadel had held out for him, how they were ready to force the invaders from their city like lancing poison from a boil and now he had arrived, to save them all, victory was certain.

This is too much for the Lionheart. How could he refuse this request from the fearless priest? Richard knew it would be foolhardy and incredibly dangerous to attempt a beach landing in full view of the Saracen defenders, but The Lionheart was going to do it anyway.

"Men, to your oars, we are taking back what is ours," the Lionheart roars.

Richard's ship is the first to beach and he throws himself over the side. He does not wear full armour, for that has proven the death sentence of many a warrior at sea who has fallen overboard. Waist deep in the swell, The Lionheart booms his battle cry and begins racing towards the beach. After a prolonged period of inactivity, the defenders had begun to relax in the midday heat and they are somehow taken by surprise with Richard's sudden charge.

What should have been a thunderstorm of crossbow bolts raining down upon The Lionheart, is actually just a trickle of badly placed shots that miss by a wide mark. What should have been an organised defence of regimented pike men, is in reality just a smattering of panicked soldiers frantically grabbing at their weapons and trying to form into a line.

Regardless of the lack of Saracen organisation, this is the stuff of legends. King Richard The Lionheart has personally reached the first line of Saracen defenders before most of his army has even managed to get off their boat. The Lionheart fights with his familiar Danish war axe. He cleaves from left to right in wide, arcing strokes. There is no lithely dodging the speed of his flashing axe head and nor is there a chance for the defenders to block, such is the power The Lionheart imbues every blow with. It does not take long for the venom of this attack to become too much for the Saracens who turn and run. Richard is not done though, he now takes up his crossbow and not a single defender of the beach manages to escape his pinpoint accuracy. The Lionheart laughs manically as he shoots the runners in their backs.

Those Crusaders who have not yet managed to disembark from their ships are becoming increasingly frantic, lest there be no glory left to claim. From the momentum of his initial charge, The Lionheart manages to lead his personal bodyguard and a handful of men well into the city. He makes straight for the former Knight Templars' garrison, a symbolic figurehead of the city. Richard fights his way through the narrow corridors of the crooked house, his burly form violently smashed through narrow doorframes and partition walls. Crossing blades and bellowing orders, Richard takes control of the roof and victoriously flies his legendary, Three Lions flag high above the city.

Word spreads quickly amongst The Saracens, The Lionheart is an unstoppable God of War, run now to save yourself.

What begins as a rout turns official, as Saladin endorses the retreat. What else can he do? He can't stop The Crusaders, they are too venomous, organised and everyone is terrified of Richard. Saladin and his men retreat back into the hills and once more Jaffa, an outpost just a few miles from Jerusalem, is back under Crusader control.

The Lionheart was understandably ecstatic. Richard declared to any who would listen that with only a fraction of his army deployed and whilst wearing only his boating shoes (it's unclear exactly what boating shoes are…), he had routed Saladin's entire army. It was fights like this that were the very reason Richard had got into Crusading in the first place.

But let's not get ahead of ourselves. This was a city that, until a week ago, had been under their control anyway. They had not captured the True Cross nor really got any closer to invading Jerusalem. The Lionheart still needed, urgently, to return home. Once more, Richard sent an envoy to Saladin to discuss peace terms albeit this time on the heels of victory.

There is a back and forth of messages between the Lionheart and the Sultan. Once more negotiations hinge on The Lionheart giving up the Castle The Crusaders had built in Ascalon and once more, Richard says no. The negotiations are smoke and mirrors though, in reality, both leaders are playing for time. The Lionheart is secretly reinforcing his army from Acre. A column of men is marching South, he would like them to arrive untroubled and unmolested by Saladin.

Saladin is playing the waiting game too. He knows The Lionheart is a young man who is many miles from home. He also knows that Richard's brother, Count John, is treacherous and if left unchecked, could bring serious harm to the Plantagenet empire. Saladin believes that soon the day would dawn where Richard would have to piss off home, turning his back on all that he had achieved in the Holy Land. The Sultan's instinct, which was not normally wrong, told him that this day would arrive soon. Once The Lionheart left and The Crusader's lost their mighty leader, maybe it would take one year, perhaps two, but sure enough, every yard of Saracen soil that had been claimed by Richard would be taken back.

Saladin was wrong. When he learns of the reinforcements on route from Acre this confirmed it. This Western King was like an ungodly rash that would not go away. The road to Jaffa was, apparently, lined with soldiers who would fight under The Lionheart's banner and reinforce the city. If Saladin was going to expel Richard from Jaffa, he would have to do it quickly.

Well, shrugs Saladin, every strength is a weakness and every threat is an opportunity, as he stands outside the city of Jaffa and gazes upon its defenders, it doesn't look well manned. Richard, in his hurry to arrive, has not waited for enough soldiers to properly defend such a city, especially when sections of the wall were already reduced to rubble, thinks Saladin.

The Sultan was right, Richard was ridiculously low on numbers. He had fifty knights, although only fifteen of these had their own horses and two thousand infantry soldiers.

The force looks pitifully small. They plant themselves plugging the gap in the walls of Jaffa ready to receive a cavalry charge from the Saracens. The infantry men are placed in pairs, like cacti dangerously in the desert. They drop to one knee and grimly plant their spears forward, behind their interlocking shields. Each pairing is supported by a single crossbow wielder.

The Lionheart rides back and forth across these isolated pickets of defence waving a sword wildly in the air and shouting defiance at the Saracens, he is supported by his fifteen mounted knights. If Richard is concerned the defence he mounts is pitiful, he gives no indication of this.

The first charge from the Saracens is received, with a deafening din across the battlefield. Fighting is immediately toe to toe and too close for the crossbowmen to be deadly. The Crusader line somehow holds against the superior Saracen numbers, they retreat, but not far. They quickly regroup and charge again, smashing down upon the prickly defenders. The Crusaders largely ensnare the cavalry and those that do fly past are shot down by the crossbowmen who have a clear line of sight this time. It is another stalemate.

As the Saracen soldiers recover and charge for another attack, as they have almost ten times before, the Crusaders change tactics. The crossbowmen step forward, this time in front of the kneeling Pikemen and manage to blast three volleys into the faces of the charging cavalry units. They inflict terrible and brutal carnage onto the attackers and the majority of this charge are killed and yet still, the Saracen forces thunder on towards the wall of shields the infantry men cower behind. At the last second, the Pikemen calmly step aside, the attackers, who were braced for impact, fly past towards the city.

Now that Saracen numbers had been sufficiently depleted, the trap was sprung. The Lionheart and his fifteen horsed knights tore into the Saracen forces. Once more, the King lashes out left and right with his great axe and once more everything he touches is decimated. The fighting is close quartered and bloody, Richard is certainly in the thick of it. At one point, his horse is killed from underneath him.

The Lionheart finds himself, alone, in the carnage of

horseflesh and maces, swords and screams, he carves like a woodcutter desperately around himself trying to clear some kind of space and avoid being trampled on by hooves that thunder about him. Saladin, from his vantage point on the hillside, spies Richard fighting on the ground like a commoner and takes pity on him. Weirdly, he sends one of his men with a spare horse into the midst of the combat and gifts the equine to The Lionheart, who receives it graciously.

As the day draws to a close, The Crusaders retain Jaffa and line up on the breached walls. They are greatly outnumbered by the Saracen army, but Saladin's men have lost their stomach for the battle by this point. Every attack has been met by well-organised discipline. The Crusaders have been managed by the unflappable Lionheart who rides about the field, chivvying up men here, joking with soldiers there, taking any opportunity to fire a crossbow bolt at attackers that stray too close. When the Lionheart does enter the combat himself, he is a terrible God, wreaking destruction and never tiring. His very presence raises the blood in all near him who fight with twice the vigour. Saladin begs his men to attack once more but they refuse.

At one point, the Lionheart even rides out in front of the city alone, his lance at rest. He rides up and down the Saracen line multiple times with a single fist held aloft high in the air in defiance. Even this does not tempt the attackers. Not a single Saracen soldier is prepared to try and capture or kill the Lionheart, so great is his presence and so feared is he.

Saladin is furious. These men have twice failed him in fighting the outnumbered Crusaders and now the Plantagenet King openly mocks him in his own backyard. Saladin may be angry, but even he himself does not dare to challenge The Lionheart. Perhaps, in Saladin's younger days, he may have charged in, but the Lionheart was twenty years his junior and is one of the most formidable warriors of the age. Though it galls Saladin, he does not have the stomach himself to ride out and fight the isolated Western

King.

The Crusaders on the wall cheer Richard's boldness. The sound of their chanting washes over the Saracens, "LIONHEART, LIONHEART, LIONHEART, LIONHEART".

As The Lionheart's men travelled from Acre to reinforce Jaffa, work was frantically conducted to repair the breach in the outer walls. With each foot the masonry raises in height, The Crusader's position was becoming ever more entrenched as once more the occupiers of Jaffa. Saladin wasn't happy about this, he sent summons to Egypt advising his ranks needed inflating immediately by experienced, veteran soldiers.

An arms race began between the two sides and battle plans were drawn up. Saladin continued to keep pressure on Jaffa whilst also concerning himself with the defence of Jerusalem, after all, odds were favourable that The Lionheart would, at some point, make yet another play for the city.

The eighteenth-century poet, Robert 'Rabbie' Burns, wrote about how the best laid plans of mice and men oft' go awry, the late and idolised songwriter John Lennon offered a similar sentiment when he surmised that, 'Life is what happens whilst you are busy making other plans.' Both of these poetically framed observations prove true in this instance. As Richard and Saladin plot, scheme and jockey for position, the Lionheart once again falls ill.

As is often the case with the most serious of fevers, it takes a grip of The Lionheart swiftly. When he beds down one evening, The King feels slightly out of sorts, a little fatigued perhaps and his eyes oddly dry, but otherwise fine.

"Nothing that a good night's sleep won't fix," Richard slapped his thigh haughtily as he declared this to his dining companions. The Lionheart wakes though in the early hours of the morning whimpering like a kitten. His sheets are drenched, he is burning a high fever and yet he shivers violently, claiming he is cold. Sick, exposed and in the middle of the desert surrounded by enemies, The Lionheart can do little but send urgent messengers to Saladin to sue for peace.

If you are thinking The Lionheart seems particularly susceptible to suffering bouts of illness, I know what you mean. Three years ago, when the crusade began, he had been similarly incapacitated. The Lionheart did suffer from some kind of underlying medical condition, although it is unclear exactly what this was. He was often described as having a slight shake, or tremor. This affliction is unlikely to be early onset Parkinson or a result of a drinking problem, as whatever caused it did not seem to affect his ability to don plate mail armour nor wield heavy weaponry with devastating accuracy. It has been hypothesised that whatever did cause his tremors, was some kind of autoimmune disease that made him more susceptible to other ailments.

Equally though, The Lionheart was not an old man at thirty-five, but nor was he young. He had spent his adult life fighting his father, his older brother, his father again and now Saladin. The Lionheart was exhausted. Granted, the King never looked flustered nor out of his depth, but in reality, he was a swan, calm and poised above the surface whilst frantically paddling underneath. This constant stress and regular release of adrenaline undoubtedly took its toll.

Whatever we may speculate to be the underlying cause of his fever, does not change the situation that we find ourselves in, The Lionheart is sick and seriously so. His fever will not stop burning and even his own allies don't know what should be done. Henry of Champagne, Richard's nephew, unhelpfully declares that should The Lionheart die, he will not personally attempt to keep Acre or Jaffa from the Saracens and thus secure The Lionheart's legacy in The Holy Land.

Richard's enemy Saladin is also unsure what action is appropriate in this instance. The Sultan has pictured the death of his adversary a thousand times in a thousand different ways, but never like this. They had played cat and mouse across a chessboard that spanned deserts and oceans. They had played their game at the expense of so many lives and for it all to end like this, seemed unsatisfying to the Sultan who wished for closure.

Saladin's brother, El-Adin, is said to have walked through Jaffa to visit The Lionheart's sickbed. Here, it is claimed, El-Adin sobbed on the floor by Richard's sickbed and raged at the sky, screaming at the unfairness that such a great man should be taken so young. This almost certainly didn't happen, as how could the Saracens have confidence The Crusaders would not capture this important general? What definitely did happen though, which is equally baffling, is that Saladin kept sending little care packages to the dying King. He would send baskets of fresh pears and peaches to the patient; these would be packed with fallen snow from the mountains to keep them preserved. For days on end an envoy would arrive from the Sultan with Richard's potassium fix and boosters of vitamin A and B.

The cynical amongst us would hypothesise that, as the care package arrived at the King's camp, the courier who introduced himself would speak with slightly too clear a diction for a common born lowly servant. Those of us who doubt the intrinsic goodness of man, would question the courier's muttering as he passed each guard station. Were these prayers to the prophet Mohammed, or, was the courier trying to memorise the defensive fortifications and garrison assignments of the city? What was that he was repeating, "three by three cover formation, crossbowmen with pike support behind a wooden barricade? Three by three cover formation crossbowmen with pike support behind a wooden barricade?"

Had The Crusaders taken the time to follow the courier, would they have seen that once he was out of sight, he frantically retrieved from his pack a piece of parchment and started sketching palisades, detailing armaments and doing everything possible to map The Crusaders' defences each day? We will never know, for nobody followed him past that first sand dune.

The Lionheart will make a full recovery, but at this point, he barely has the strength to read the terms of the contract, let alone negotiate the small print. The Lionheart signed off on a three-year peace treaty with the Saracens. The Crusaders would retain Jaffa and Acre, however, Ascalon Castle was to be torn down. Jerusalem would of course remain with Saladin, but supervised pilgrimage would be permitted for Christians to the city. It was basically the same deal that had been on the table twice before.

Henry of Champagne managed to somehow retain his excellent title as King of Jerusalem despite being based in Acre and not allowed to reside in The Holy City. The Lionheart will never actually visit Jerusalem, nor will he ever sit at a table and have a face to face with Saladin.

Richard will send a final message to the Sultan though as he leaves, advising him that when the three-year peace treaty is up, he will be returning to claim Jerusalem. Saladin reads this with a smile and shakes his head in wonder at this Western King's gumption. Saladin wrote a number of replies that he scrunched up and cast into the camp fire, before eventually settling on a civil response to Richard. Saladin replied that there was nobody he would rather lose his land to than Richard and he eagerly awaited his return.

The Lionheart will not wage war against Saladin again though. The Sultan will himself succumb to a fever, just one year later at the age of fifty-five. For the time period, this wasn't a bad run. Few men on their deathbed can have been more confident in their legacy being remembered and their name living on eternally, than Saladin. He had achieved the impossible.

The Pope had issued a plea for help to the Christian world that had been answered by heroes such as Leopold of Austria, Philip of Flanders, Guy Lusignan, Henry Champagne, Philip II Augustus, The Lionheart and many more besides. Richard brought tens of thousands of troops to bear in the Holy Land, a significant amount of whom will never return from the desert. The Lionheart will be forced to apply heavy taxation across his homeland to pay for this relentless campaigning. All of these resources, all of this expertise and all of this human capital was levelled at the Sultan, still though, Jerusalem remained under Saracen control. Saladin died both peacefully and proud.

The Lionheart, though not dead, was more than a little concerned about his own legacy. Yes, he had captured two coastal points in the Holy Land but in reality, that was about it. Richard had not even succeeded in returning The True Cross to Christendom. It's believed a Saracen rider rode with it to Damascus following The Massacre of Ayyadieh, after that, it's never heard of again. It could have been destroyed in retaliation, or lie forgotten in a dusty Damascus vault somewhere, maybe it was all a bluff and Saladin's men never even held the relic?

However you looked at it, The Third Crusade had been a spectacular failure. Perhaps the greatest cost was not even the devastating tally of human lives or the significant dent in the royal treasury, the greatest cost, may have been the absence of the Lionheart in his own land.

Richard's brother, Count John, was running the country into the ground, to the point where it was becoming populated with mythical, Marxist figures such as the infamous Robin Hood. The Plantagenet empire was in a bad way and needed a hero now more than ever.

The Lionheart set sail from Acre and departed for the shores of his homeland.

An Intermission with a Magician: Eustace the Mercenary Pirate Monk

As Richard sets sail once more for Europe, he takes the time to recover from his sickness and rest from the ceaseless campaigning he has endured over the last decade. He stares moodily across the eerily still, glasslike water with his eyes scrunched tightly against the glare of the sun. Richard had pictured his return home a thousand times, but never like this.

Whilst The Lionheart is licking his wounds and learning to reconcile his failures with his own exacting standards, we should afford him a little privacy. As he sails home, we are going to learn about another interesting figure from this period, we are going to learn about Eustace the Mercenary Pirate Monk.

He will pop up very briefly in ten chapters time, but in our tale, he will be just a footnote. You will hear of him only in the following line:

"Even Eustace the Mercenary Pirate Monk defaulted from the Plantagenet King and allied with the Capetian One."

It would be implausible and impractical to give the backstory of every figure in history that shares a stage with The Plantagenets, but for Eustace, it's important we make an exception. As his name would suggest, he's a seriously interesting guy.

Eustace is a man of legend, however, he does get referenced in enough respectable sources corroborating his movements for us to be confident that he did, indeed, exist. As for books solely about him that were readily available, there were only two that I could find. One, was a vivisection of an epic poem written about Eustace. It diligently tore apart each stanza with forensic detail and meticulous references. The study painstakingly explained the background to every verse and rhyming couplet. Whilst it was extremely useful for piecing together the movements of Eustace, it made for fairly dry reading.

The second book solely dedicated to Eustace more than made up for this though. Released in 2012, *The (True?) Story of Eustace the Pirate Monk*, published by a boutique outfit operating from a PO Box in Durham, was penned by author Kathryn Bedford. Bedford's picture book is aimed at early primary school readers and Kathryn does not shy away from setting a challenging task for her young readership. She asks her third-grade learners to infer which of the stories about him are true and which are made up. This is no doubt a useful skill for Bedford to instil in her pupils, however, I would implore that as you read this chapter, you do the exact opposite.

The reason this chapter requires such an introduction, is that over the next few pages, we are going to see Eustace the Mercenary Pirate Monk actively engaged in wizardry. This presents a problem for the sorcery can become a distraction, causing us to analyse and question every detail of the man's life as opposed to just enjoying the tale. Whilst we can accept that magic was readily believed in during the medieval times, it is impossible for us to credit the same today. When we look a little closer though, much of the "magic" Eustace will engage in, is in fact, not magic at all. Eustace's spells will take the form of influential mind tricks. He will convince his victims what is true is false and what is false is true, now this *magic*, I can assure you certainly does exist – today you will often find high level wizards of this discipline working in politics.

Where we do see Eustace casting spells of a completely fictitious nature, it's important to remember Eustace's ability to get inside people's heads. Eustace was also very busy throughout his career creating his own legend, he was his own PR agent, hype-man and biographer. He could be found late of a night, whispering unlikely tales in taverns about his arcane and occult powers that in turn would get passed on to others. He will build a reputation that he will trade on throughout his career.

Enough, let's dive into the wonderful world of Eustace the Mercenary Pirate Monk.

Eustace was born around 1170 at the age of zero in a small coastal village ten miles from Boulogne. Although Eustace is often referred to as a knight, no records survive confirming he actually earned such pips. Considering his aptitude for combat and military leadership though, he must have spent at least some of his formative years undergoing martial training. It was around then he began to learn the arts of seafaring and navigation, by sailing small cogs along the Northern coast of France on fishing expeditions.

We also know, that at some point, Eustace expanded his horizons and took a gap year to Toledo, Spain. Visitors to Toledo today can expect to be blown away by the cannons of the military museum, gaze in wonderment at the Santa Iglesia cathedral, or lose oneself down the many snickleways and tapas bars the city is blessed with. Back when Eustace visits though, Toledo had something of a more seedy reputation. Not brothels or ladies of the night, although I'm sure there was a bit of that, this was something much darker, much more disturbing and much more unnatural. The city is said to have had the world's finest school of necromancy.

Necromancy is an umbrella term used today for any kind of magic that can communicate with the dead. This ranges from the "maybe okay" forms, such as a séance speaking with your dearly, departed nanna-nan, to the absolutely abhorrent re-animation of corpses with the intent to weaponise these cadavers. You won't be surprised to hear, that Eustace spent his time learning about the darker end of this spectrum. During his studies he is even rumoured to have met with the devil himself and somehow made him an ally to his cause. Exactly what Eustace's cause was at this point in his career, is anyone's guess, it seems unlikely that Eustace knew himself.

After travelling and "finding himself" on his gap year, it was time for Eustace to embrace a semblance of responsibility and get a job. For a man who has the devil's number in his phonebook, Eustace makes the rather unlikely decision to become a monk. This doesn't seem like a natural career progression for him, perhaps in being near God he was attempting to keep his friends close, but his enemies closer?

Eustace was not a great monk, he found the lifestyle boring. Prayer three times a day, abstinence from booze and an absolute ban on doing the five knuckle shuffle…. There was just no release for a man of Eustace's vices. They say that an idle mind is the devil's playground and this proved to be the case for our monkeying Monk, who quickly set himself to causing mischief throughout the monastery.

Some of the examples we have of Eustace's skulduggery seem a little mundane. He is referenced at one point as having used his superior skills of manipulation to trick the monks into taking off their shoes. Those watching apparently howled with laughter… I guess you had to be there.

On a more sinister note, he also cleaned out the abbey of all valuables and took them to a local tavern to spend the night deep in cards, cups and dice. The monastery never did get their valuables back teaching us, presumably, that even if you are a great and evil wizard, the house still always wins.

Eustace is having fun, but it is time for the frivolities to come to an end. His father has recently died under suspicious circumstances following a public and heated rivalry with his local neighbour, Hainfrois. Hainfrois had coveted Eustace's dad's heifer for years and it all seemed a little convenient that he had now died. Yes, I'll repeat that, Eustace's old man may have been killed over a cow.

For all of Eustace's supernatural abilities and close connections with Lucifer, he still opted to follow the correct channels in raising a grievance against Hainfrois. He paid a visit to the Count of Boulogne. To this man of power he respectfully and coherently outlined the peculiarities surrounding the death of his dad. Eustace went on to explain he was certain Hainfrois was responsible for this and he demanded justice. The Count did what most medieval leaders did when they didn't really know the answer to a judicial decision, he decreed trial by combat.

A trial by combat is, as it sounds, Eustace and Hainfrois would have to get armoured up and throw down in a ring of death before the entire court. God would support the righteous and ensure their victory, even if he didn't, the whole thing would be tremendous fun and a bloody good day out. Though the fight would be the main event, the spectacle wouldn't end there, there would be jugglers, jesters, a hog roast, strong men, heavy drinking and public debauchery…come along this Saturday and bring the kids.

Eustace is a good fighting weight and has youth on his side. He skips about throwing shadow punches into the air. Eustace is trained in the dance of death and is well up for the fight. That being said, he is largely untested. Being trained in swordplay is a very different affair to swinging a blade in anger against an opponent. Even so, the bookies like Eustace and he is the odds-on favourite for the win.

Hainfrois has certainly fought in a battle or two during his time but equally, he is disgusted at the idea he should fight Eustace. He approaches The Count and argues with his decision, "I am sixty years old. I am not about to get in the ring with somebody a third of my age who is said to have the devil as a pissing godfather!"

The Count, reluctantly, concedes that Hainfrois has a point, it probably isn't fair to make him duel a man forty years his junior in a fight to the death. With a sigh, The Count gives the okay for Hainfrois to appoint a champion in his stead, providing he gets on with it quickly.

Hainfrois selects Eustace de Marquise as his champion. To avoid confusion moving forward we will just refer to him as Marquise. In contrasts to Eustace's lack of practical combat experience, Marquise has tons of it, he is a nationwide renowned warrior.

Eustace begins to do the hokey-cokey, he has already put his left foot in and now he is frantically trying to take it out again.

"My back feels stiff," he advises The Count.

"I am sure it does, stiff with the pride of carrying out justice in front of this great crowd," The Count replies holding his fist aloft. The audience cheer.

"I think I have left my cooking fire on at home, I should probably go and check on it."

"In case you died in combat, I took the liberty of sending one of my men to go and appraise your home yesterday. You will be delighted to hear your fire is not alight and we have fed your cat. Rest your mind of these mortal matters and prepare for combat," declares the Count with a wink.

"I'm a monk, my vows mean I cannot shed another's blood," Eustace had him now.

What should have been a fun and simple trial by combat, was turning into a faff for The Count. He couldn't really argue against Eustace's Monk argument though, "fine, you can appoint a champion too."

Whilst Eustace is happy he no longer has to face Marquise, he is also a little frustrated. Apart from the devil, who wasn't taking his calls, he doesn't know anyone as competent as Hainfrois' champion. Eventually, Eustace settles on his man, one of his cousins by the name of Manesier.

Whilst Manesier is a tall, strong and steady fighter, he is clearly enchanted in the thralls of one of Eustace's spells for the man is accepting a death sentence in agreeing to fight Marquise. They are warriors of a completely different league.

Eustace does not need to use his skills of divination to

see the future, he advises The Count he does not acknowledge the outcome of this fight before it even begins. Marquise cuts down Eustace's cousin brutally in front of the cheering crowd and is declared champion. Hainfrois is innocent in the eyes of both God and the people.

Eustace was upset but he wasn't going to waste this opportunity. Eustace uses this proximity to The Count to somehow successfully wrangle a job as seneschal of Boullonnaise. This was a big job, it was essentially chief of staff, finance, operations and HR for The Count's affairs. It is a position that will allow Eustace to well and truly probe all kinds of hot pastries with his sticky little pinkies.

Eustace has quite the reputation already by this point. He has walked with the devil, ripped off a monastery, survived a trial by combat only to be appointed a senior manager with executive powers for The Counts' interests. Eustace feels invincible.

The next steps he will take are a tale as old as time itself. Drunk on power and unchecked responsibility, Eustace begins to divert the Count's funds into anonymous, off-shore bank accounts controlled by his primaries. He embezzles misappropriated funds and self-approves outrageous personal expense claims, clearly in blatant disregard of The Count's, already generous employee reimbursement policy.

Hainfrois, Eustace's rival, is one night burning the midnight oil when suddenly, he begins to rub his hands together in glee. He has been pouring over Eustace's expense accounts and found an outrageously inflated nominal code.

"Over 100,000 marks on feather quills, Eustace, my my, you have been a busy boy," Hainfrois mutters, he has got him.

Needless to say, The Count is not impressed. Eustace is forced to flee to avoid incarceration but before he leaves, he declares The Count his sworn arch enemy and advises him that it will cost 10,000 marks in damages to be rid of him. The Count is unsure where Eustace has come up with this figure and bemused as to why Eustace seems to consider his dismissal for stealing unfair?

News reaches The Count that Eustace is hiding out in the forest of Boullonnaise, no doubt he would be spending his time reflecting on his actions and relieved he had escaped, surely, he couldn't be intending to antagonise The Count further?

"We need to antagonise The Count further," declares Eustace as he holds court in the middle of the forest. If you are thinking Eustace has some parallels to Robin Hood, you'd be right, he is said to be one of three people the fictional, heroic righter-of-wrongs was based on.

"Allow me to repeat myself, we need to antagonise The Count further," Eustace's people look nervous, for by now he has people. His underlings are inspired by Eustace's fearsome, arcane reputation and his ability to turn profit off the back of almost any scam.

Eustace goes straight for the big guns against The Count, he burns down four of his windmills whilst The Count is enjoying a wedding. Eustace continues with all other kinds of mischief intended to both demean The Count and leave him out of pocket. One day, bold as brass, he approaches The Count himself whilst the nobleman is leading a stud of horses through a valley in Northern France. What is Eustace thinking, approaching the very man who would see him killed? Fear not, for Eustace is disguised…as a monk. Yes, Eustace the Monk, is disguised…as a monk. Okay, Eustace is disguised as a white monk and previously he has always adorned black robes, but still, it doesn't seem the most creative of disguises.

Eustace approaches The Count, a man of whom he has worked with for many years and somehow, isn't recognised. They talk for a time, mainly about the infamous villain "Eustace the Mercenary Pirate Monk". Eustace then sneaks off and steals one of The Count's fastest horses before declaring in a booming voice his real identity to all gathered.

Recognition hit The Count like a slap to the face as Eustace whipped off his virginal white robes to reveal black underneath. Deceptions like this become common place in the rivalry between Eustace and The Count, usually involving some kind of dress-up on the part of Eustace, he loves it.

With each farthing and pfennig Eustace took from The Count, the price on his head was rising. Things were getting hot for him, the Capetian Kingdom was not a safe place for Eustace to be anymore. Under the cover of moonlight, he makes a run for the border. He succeeds in reaching the safety of Normandy, heartland of The Plantagenets.

Here, Eustace offers his services to the King, initially, he is tasked with leading a raid against one of Philip Augustus' most important barons, a man by the name of Cadoc. Eustace stealthily, sneaks his way up the coast, leading a small band of men spread across a fleet of ships. The monk strikes under the cover of darkness, creeping into Cadoc's fortified town. Eustace and his men loot, plunder and capture a number of high profile, valuable hostages. As bells ring and the defenders form up into ranks, Eustace lets out a shrill whistle, his men scuttle back to the boats and like that, they're gone, gliding away across the inky black water.

Cadoc is furious and immediately gives chase. Now Cadoc is an accomplished seafarer himself. Accomplished though, is very different to being a master. Just as Eustace has humiliated him on land, he does exactly the same at sea, competently commandeering five of Cadoc's greatest warships. The Plantagenets are delighted to hear of the defeat of Cadoc. The King permits Eustace to build a grand palace in England even loaning him the money to get the ball rolling with construction.

Eustace continues to work for The Plantagenets, spending a considerable amount of time fighting in the Channel Islands in a bid to bring these under the family's control. Eustace enjoyed military success over this period through a solid understanding of troop manoeuvres, a mastery of naval warfare and being the possessor of a bloody big axe.

We should not consider Eustace to be an officer and a gentleman though, not by any stretch. Eustace can be likened to one of Atilla the Hun's great war elephants. Whilst their presence on a battlefield was tangible, they were also unpredictable and notoriously difficult to control. These great mammals were just as likely to trample allies as enemies and by this point, Eustace is trampling on everyone.

At one point, his lands in Norfolk were seized by the sheriff of Nottingham for non-payment of a debt owed and arrest warrants were signed for Eustace. Eustace was effectively now, unable to return to England. Shortly after this the Pope wished to visit Western France and was told he would have safe passage from The Plantagenets' soldiers, but no guarantees could be made for what Eustace would do. To make matters worse, he commandeers five war galleys from The Plantagenet King to complete a raid on the Capetians, which to be fair to him he does, but he then decides to keep the ships. This was beyond pushing boundaries and flexing muscles, this was treason.

At this point, Eustace does what any self-respecting pirate captain would do, he sets up his own pirate colony on the Isle of Sark. This channel island, with its battering winds and rugged coastlines was perfect for what he intended. Eustace set about creating a paradise for his swashbuckling band of buccaneers. There was a strict schedule, each day would start with a shot of rum as an eye-opener, followed by sea shanties in the round, knot-tying in the early afternoon with a dagger clenched between your teeth, followed by more rum, dice, some whoring, rum, bit more sea shantying, rum, nap, rum, rum, rum, dinner of fish and sea weed (with rum), before doing it all over again the next morning. Eustace had created his own piece of heaven on Earth.

Alas, all good things must come to an end. The Plantagenet King wanted his boats back. He launches an attack on the island. It's hopeless for Eustace, he and his men are so outnumbered and outgunned, it isn't even a fight. The pirates surrender the city and the thirty or so off-the-grid adventurers are taken hostage, not Eustace though. At the last minute, he manages to sail away to safety on his fastest galley.

The political landscape was shifting in Northern France. Although Philip is still alive and ruling, his son, Prince Louis was becoming ever more influential. Not in the farcical display of family feuding and usurping we witnessed during The Old King's reign, Philip enjoys a good relationship with his protégé and is amicably handing power over to his son.

With this subtle, but seismic shift underfoot, Eustace spies an opportunity. He meets with Louis and pledges his services to him and his Household. This is where we must rejoin Eustace, in danger of becoming too much of a respectable figure of Admiralty for the Capetians, Eustace is delighted to find himself once more, on a pirate's mission. The Monk has been tasked with smuggling siege equipment and other heavy ballistic weaponry from Calais to the English shores for the front runners of the Capetian army.

Even for a sailor of Eustace's considerable experience, crossing the English Channel wasn't safe. There were rogue waves, howling winds and tentacled kraken. These were not the risks Eustace is worried about though, he is concerned with the Plantagenet naval blockade of warships that protect the coastlines of Albion. Eustace will need to prove his mettle by sneaking a fleet of sixty cargo ships and ten war galleys past the itchy-trigger-fingered English who lay in wait.

Eustace calculates cost by the length of the smugglers route he intends to run. Understand, when we talk about cost here, we are not talking money, Eustace concerns himself primarily with the risk involved in any given expedition.

As Eustace watches crate after crate being loaded into the too-small a fleet he commands, he notices with a professional eye the ships sit lower and lower in the water. He mentally falters for a moment, would two trips be more appropriate? Two trips meant more manoeuvrability for the vessels and it would certainly be safer should the weather turn, but, it also meant double the risk.

"Best to do it in one trip," Eustace mutters this mantra over and over as the daylight fades and his men load the last of the crates onto the fleet. He smiles briefly as he notices Dockers withdraw away from his muttering, for fear he is preparing some kind of dark incantation. Eustace sincerely wishes he did know how to cast a spell, if he could, he would guarantee all safe passage and a happy life after this final hardship was endured. He would conjure eternal summers and comfort for all of his sailors and their loved ones.

Eustace sighed, for he could do no such thing. Although people believe he has sorcerous powers, he does not, although people believe he has walked with the devil, the closest he has come is The Plantagenet King.

Eustace does not let any of his self doubt show to his followers. His special brand of magic has always been built on deceit, falsehood and bravado. Eustace's power, is to embody others with courage based largely on The Monk's own tall tales and showmanship. Crucial to the success of this practiced performance, is conveying no fear himself, even though inside he is terrified. Eustace ascends precisely a third of the way up the rigging of the primary war galley's vessel, lazily, he wraps his forearm tightly to the rigging and leans out precariously, his balance is perfect as he leans out forty-five degrees, all eyes are on him. Welcome to Eustace's stage.

"This is the part, where I should tell you about the dangers of the crossing, the perils of the sea, the squid and the psirens, the risks we are all taking. This is the part where I tell you we should kiss our loved ones and put our affairs in order," Eustace has the gift of being able to project a whisper.

The crowd can simultaneously hear perfectly yet are also forced to lean closer, it is somehow both spectacular and intimate.

Eustace's drops his voice, "This is the part, where I tell you to remember the smell of your sweetheart, the softness of your baby's cheeks, or, that we will drink rum upon our victory," the men gathered before Eustace nod sombrely, "Well, forget that! We will drink rum now!"

Across every boat on Eustace's fleet, flagons full to the brim are brought out and passed around. Experienced naval veterans baulk in surprise, normally this would happen at the end of a voyage, not the beginning.

Eustace continues, "We will drink rum now, for we have already won. We will not say goodbye to our loved ones, for we will see them shortly."

"But the English blockade," spluttered a sailor with one eye, emboldened by a deep swig and the fire coursing down his throat.

Eustace smiled in a kindly fashion, a kingly fashion, a godly fashion, "I, Eustace, The Monk who has walked with the devil and possesses power no other mortal can ever dream of, has dealt with that. I have commanded the wind to blow us swiftly and safely to port. I have cast a spell to ensure the Plantagenets are drunk and confused...more so than usual," that got a few laughs which reassured Eustace, "I have cast a spell to ensure you are all safe and will return to your wives rich and horny! I guarantee all of your safety"

The man's eye crinkles, he smiles and it is a true smile, it is a relieved smile. He triumphantly shouts his approval of Eustace, pumping his fist aloft into the sky. Eustace climbs down from the rigging and hears the three thousand gathered sailors who were previously terrified, cheering, they are exalted that a powerful wizard such as Eustace would personally intervene ensuring their own safety. They are not scared to cast off nor are they worried for the journey. They do not feel the cold nor do they fear the enemy, they are ready to perform whatever duties are required for they know, without doubt, that they are safe and protected by powers they do not understand.

Eustace feels a dull ache in his heart as he climbs down from the rigging amidst his cheering and inspired troops.

Tell me what we have just witnessed isn't magic, tell me it isn't real.

By the time Eustace and his cargo train spy the Plantagenet fleet, there is little they can do. The wind has been against Eustace the whole way and the enemy warships materialise from nowhere. Now would have been a good time to turn, to sharply shift masts and spin 180 degrees, but to attempt it with a convoy this fully laden and in these conditions, would have scuppered the fleet. Eustace knows he has lost, although if you looked at him now, you wouldn't have been able to tell. His head tilts slightly and he mutters unheard words and holds his hand out towards the Plantagenet ships. The men aboard the fleet gain strength from his actions and row harder.

The Plantagenet fleet sit up wind of The Monk's convoy. They spy how Eustace's boats' sit in the water, how few war galleys guard their approach and they wait, they wait. Once they are close enough, they unfurl their sails which immediately catch the headwind propelling them forward and onto the sad smugglers in a matter of seconds. Nobody is left alive, including Eustace.

We must return to our main timeline and to The Lionheart, who is still sailing across the Mediterranean Sea returning home from his failed crusade. It is 1192, two decades before Eustace will fail to pull a rabbit out of a hat in the most important spell he ever attempted. Aside from the brief mention Eustace will receive in a few chapters time, he will not feature again in our tale.

When you do reach the line that triggered this intermission:

"Even Eustace the Mercenary Pirate Monk defaulted from the Plantagenet King and allied with the Capetian One."

Pause, just for a moment. Raise a small dram of rum to Eustace the Mercenary Pirate Monk and whisper into the air, "I believe in magic."

Chapter 22: Fetch the hounds, the hunt is on!

The Lionheart was not having a good trip home. Every Capetian port he attempted to dock in was closed to him. Richard got it, he may have fought shoulder to shoulder with Philip on many occasions but he had just spurned his sister. That was a slight that would not be soon forgotten. The Lionheart is a little surprised though, as a returning crusader he was supposed to enjoy free travel and protection by order of The Pope, he should have been able to dock anywhere in the Christian world he damn well pleased.

The journey continued to spiral, when The Lionheart and his men hit bad weather and were forced to wreck their ships upon the coastline of Austria to avoid perishing at sea. There was nothing else for it, Richard would have to walk home. Considering the recent frosty reception he had received in the ports of France, The Lionheart decides to keep his head low for his ramble. He is fast suspecting the parchment the Pope had signed that guaranteed his safety, was not worth the paper it was written on.

The Lionheart *should* be worried, for he is not a man without enemies. There were many who would wish to capture Richard; Philip, The Barons of Aquitaine, Sultan Saladin. All of these had plenty of motive to take advantage of the vulnerable position The Lionheart finds himself in, but it is not any of these who will make a move against him.

Do you recall when The Lionheart strode into the city of Acre following the siege? He himself spent much of this conflict on his sickbed shooting at people. Do you remember his fury at seeing the Austrian flag, flying high alongside Philip's and how Richard tore it down? Behind the scenes,

Leopold of Austria has been working tirelessly to make things very difficult for the returning Crusader King.

Leopold found convincing Philip to close his ports easy, they were rivals anyway and Philip was seriously annoyed about the whole, *not marrying his sister* thing. Harder to do for Leopold, had been to secure other European monarchs' support in hunting down Richard whilst under the protection of the Pope. Leopold begins raking up the dead and pulling skeletons from Richard's closet, he lobbies for his arrest on the grounds Richard arranged for the murder of Conrad of Montferrat, the former King of Jerusalem who had been stabbed to death by members of the Assassins Guild. This was an interesting argument. Conrad had been cousin to the former Pope and had influential connections to key figures all over Rome. If Richard was indeed guilty of this heinous crime, of course The Pope would like to see him detained.

The evidence did seem to point towards Richard. They had a confession from one of the Hashashins' Guild that Richard had ordered the killing. Granted, the confession had been made under severe torture, but hey, it was still a confession. They also had though, a letter from the guild that was not written under duress that explicitly advised Richard had sponsored the murder.

Leopold thought he had enough, so did the King of Germany. Despite being angry, Philip was being his usual, non-committal, lackadaisical, red-wine drinking self, but he did agree to close his ports to Richard. These men of power knew that Richard had left The Holy Land, they knew he had not been able to make landfall in France, they knew he was either still adrift at sea or was scurrying in shadows across the continent in a bid to return home.

"Fetch the hounds," shouts Leopold. The hunt is on.

Richard knows the game is afoot and has taken his covert operations to the next level. Aside from avoiding main roads or settlements, he has increased security protocols by travelling in disguise. He decides to conceal himself by donning the costume of a rotisserie of chicken. Presumably, rotisseries of chicken were far more prevalent and recognisable in the medieval times than they are today, as source materials assume a lot of prior knowledge from us in terms of what that would actually look like.

To successfully pull off a disguise though takes a certain personality type. Simply putting on the clothes of a man who rotates poultry for a living, will not render you unrecognisable. If you are to go undercover in this manner, you must carefully consider your character, the way you walk, how you hold yourself, you must perform. Richard is not the only king to have ever adopted this strategy.

In the seventeenth century, King Charles II will be forced to go on the run following the regicide of his father by the people and one Oliver Cromwell. Charles will disguise himself as a farm labourer, a friar and even a young peasant girl during his time on the run escaping England. The six foot tall Monarch, who was a giant for the period, will at one point have to comically climb an oak tree, elbow over heel, knee over shoulder, to hide in the branches of a Worcestershire Oak as Cromwell's soldiers search for him below.

Upon his return from exile, Charles II will reinstate Christmas and kick off the greatest party England has ever seen. This party will last for twenty-eight years and come to be known as the restoration period. Charles will exist at the centre of this movement, holding court at every major feast and festival of the age. He will sit at the top table, cheeks a-glowing and goblet full, presiding over his subjects, regaling them with comic tales and witty banter. Charles is an extrovert that loves nothing more than performing. One of his favourite after dinner speeches, would be about his time on the run after the execution of his Father, it is a story Charles tells very well.

He will put on a tiny tinny voice, as he re-creates the

moment he is disguised as a young peasant girl and questioned by Cromwell's soldiers, he will raise his lanky legs as he explains, in a self-deprecating way, how his big clown feet were too large to fit in the dainty lady's shoes and the sides had to be split. Charles will mime, both to the amusement and growing suspense of his audience, his awkward scrambled ascent against the rough bark of the infamous old oak tree in Worcester and how he hid, legs and arms wrapped about a sturdy branch, shaking, as his would be killers prowled below. Charles depicts a time of his life that must have been terrifying for him with a visceral energy, a dry, self-flagellating wit and natural charisma that left audiences enraptured. Charles' one man show was a tour de force.

It is this very kind of energy and showmanship that Charles possessed in abundance, that makes him so good at pulling off a disguise. For concealing ones' identity is more than simply pulling on a chicken rotisserie's clothing, you have to live it. You have to walk the walk of a man who has plucked a bird or two in his time, you have to come alive with passion when you describe how consistently you can brown a carcass, you must have a believable backstory, you must be charismatic. You must perform.

The problem is though, The Lionheart is no good at any of these things. He doesn't have a sense of humour, self-deprecating or otherwise, he is deadly serious, all of the time. On the rare occasion we do see The Lionheart indulging in a joke, it is usually cruel and at somebody's expense, like when he had golden chains made for the King of Cyprus. The Lionheart also does not possess the energy or showmanship of a performer, he is wooden and frankly too terrifying for an audience to engage with. Even with his disguise, The Lionheart is recognised twice before even reaching Vienna, on both occasions he manages to move swiftly enough to evade his would-be captors but it is a narrow escape.

As he hides, on the outskirts of Vienna, the Lionheart realises he needs to purchase supplies but is facing something of a liquidity problem. He sends a young boy down into the city to flog some jewellery and raise funds to purchase the essentials, flour, salted meat, wine, that sort of thing.

There were a couple of issues with The Lionheart's plan, firstly, the old knick-knack trinket the boy was sent to sell, was solid gold and absurdly valuable for a peasant boy to be in possession of. The second issue, was that it bore the Lionheart's signature emblem. It didn't take long for people to piece together this French speaking stranger who kept mumbling about chickens, wasn't who he claimed to be. The Lionheart will be apprehended and arrested as he attempts to lie low in a tavern in Vienna.

It is January 1193 and Count John enters the city of Paris with just a skeleton guard, his hood is drawn tightly about his face for The Lionheart's little brother does not wish to be recognised.

Being King was not a dream The Count should ever have dared to dwell upon and deep down he knew that. As the fourth son of The Old King, Count John had grown up with the rather mean, if factually accurate title of, "lackland," a nickname that prodded fun at the absence of titles or deeds attached to his name. As his brothers kept dropping like drunks at a wedding though, Count John found himself tantalisingly close to being the last man standing in this Royal Rumble.

Young Henry had been an impatient fool, Count John thought unkindly, had he just waited for The Old King to die he would have inherited everything. Geoffrey hadn't been the sharpest sword in the armoury either, come to think of it, getting trampled to death in a jousting accident, I mean talk about pointless.

The latest development was just unbelievable. The Lionheart, the last remaining brother standing between John and the throne, had somehow been captured by Leopold of Austria. The Lionheart certainly wasn't a fool, at least John didn't think so, but he also wasn't smart. I mean who the hell spent all of that money, risked their own life and endangered their kingdom just to engender themselves to a Pope who couldn't even keep you safe on your way home? John has a fair point.

Yes, there was a chance the Lionheart would be released safely, but there was also a chance he wouldn't. There are examples of History changing when an elder son dies and the younger sibling steps into the breach, Henry VIII is an example of this. Had the infamous, bloated Tudor monarch's elder brother not died, England would look very different today and Anne Boleyn would still be alive (well, probably not after all this time, but her remains would at least be intact).

Though there are instances of an elder sibling dying, there does not seem to be any other instances of three such deaths, falling neatly into place like collapsing dominoes to allow the fourth youngest son to take the throne. To John, it seemed like divine intervention, it was written in the stars that he would be King.

Besides the fact that The Lionheart wasn't dead, only imprisoned, there was another fairly significant barrier to Count John's ascension. When I wrote earlier that John;s elder brother Geoffrey died without a male heir, this statement was something of a Schrodinger's cat, it was simultaneously both true and false.

Geoffrey's death, six years earlier in Paris, had been sudden and unexpected, that much is agreed upon, although this is where consensus ends. There are two versions surrounding Geoffrey's death. The first, is that he died trampled to death in an accident at a jousting tournament. The second telling of the tale, places Geoffrey in the Parisian court addressing Philip Augustus and his closest advisors. Geoffrey is in the middle of declaring his intentions to go to war with his father, The Old King, when he is hit with a sudden and crippling chest pain. At twenty-seven, Geoffrey should not have been at risk for a heart attack but it isn't an impossibility. Chroniclers of the time who subscribed to this theory, attributed this sudden death to Geoffrey's intent to rebel against the blessed Old King, they see it as an example of God, or perhaps Becket, smiting him down from heaven.

As Geoffrey's casket is lowered into the earth, his wife Constance throws herself upon it, wailing uncontrollably. Her tiny fists rain down on the slap of stone that separate her from her deceased beloved, she feels numb and wishes to be buried with him. Would it have eased her grief at all to know, that Geoffrey was not completely dead? A part of him, unbeknownst to Constance, lived on within her womb, the spark of a fire, the seed of a sapling. Constance is pregnant with Geoffrey's progeny.

Not only does Geoffrey manage to posthumously Father a child, from his loins spring forward a healthy son that was built like a Little Lionheart and had the charisma of a Young Henry, Constance named him Arthur. By now, Arthur is six years old and alongside Richard, represents a barrier in John's play for the throne. Even if Richard was indeed out of the way, which was by no means a certainty, technically, the six year old Arthur would have a better claim for the throne than John.

Despite himself, John quite liked his little nephew, his sense of entitlement and constant demand to do whatever he wanted and only that, was truly an inspiration. John had played wooden swords with his nephew during a recent visit. After a brief spell of clattering swipes, parries and laughter, Arthur had spied a pile of great stones intended for the maintenance of part of the castle walls.

With the speed of a cheetah, he had dashed towards the rubble and leapt majestically, climbing towards the sky like Icarus, higher and higher. He turned with a snap, laughing manically, in a sing song voice he shouts, "Uncle

John, I'm the King of the Castle and you're a dirty rascal."
Count John laughed along, perhaps a little too
enthusiastically for he doesn't find it very funny.

It was these concerns that brought John to Paris. He
had received a letter from Philip saying they should meet.
The timing made it clear it would be about his brother. The
price tag placed on Richard for his release was insanely high
and raising such a sum seemed insurmountable. It was
looking increasingly likely that Richard would remain in his
jail cell for a considerable time.

Not that John wanted that you understand, the last
thing he wanted was to seize control of the Plantagenet
Nation whilst Richard was still alive, of course not. That
being said, the country did need leadership and John was
open for business.

John views his visit to Philip today as by no means
treasonous. John simply wants to put a contingency strategy
in place, a "plan b" if you will, should Richard not return,
which he almost certainly would… probably. The only
reason John is arriving in Paris under the cover of nightfall
and in disguise was purely logistical so as not to get waylaid
on route.

John had other reasons to be cautious too though.
Eleanor of Aquitaine, for one, she seemed to suspect he was
up to something and scheming for the throne. Unbelievably,
somehow, the talking wildebeest Sir William Marshal also
seemed to have suspicions of him. Whenever Philip's name
was brought up in the Plantagenet court, he would look at
John with his big, wide, stupid doe eyes, how John would like
to put a crossbow bolt between them. So yes, there was more
than a little need for caution before his meeting with Philip
Augustus.

John will parlay with Philip and their deeds will be as
dark as the night on which they met. The terms drawn up
were fairly simple.

Firstly, Philip will support John in becoming King of

the Plantagenet empire. This is more than a little dodgy, after all, The Lionheart isn't dead and even if he was, his nephew Arthur was next in line.

Secondly, it was agreed John would marry Philip's sister. Philip is determined to get his Capetian Plantagenet wedding that had been so rudely snubbed by Richard across the line. A union between the two dynasties was probably not a bad idea, the families had spent an inordinate amount of time, money and resources fighting each other. Cementing some kind of peace through marriage could be a positive for both empires.

There was a problem here though for John was already married. To fulfil this part of the bargain, John would somehow need to convince the Pope to nullify the union between himself and his existing wife.

The final agreement reached, was that John would assist Philip to buy The Lionheart for the hefty sum of 100,000 Marks. If point one of the deal was a little dodgy, this could be tantamount to regicide. Philip was hardly likely to release The Lionheart if he were to gain custody of him, especially if he has also pledged to assist John in taking over the family business.

Owning Richard would effectively leave Philip with the choice of whether to campaign against John, or the Lionheart, when you put it like that, it was no choice at all. Count John has just signed a death sentence for his brother.

As John leaves Paris, the rain lashes down. He draws his cloak closer to him and his hood remains up. Does he pause, just for a second? Does he reminisce on endless childhoods of Summers spent playing in the Aquitaine rose gardens with his mother and Richard? Does he recall his little nephew's smile, or wonder what Young Henry would do in his stead?

No. Count John doesn't wonder any of those things. Under his hood he is grinning from ear to ear, he is the cat that has got the cream, he is the brother that has taken the throne.

Over the next few months, Count John will all but openly move against his brother. He will use emergency powers to seize castles across England, re-appropriate seats of government and manoeuvre himself into position to take the reins from the imprisoned Richard.

Chapter 23: The Unhappy Economics of Richard's kingdom

This unfortunate capture of Richard provides an opportunity to blur the lines between History and Philosophy. Namely, we can answer the question of how much a man's life is worth, not just a man but a King no less.

Today, in the United Kingdom, were you to lose your little finger in an accident at work that was not your fault, you could expect to receive in the region of £9000, a thumb, however, would pay out upwards of £30,000. On the other hand, excuse the pun, were you to lose an entire hand, you would be in for a six figure payout of £100,000+, limb(s) you're looking at least a quarter of a million.

A life though, that's harder to value. The United States were forced to give it a go following the attacks of 9/11. In the wake of this atrocity, $2 million dollars seems to have been the average pay out to families who lost a loved one, although, compensation ranged significantly for victims based on variables such as age at death and anticipated future earnings potential. In the words of the great political novelist George Orwell, "All animals are equal, but some animals are more equal than others," if this is the case, than The Lionheart must be the most equal of us all.

His ransom was eventually agreed at 150,000 marks. In today's money, this is a figure of about £2 billion, it was an absurd sum. It wasn't as easy in the Medieval times to debase currency and "print" money. This kind of figure was going to require rounds of funding the likes of which the medieval world had never seen before. It would need draconian levels of taxation and a massive PR campaign on behalf of The King. To pull all of this together with minimal alienation of either The Barons or the lay people, would need a leader of magnetic charisma, political clout and inspirational gravitas.

Eleanor of Aquitaine does not miss a beat and hits the touring circuit to raise the cash, she is ably supported by William Marshal and Earl Hubert Walter. It's a big task, for Eleanor didn't start with a lot in the coffers to begin with. The Lionheart had put everything up for sale to pay for The Crusades already. Remember William the Lion, the crazy Scottish monarch who had been forced to sign a humiliating treaty under The Old King? That treaty had been ripped up under Richard in return for the tidy sum of 10,000 marks. William had even been offered his beloved Northumbria for the right price, it was a deal The Lion declined for the small print dictated he would not be granted control of the castles in the region, which was the bit of Northumbria he really wanted. The Lionheart even declared he would have sold London if only he could someone foolish enough to buy it.

The pressure was on for Eleanor of Aquitaine for she is not the only one interested in buying The Lionheart. Philip was sniffing around, making low ball counter offers for the Plantagenet King. The chance to have his arch rival as a captive, was just too appealing a notion for Philip. Whilst Philip was not able to offer the full amount, his early substantial tender was sparking a bidding war and just about justifying the Lionheart's eye watering valuation.

Eleanor and Sir William Marshal were travelling across the Plantagenet empire enforcing extortionate taxes across the people and churches of the land. The Jewish community were hit particularly heavily. They were ordered to extend significant lines of credit to the crown, this in turn forced them to doggedly claw back any outstanding debts that were owed to them. This redirected much of the people's anger away from the Plantagenet family and towards the Hebrew community.

Bags of silver began to pile up in the cellars of St. Paul's

Cathedral, although it was painstakingly slow and the Plantagenets were in very real danger of losing this high stakes auction. The problem is fairly obvious. They are trying to raise otherwise unheard of sums for a raping, murderous psychopath who had already lost a lot of their money not winning the Crusades. It was time for Richard to get a rebrand.

Eleanor of Aquitaine sets about weaving a tapestry that will persevere even today. The PR persona of, "The Good King Richard" is born. Much like when in her early career she ordered burly knights to recite poetry, she now has little white rabbits running about the kingdom telling tales of her son's great chivalry as a knight and the countless acts of heroism he had conducted in the Holy Land on behalf of us all in the eyes of God. The King becomes a paradigm of honour and piety.

The Lionheart's new face, with its easy going smile and good-natured eye crinkles, proves far easier to raise coin for than the snarling, feral beast he truly was. St. Paul's cathedral cellars are eventually filled to bursting point with hessian bags crammed with silver, Eleanor of Aquitaine had done it. She personally saw to the transfer of funds, which was to be "At the King's Peril," meaning, in short, that if the money were to go astray in transit it would be The Lionheart's problem and his alone.

Eleanor's achievement should not be underestimated, it was crowd-sourced fundraising on an unprecedented scale. For the Lionheart's ransom, Eleanor had successfully removed a quarter of coinage from circulation in the Plantagenet kingdom. This, in turn caused mass deflation of their currency and barter to once more prevail in many areas of the country that had literally ran out of money that could be used.

Richard emerges from his imprisonment as the legend his mother has created. He embraces his new found popularity and happily steps into the shoes of, the Good King

Richard. In reality though, he is anything but. The Lionheart's failed Crusade and King's ransom, has pushed his lands to the brink of financial ruin.

The Old King had proven himself to be both frugal and financially dexterous. For all of his constant travelling, muscle flexing, snarling, intimidation and howling at the moon, he didn't actually conduct that many out and out military campaigns - he didn't like them. He felt the outcome wasn't predictable enough and The Old King was a stickler for being in control of everything. He also, quite rightly, identified that they were money pits.

The Lionheart had inherited a kingdom that annually would raise around £15,000 from its subjects. A few short years later Richard will have stepped on the gas and be squeezing double that from his populous. This additional revenue was not the result of a nationwide increase in GDP, it was borne simply from taxing his Barons and Earls more than will prove sustainable. This was fine though, it was explained away as an extraordinary, atypical cost appropriated for The Crusades, a "Saladin tithe".

The problem was though, these extraordinary, atypical expenses were becoming both ordinary and typical. If it wasn't crusading, it was Richard's ransom, once the ransom money had been raised, The Lionheart will go back to war with Capetian France. The nation will never see a return to the taxation levels Richard's father had successfully managed to run his Kingdom at. Perhaps if this enforced austerity had delivered Jerusalem, or was part of a short-term plan for a brighter future, the people could have understood, but there seemed no end in sight.

The Lionheart is crippling the economy and spending all of the money on military campaigns, whereas rival nations were re-investing across their own lands facilitating growth. Consider the market share of the Plantagenets vs. The Capetians, in 1180, under The Old King's stewardship, annual revenues were £15,467 whereas the Capetians were raising around half that. By the end of the Lionheart's reign, the Capetians will be raising more than the Plantagenets through their own organic growth and successful expansionist policies.

Whilst The Lionheart is keen to shore up his borders and reclaim lands that have been nibbled away at during his absence by Philip, more on that shortly, Richard does not seem to recognise or understand the growing need to take an interest in the financial management of his Kingdom. The insanely high taxation he is inflicting upon his Barons trickles down to every subject in his kingdom and the empire is miserable.

Chapter 24: Beware, for the devil is loose

Philip was the first to hear about the Lionheart's release. He sent word to John advising him to watch himself, "for the devil was loose". Upon returning to his kingdom, The Lionheart was horrified at what he found, for his lands were in a sorry state. His loyal(ish) band of barons, were fed up of being taxed extortionately and were no longer feeling particularly loyal. John had seized control of a number of castles and Philip kept stealing bits of Normandy. The Lionheart decided, it was probably time for a party.

Yes that's right. The Lionheart decided to have another coronation in Winchester, England. This was definitely a party, although it's unclear whether it counts as a coronation. The Lionheart had, after all, already been crowned. The only other King of England who will ever be crowned twice will be Henry VI, who at least had the decency to rule for a bit, be forced out for nine years and then come back to rule again. The Lionheart's second coronation was purely an attempt to live up to the legend his mother had created. Richard spends time kissing babies, shaking hands, kissing shaking babies, probably shaking babies knowing the Lionheart as we do.

He hates this necessary, but sedate period. For The Lionheart there has to always be a battle on the horizon, a war to win. There needs to be a fight and the Lionheart is spoiling for what will no doubt be his biggest yet. He is going to fight for his legacy, lands and birth right against his own flesh and blood, his brother John.

As The Lionheart prepares to march on Tickhill Castle in South Yorkshire and evict his brother's men from their walls, it would be reasonable to ask if this is a castle that generates significant revenue, or, perhaps is it one that holds a geographically strategic location? Not really, it's just a castle The Lionheart had explicitly told his brother to leave alone. In Richard's absence John had taken it anyway, sibling rivalry stuff, you know how it is.

In the Holy Land, The Lionheart sometimes felt like a fish out of water, here, in the Plantagenet kingdom, he is a shark very much in his element. The great military leader begins completing all of the due diligence and preparation you would expect from an operator of his level. The great siege weapons from The Crusades, "God's own Catapult" and "Bad Neighbour" are serviced, greased and loaded up onto wagons ready to rain thunder and death down once more, under The Lionheart's flag.

The army bed down for one final night of calm before the inevitable storm. They serve one of the greatest war time Generals on the planet, but even so, Count John is an unknown commodity. He has proven himself adept at navigating the murky waters of political court, who knew what he was capable of on a battlefield?

Any soldier will tell you the night's sleep before a conflict is bittersweet. Though your alert and anxious mind prays for the release of unconsciousness, you fear that it will become your eternity and you cling fast to what could be your final wakeful hours on this earth.

Tickhill Castle is not the largest of castles, but that doesn't mean a lot. In fact, smaller castles can be easier to defend, less wall space to man and a more concentrated splash zone of fire. These are all thoughts that are going through The Lionheart's mind as he marches towards a decisive and bloody conflict with John.

England is not the sparse deserts of The Holy Land and across windswept Albion, word travels far faster than the deserts surrounding Jerusalem. Count John's spies had departed Winchester before The Lionheart and his armies had been able to mobilise. They ride swiftly, by cover of nightfall, their horses' hooves gliding over the dew flecked grass and rocky outcrops. They will urge their horses ever faster as the enlightened city of Oxford passes them by in a blur.

The Tickhill Castle Warden reads the note warning him of Richard's approach, he shakes his head with a wry smile. This wasn't a complete surprise. He had suspected they would be a target the moment orders had arrived from Count John advising them that they must defend, resist and repel at all costs. The castle was well prepared. The walls had been checked for breaches or weaknesses and had not been found wanting. Arrow quivers were stuffed and the dungeons were lined with vats, filled to the brim, with boiling oil. In other words, the castle was ready.

Forget that though for a game of soldiers. The Warden follows the only course of action he believes realistic, he unequivocally and without condition surrenders to The Lionheart.

The Lionheart's father, The Old King, could terrify and intimidate people with a stare, an angry word or some kind of posturing, often negating the need for actual combat. We saw him do this on the Welsh Marches with great success. The Old King would though, usually have the decency to be within shooting range of the castle he is trying to steal when he attempts this kind of intimidation. The Lionheart over two hundred miles away secured the surrender of Tickhill Castle by his reputation alone and this is not underserved, The Lionheart is a terrifying military commander with more campaigning hours under his belt than any other living General.

A few of Count John's castles will hold out for a little longer than Tickhill manages, but not much so. Nottingham Castle dug in the deepest, managing to keep Richard at bay for a whole two days. The Lionheart mops up this resistance with relish, swiftly resuming control of England once more.

One evening, as The Lionheart rests in his court in Normandy, John visits and prostrates himself at his feet. The Count begs for forgiveness, he howls, he weeps, Richard sits stoically, his face gives nothing away. Finally, after what feels an eternity, The Lionheart stands to speak to his grovelling, snivelling excuse for a brother.

Succinctly, Richard will summarise rather patronisingly that he does not consider his little brother John (aged twenty-eight), to be anything but a child. The Lionheart felt that John had fallen prey to bad advisors, he makes it clear it is they who shall bear the brunt of his wrath. Richard's uncharacteristic good grace could be attributed to a number of motives, he had never been particularly bothered about England anyway, he thought his brother John a paper tiger, Richard considered John's rebellion to be an appetiser compared to the main course that would be Philip Augustus.

For whilst The Lionheart has been incarcerated and dealing with John, Philip has conquered much of Normandy and the Plantagenet interests in France. It is time for Richard to once again pitch his prowess against a worthy opponent, The Lionheart needs to sort out Philip. To do this, he will need strategy, he will need resources, he will need allies that he can trust. It is time for the Lionheart to have an awkward conversation with the great knight, Sir William Marshal.

Sir William Marshal, well that's a character we haven't heard from in a long time, a very long time.

Come to think of it, why didn't the Lionheart take Marshal with him on The Third Crusade? After all, Richard was about to plunge himself into unfamiliar surroundings against the Sultan Saladin, the greatest foe he will ever face, who wouldn't want the giant of chivalry at his side grinding his teeth and grinning demonically? Marshal had served The Lionheart's family loyally and with distinction after all, proving his fealty to Eleanor, Young Henry and the Old King. It seems inconceivable Marshal would have been anything but an asset in the Holy Land.

We can't know with certainty why Marshal was not picked to accompany Richard on his Crusade and we are left to speculate. Perhaps, Richard does not want the tournament celebrity Marshal who is already established in Jerusalem and closely connected with the Knights Templars to overshadow him in the desert? Or, The Lionheart is worried about his mother. He does care for her after all, perhaps Richard felt better leaving behind a stalwart rockstar such as Marshal at her disposal?

At this point though, it is worth us revisiting the last meeting these two great warriors shared, if you recall, Marshal had been charging hard downhill at the unarmoured Richard, his lance had been clenched overhand in a vice like grip and was aimed for a killing blow.

The Lionheart was exposed and unprepared, his life was in Marshal's hands. At the last second, Marshal dropped his aim just a fraction, he smashed into the King throwing him from his saddle and ran through his war horse.

The Lionheart prepares to meet with William Marshal once more. When he does, Richard cocks an eyebrow in surprise. Marshal's previously jet-black hair, is now silver as a badger and a small bald spot adorns his crown, The Lionheart can't help but smile. William Marshal has gotten old. On closer inspection though, he still looks in fantastic shape, thinks The Lionheart, if anything, he looks fitter than he did five years ago. His paunch was gone, he stands taller and his limbs move with a fluidity that a man half his age would envy. How is that possible? Do the sands of time not ravage this giant of a man like it does the rest of us, wonders Richard?

Marshal is proud of his physique and age defying body, whereas previously Marshal had been partial to a party or a glut of gluttony, he now understands that a gentleman of his advancing years needed to look after himself. Marshal endeavours to drink plenty of water each day and usually gets a good night's sleep.

When Marshal does feast, which these days was none too often, he will pour himself a full goblet of wine before publicly taking a herculean swig, he will then discretely leave the remainder on an unoccupied table somewhere no one would notice. Marshal also works hard hours every day in the training yard, mercilessly swinging his great, heavy practice sword against the wooden tilting post, sweat pours from his face and splinters explode in the air around him.

Marshal and The Lionheart size each other up. The two men circle one another, snarling slightly. The Lionheart looks tanned, thinks Marshal, recalling the unrelenting desert sun that beat down on him in the Holy Land all those years ago when he had taken the cross. Marshal also observes, that whilst there is still death behind the eyes of the Lionheart, he carries himself with a discipline and prestige that was not there before. There was a hint of humility, a whisper of wisdom, perhaps the man has changed, perhaps he has grown?

"Shall we ride." The Lionheart asks, in a way that makes it perfectly clear this is no question. Marshal nods.

The two heroes ride but do not speak. Eventually, after their horses' gallop has eaten up much of the French countryside and they are well and truly alone, The Lionheart pulls up his mare, "Had I not deflected your lance and glanced it down towards my horse, you would have killed me that day Marshal."

We should bear in mind that this statement isn't true, the Lionheart knows it isn't true as does Marshal. We know it is not true. Marshal had Richard that day in the valley and chose to spare him.

Marshal is facing an impossible choice though in which there is no right answer. Does he suggest, that actually, Richard the Lionheart is a liar? That wouldn't go down well. Equally though, does he agree that the King deflected the blow, in which case Marshal had attempted to kill him? That also didn't sound too good. Marshal wrestles with his options and reaches his conclusion.

Marshal would have nobody, not even Richard the Lionheart, King of the Plantagenets, doubt his skill or knightly prowess, "I have enough strength and control over my lance to have killed you had I wanted to," replies Marshal.

The exchange wasn't going quite how the Lionheart would have liked it to, but there wasn't much he could do, he needed Marshal. Richard advises the great knight that he is forgiven and is to be enlisted immediately in his armies for the war in France.

The Lionheart wasted no time getting to work reclaiming castles and towns that John had surrendered to Philip. One of the Lionheart's first moves, was to win back the town of Vendome, an isolated settlement that was of strategic importance as a launch pad into the Loire valley. Vendome was not a fortified town, so the Lionheart's men set up a defensive encampment just outside the city. They finish this in the nick of time, just as the final trench is dug and the last wooden palisade erected, Philip and his men appear on the horizon.

There are uncomfortable murmurings across The Lionheart's camp as the men digest the size of the Capetian army. The Plantagenets expected to command numerical superiority, but in reality, the armies are pretty evenly matched. The meagre defensive ditch and barricades the Lionheart's men had worked on would offer a negligible advantage, but even to experienced Generals, the whole thing seemed as sure as a coin toss.

The Lionheart isn't concerned though, not because he feels particularly lucky today, but because he knows something that his men do not. Richard has the relaxed demeanour about him of a Grand Master Chess Player that can see into the future, he knows that in ten moves time he will win a sure-as-day, check mate victory. Word is brought to him that there is a messenger from Philip in camp who wished to speak with him, "I'm sure he does..." the Lionheart mutters distractedly as he pulled on his iconic, Crusader tunic.

How could The Lionheart be so certain of his victory, what does he see that we cannot? Richard knows he has won, for Philip has walked into a trap. If anyone should be able to spot this trap, it is Richard, for he has seen it many times before. It is the very one he himself nearly fell into multiple times when crusading in The Holy Land. Not once, not twice, but three times Richard and The Crusaders rode to within spitting distance of Jerusalem, only to decide that the isolated approach, the exposed supply chain would see the battle lost before it began.

Though only a handful of miles separate the two armies, the narrow road and indefensible open fields that surround Vendome, mean that Philip and his men must run a gauntlet of death before they could even engage with The Plantagenets. The Lionheart knows this and he intends to harry the Capetians every step of the way, his archers will advance, fire three disciplined volleys before disappearing off into the country side. Philip's men will be unable to give chase for fear a larger force awaits ready to ambush them just over the next horizon. Philip cannot even easily reverse out of the jaws of this trap, for if he does, he must still traverse miles of open road with the Lionheart and his men snapping at their heels.

Philip has, by now, realised what a terrible mistake he has made by coming to this isolated town and how tenuous his vulnerable foothold really is. He has trod on a pressure plate and heard the ominous, metallic click of the trigger, he is fully aware, that even a hairline movement could see the landmine go off beneath him. He had banked on the Lionheart riding out to meet him in open combat. Philip had reasoned that Richard was hot headed, impulsive, rash, under no circumstances did he picture The Lionheart calmly sitting back and doing nothing. Philip has marched his entire Capetian army into an indefensible no man's land.

Philip does what any poker player would do when he is caught without decent cards, he bluffs.

"We will attack at first light," the messenger announces to the Lionheart.

"See that you do, we will be waiting for you and if you do not, well, we may just pay a little visit to your camp," The Lionheart speaks softly with the clarity and conviction of a man who knows he has already won.

The Lionheart's scouts keep a watchful eye on the Capetian camp all night, but no attack is forthcoming. At first light, the Lionheart forms his men into ranks, this is too much for Philip who loses his nerve and gives the order to retreat. The hunt is on, The Lionheart forms a strike party and rides out hard to engage with the retreating Capetians. This strategy is not without risk to Richard, if the Lionheart loses control of his men in the advanced party, they could leave themselves vulnerable to a counter-attack. The Lionheart attempts to mitigate this risk by commanding Marshal lead a secondary force behind the Lionheart.

Sir William Marshal's men will be ordered to march slowly, with a rigid discipline, mopping up any Capetians that manage to slip past the Lionheart's riders, but more importantly, they will provide a safety net for Richard and his men should they need to withdraw behind it. This was no easy task, Marshal's men must watch their comrades in Richard's regiment, winning both glory and plunder, looting and raiding, swooping and harrying whilst all the while continuing their steady, rigid advance. The fact Marshal can pull it off and hold the line, is a testament to the respect he commands and his abilities as a field general.

The safety net was a sensible precaution, but in the end, it wasn't needed for the Capetians never manage to rally. In fact, as more of the rear guard are killed, it turns from a semi disciplined retreat to pandemonium. Blindly running was the worst thing The Capetians could have done. The Lionheart and his men fall upon them with a renewed vigour, incarcerating and killing hundreds of Philip's soldiers as they hunt for the man himself. The night is still young and The Lionheart is desperate to capture The Capetian King.

It is all rather embarrassing for Philip. The Lionheart and his men have completely routed his forces and destroyed a significant proportion of his army. They have stolen a huge amount of plunder having captured a supply train, including some of Philip's personal artefacts. Richard can smell blood and is desperate to go for the kill and end this. He comes seriously close too, missing Philip by the slightest of margins when the Capetian King goes off-road to hide inside an abandoned church.

Philip listens in the dark and empty church to the horses' hooves travelling towards his hiding place. Philip's heart pumps so loudly in his ears, he is sure his would be captors could hear it, even outside the old stone walls. He tries to control his breathing, but is hyperventilating as the column of horses stop right outside the church door. Philip gasps for air like a drowning man who has just broken the surface, he clasps both hands to his mouth to try and silence his panting and whimpers, tears stream down his cheeks.

He can hear the men shouting to one another, though he cannot make out what they are saying. He is certain, that at any moment, they will kick in the heavy door of the church and he would feel a metal gauntleted hand grasp upon his ankle, unceremoniously, he imagines he will be dragged from under the pew he cowers beneath.

Miraculously though, the church door does not explode in splinters and an armoured hand does not clasp about his exposed ankle, after what seems an eternity, the hooves start up again and fade off into the distance. Philip breathes a sigh of relief and begins to crawl out from beneath the great wooden bench, he steadies his gasps and leans heavily against the wall, slowly, he slumps to the floor. The all-encompassing terror he had felt before has now passed, it is replaced instead by a bottomless pit of despair. Philip clenches his jaw, he is the King of the Capetian dynasty, he was the stock of men who had always commanded their own destiny and that of their subjects, he would be no different. He swore to God in that dark and abandoned church that night, he would beat this Lionheart.

Philip stands tall, he arches his back, he snarls into the blackness, "I am coming for you Richard." The balls of Philip's feet hum with anticipation, he can hear the marching drum in his mind that his men will move to, the communal wine in the font quivers and jumps to the beat.

The communal wine in the font quivers and jumps to the beat, Philip thinks with a panicked pang, that drumming was not in his mind at all, it was outside the church he sought sanctuary in. Philip dives back beneath the pew.

The shocks Philip can hear, is thousands of fully armoured Plantagenet men marching in a slow and disciplined fashion along the abandoned road, it is William Marshal's rear guard. Philip does not know it but these men are under strict orders to neither loot nor deviate from the main path.

The Capetian King waits for the rumble of marching soldiers to pass, before running off into the inky black night.

Over the next four years, The Lionheart will systematically and systemically take back the lands that Philip has nicked. It will be a slog, it will be non-stop campaigning and The Lionheart loves every second of it. John, to be fair, proves himself to be a valuable asset to Richard. He is diligently committed and reasonably effective against the Capetian forces.

Early in the conflict, John will secure a fairly cheap victory, demonstrating both his cunning and ruthless nature when he rides into the town of Evreux. He is welcomed into the garrison by the Capetian forces with open arms who do not yet know that he has switched sides. Once the last of

John's men are ushered in, they swiftly turn on the surprised occupiers and brutally slaughter them.

Another fight of note involving John, was the battle for Castle Milly. John was supported and monitored by Sir William Marshal, who by now has become the Lionheart's right-hand man. John and Marshal arrive at the castle to find the defenders lined up on the walls, geared up and ready to fight. The pair elect to breach the walls but lack the necessary siege engines to collapse the masonry, instead, great ladders are readied and the generals give the order to charge.

The onslaught from the defenders was intense, large blocks of wood were dropped although arrow fire was sparse, the castle seemed under resourced. Despite this, each time the attackers manage to get a ladder up against the wall, the defenders would push the bloody thing back down, it was infuriating.

Eventually, one of the ladders sticks long enough for two of the Plantagenet knights to crest the battlements. Marshal whoops and cheers although his cries soon turn to dismay. Marshal watches their silhouettes fighting atop the ramparts, alone and isolated, he knows they are in serious trouble. With a great war cry, the fifty year old Marshal sprints in full armour thirty metres to the wall, it feels like three miles to the ageing warrior. Somehow, Marshal manages to scale the ladder unmolested with an impossible speed for a man of his age and armoured encumbrance.

By the time he has reached the top of the wall, he is so out of breath he can barely stand. Feebly, he manages to parry the first blow that is aimed at his head. It is around now that Marshal worries he may have made a foolish error. He is completely winded and can barely stand up straight, a sea of enemies wash along the ramparts towards him, eager to capture such a high profile prisoner. Marshal needn't have been concerned though, the sight of the legendary leader bounding across the killing fields and rocketing up the ladder had so inspired his men they were but a metre behind him.

The day was won by Marshal's typically brave but uncharacteristically reckless behaviour. When the Lionheart hears of this much later, he will chastise Marshal, advising him to save deeds like that for younger men. It was a fair comment from Richard, Marshal is too important a cog in the Plantagenet machine to be taking risks like that.

As Spring blossoms in the final year of the thirteenth century, Richard takes a moment to reflect on what he has accomplished and to think on his future. Over the last four years, The Lionheart has restored the great Plantagenet empire, reclaiming land and pushing back the Capetians. Granted, his enemy still retained an annoying amount of castles across the continent, but they do so in deed alone. Richard and Marshal have every square mile of French countryside covered by patrols, to the extent that chroniclers record Philip's men hardly dared leave any of their forts for fear of capture or combat. Supplies reaching the defenders locked behind their castle walls were sporadic, more often than not the Lionheart and Marshal's men would spot these wagons and pilfer them. It was just a matter of time before the Capetian controlled castles in Richard's realm would surrender, hungry soldiers didn't tend to be the most loyal.

The Lionheart furthered his stranglehold on the Capetians and central France by building a castle of incredible fortitude. Nestled into a meandering arc of the River Seine, general consensus agreed that Castle Gaillard was unconquerable. Aside from the natural protection it was afforded by the river, it also boasted seventeen towers and walls that were four metres thick. These walls scarred the hill it was built atop in wide, concentric circles. Chateau Gaillard was stunning, terrifying and a complete overkill. The Capetians were already hiding in burrows, The Lionheart already *owned* the roads, but it sent a clear message. Richard was back.

Further afield, things were also looking interesting. Rome had a new Pope and his name was Innocent III.

Innocent and his family had turned Popeing into an ancestral business, a "Pope & Sons" set up if you will. Innocent's Uncle had been Pope before him, Innocent's nephew will be Pope after him, even Innocent's nephew's nephew will one day adorn the pointy hat. In fact, over five centuries Innocent's family tree will boast a staggering thirteen Popes, forty cardinals and three anti-popes. An anti-pope is as it sounds, a nutter who acquires his own followers and declares himself to be Pope in contempt of the officially anointed leader on Earth of Catholicism. To say being a Pope ran in Innocent's blood, would be an understatement.

By 1199, Innocent has only been in power for a year, but already he is causing waves. He behaves less like the spiritual leader and moral compass for a worldwide faith, than he does an expansionist minded Dictator of an Empire. It's easy to see why Innocent was confused, the relationship between European Kings and the Vatican was more than a little muddy. Kings of Europe would pay tribute to The Pope, they would crusade for him, in many ways they were answerable to him. To say the Plantagenet empire was a vassal state or a fiefdom of Rome would probably be a step too far, but it would not be completely inaccurate.

The Pope lacked the military might to be able to conquer Richard, although this was something Innocent was working to resolve with his recent inception of the order of the Teutonic Knights and the relationships he was forging across Europe. Innocent's growing military clout was not the only weapon in his armoury, he also wielded the power to excommunicate individuals, regions or even entire nations. This would essentially condemn to damnation the souls of all subjects residing within, put a halt to any spiritual services, weddings, funerals, baptisms, Christmas. Excommunication was serious business and not something any Pope would resort to lightly. That being said, Richard did feel Innocent more likely than other Popes to push this big red button if challenged.

We are getting ahead of ourselves though and we are a long way away from Innocent resorting to anything quite so extreme, for at the moment, Innocent needs something from The Lionheart and is playing nice, Innocent is schmoozing. The Pope wants Richard to reconcile with Philip Augustus and launch, "The Fourth Crusade: Richard's Revenge."

The Lionheart is understandably ambivalent about this, on the one hand, Jerusalem is his high school sweetheart that moved away, the book he never finished, the song he never sung. He is also painfully aware though that last time he mobilised and went to war for Rome, Philip had pinched half of his land and Leopold of Austria imprisoned him for over a year, all whilst the previous Pope hadn't bothered to lift a finger. There was no certainty, despite his assurances, that Innocent would behave any more proactively in defending Richard's kingdom in his absence than his predecessor had.

Another issue that bothered The Lionheart when he thought about Crusading again, was that for Richard, the vision of conquering The Holy City and the fantasy of defeating Saladin had become so intertwined, it was now almost impossible to unpick. The Lionheart knows he will never get to defeat the Sultan, for Saladin had passed away of a fever six years earlier, he had died victorious, a hero and with a legacy that will echo through the ages. Maybe that was the way to go, mused Richard? He thought back to the note he had sent Saladin when he had departed the Holy Land, he had promised to return to Jerusalem and take the city from him, now he would never get that chance. The Lionheart pauses for a moment to pay respect to his long time rival, whilst also cursing the dead man for depriving him the final showdown he so craved.

By now, Philip Augustus has largely surrendered against Richard, although one or two castles still hold out. It is here that we re-join The Lionheart, at Chalus Castle.

Richard surveys the frontline, slightly bemused if he is honest that it was still resisting. A skeleton force defends the fortification, there are just two knights and less than forty infantry men.

Yesterday, Richard's sappers had completed most of the undermining work, the outer wall would soon collapse. Only six defenders had been on the wall yesterday attempting to fight off the attackers, they were so badly armoured that some were using frying pans instead of shields. The Lionheart had held them off single handed without breaking a sweat. The twang of his crossbow rang melodically across the quiet battlefield like a harp.

As The Lionheart took his early morning stroll through his camp, he recalls with sepia toned, rose tinted glasses his time in The Holy Land, he reminisces about spearheading the beach charge of Jaffa, his wedding in Cyprus. This nothing-castle that Richard is now faced with feels a far cry from those heady days of heroism that he longs for once again.

The Lionheart pauses to survey the castle walls with confusion, the stone fortifications seemed to be defying everything he knew about construction, they should, by all rights, have collapsed by now. Richard feels the cool air against his skin as he walks, absent minded he is transported to the contrasting, arid heat of the desert outside Jerusalem, with a shudder, he feels the spindly hairy spider legs of the tarantulas dance once more across his flesh.

The Lionheart rubs his eyes and looks again at the impossible walls. A movement catches his eye. A lone defender is on the battlements, it is a man by the name of Peter Basilius. He pops up like a jack in the box and loosens a single crossbow bolt at the King. The Lionheart sees it. 'Decent shot', he thinks, though he does not seem to comprehend the implications of it.

The bolt hits the unarmoured King, embedding its barbed tip deep into his shoulder.

Peter Basilius, an unknown and unheralded Capetian knight, has just killed King Richard the Lionheart.

Chapter 25: The Heart of The Lionheart

The bolt protrudes from Richard's shoulder who gasps at it in disbelief, he can't quite believe the little bugger has shot him. As well as shocked, The Lionheart is also embarrassed. How could he have been so stupid as to blindly wander into firing range of the castle walls whilst unarmoured? It was an amateur mistake. Red faced, Richard gives Peter on the walls a mocking salute and a sarcastic clap before storming back to his tent, grimacing in pain at his shoulder.

Under the cover of his canvas, The Lionheart drinks deeply from a wine goblet before biting down hard on a stick and yanking sharply at the barbed missile. Richard squeals in pain and spits out the stick, sobbing. Cursing, he drinks deeply and tries again. Pull as he might, Richard cannot remove the arrow, a surgeon is sent for.

The surgeon sets about cutting around the wickedly serrated arrow head, but it is embedded so deeply as to be in the bone. The Lionheart is no stranger to pain, but even so, he is soon writhing in agony and has to be held down. Surgery was never a picnic in Medieval times, but the medic makes a particular hash of the operation. Although he eventually extracts the crossbow bolt, he mutilates the King's arm in the process.

Richard gives the order for his men to attack the castle. The battle is fast and decisive, the castle is taken. Peter Basilius is clapped in irons and thrown in the dungeon.

Over the next few days, The Lionheart's health deteriorates rapidly. The skin around the wound went from lacerated, to red and inflamed, to black and sickeningly cold to the touch. Though the wound may have felt like ice, the rest of Richard was burning a high fever. He was dizzy and could not keep food down. As the infection began to pass into The Lionheart's bloodstream and early onset sepsis began, he sends for the young knight, he sends for Sir Peter Basilius. Richard wishes to stare his grim reaper in the face and snarl at him.

As Peter enters the Lionheart's chambers, the King can barely sit up, let alone snarl at his killer. If anything, we find Richard in a somewhat melancholic mood when he meets the man who has shot him.

Slowly, The King shakes his head, "What was it that I ever did to you, Peter?"

"You killed both of my parents and two of my brothers," replies the young knight.

The Lionheart hesitates, he has never really considered the consequences of his constant campaigning or how it has affected others. Knowing he is not long for this world, Richard is troubled by this line of thinking, "Free him, I would have done the same, free him, Peter Basilius is to be freed."

As Peter exits the Lionheart's chamber, the air has never tasted so sweet, nor has birdsong ever sounded so melodic. Those that walk such a close shade to death, will forever see life in a high definition, explosion of ultra-colour that the rest of us can only wonder at as we fumble around in our myopia. Peter wants to sing, a great weight has been lifted from his shoulders. Peter was free of the hatred that had previously entombed him in a dark and unforgiving cell for longer than he can remember. Now the deed was done, Peter does not even particularly despise the King, it was over, Peter feels born again and is ready to begin his new life. He vows it will be one that is dedicated to goodness and helping others, not hatred.

As Peter leaves the King's Chambers, the Captain of Richard's men follows him. The guards had exchanged curious looks when Richard announced Peter was to be spared, clearly the King was out of his mind and didn't know what he was saying. Peter is grabbed, re-arrested and flayed to death.

It is difficult to accept that a story as grand as The Lionheart's could end so meaninglessly. Surely, it had been written in the stars that Richard would perish trading blows toe-to-toe on the walls of Jerusalem with the Sultan, or, in a daring do-or-die dash against his old foe Philip Augustus? It beggared belief Richard could be killed like this, the people of the time felt the same and conspiracy theories began to emerge.

It was thought that the dastardly, underhand Capetians had resorted to the unsportsmanlike behaviour of poisoning their weaponry. Popular venoms of the period included *Wolfs Bane* or *Foxglove*, either could have caused symptoms similar to the ones we saw The Lionheart face in his final days. Satisfyingly enough, in 2013, we were able to get to the bottom of this particular theory and that, is a story in itself that's worth exploring.

Upon The Lionheart's death, his body was dissected to allow more of the populous to bask in his Plantagenet glory. His entrails were interred at Caruus, the pointless castle he had just been shot for. The majority of his cadaver was laid to rest at Fontevraud alongside The Old King, yes, Richard rests next to his father whom he prematurely hounded to an early grave, even in death, The Old King can get no sleep. Richard's heart though, now that was shipped off to Rouen, where it was promptly lost.

These things have a habit of turning up again though and turn up again it did. During an excavation at the end of the 19th century a lead box was unearthed amidst the cloisters and antiquities with the following inscription, "*Here lies the heart of Richard, King of the English*".

A local historian opened the little lunchbox, all that remained of the great King's heart was a brownish sludge

279

and a white powder. The advanced degradation of Richard's heart was no deterrent for forensic scientist, coroner and historian Phillippe Charlier. Charlier has quite the résumé for this kind of thing, he got his teeth stuck into Hitler's dental records and (re)confirmed his death, he turned the heat up on the remains of Joan of Arc and announced them fake. He couldn't wait to pull on the heartstrings of King Richard.

Eight centuries after The Lionheart died, Charlier begins his work separating out the gelatinous goo to answer once and for all, was King Richard killed by a poisoned arrow?

Charlier's initial findings proved controversial. Embedded in Richard's heart, are extracts of pollen from the Poplar Plant and Bellflower. Whilst neither of these are deadly, they certainly do not flower in that region until late April or early May. Chroniclers recorded Richard's death as April 6th, which is something to this day, Charlier asserts is incorrect. His protestations fall on deaf ears, the record remains unchanged.

A significant amount of mercury was found, this wasn't unexpected. Mercury was a common preservative agent and had it been absent, there probably wouldn't have been enough heart sludge left to analyse. Frankincense was discovered, now this was unusual. That being said, Frankincense did, kind of, make sense. The Lionheart seems the sort who would have wanted his heart sludge to smell nice.

Lead from the old box had dripped in, linen strands from the long since decayed cloth the organ had been wrapped in were also present.

No poison though, no hint of foul play from The Capetians. As much as we may have placed The Lionheart atop a pedestal, he is but mortal and dying from infected wounds on a battlefield was a common occurrence that could happen to anyone, King or pauper.

The other question that is also troubling, is what on

earth was The Lionheart doing at Chalus Castle? It was a nothing fight, against a handful of knights and forty infantry men using cooking utensils as shields. Richard's lieutenants would have been more than capable of conquering the castle without his direct supervision. Sir William Marshal wasn't there, he was over two hundred miles away in Vaudreuille Castle feasting and celebrating a victorious campaign, why was The Lionheart?

Another conspiracy that occasionally gnashes its golden teeth, was that the Lionheart was on some kind of Indiana Jones style hunt for an ancient relic. Treasure had supposedly been buried just outside the walls of Chalus castle. A couple of different sources make reference to this treasure, one really goes for it and the majority don't mention it at all.

The source that confidently asserts the treasure existed, goes so far as to even describe it. Supposedly, it was an exquisite golden carving of an emperor, his wife and child sat about a ceremonial table. It sounds nice, but not really the Lionheart's bag. When looking for an antique relic, Richard generally prefers something a bit more biblical.

Solid gold is always nice, but The Lionheart has never coveted nor amassed great wealth throughout his career, he just spends it. He views finances as a fuel to propel his ambitions. Any fortunes the Lionheart did win were always spent just as quickly, normally before he had even won them. The Lionheart also didn't really consider the King's coffers to be a King's concern, it was for lesser mortals than he to keep up with his expenditure requirements.

That being said, The Lionheart liked an adventure and was an adrenaline junkie. With the campaign against Philip wrapping up, this may have been the most exciting thing on his radar at that moment in time, so Richard jumped on it, insisting on overseeing it personally. If this was what brought Richard to the place of his demise, he was trading on bad information, the statue of the emperor sat with his family was never found.

It is difficult at this juncture not to compare Richard to his father, The Old King. As we weigh the two monarchs up against one another the scales dance wildly and it is unclear whose crown bears heavier. On the side of The Old King is Thomas Becket, judicial reform, law and order, a stable empire and a solvent nation, with the Lionheart though we have heroism, style, the recovery of the empire, The Third Crusade and irresponsible fiscal management.

We remember The Lionheart as one of the greatest monarchs England has ever seen, although much of this legacy is the result of the PR machine hand cranked into life by Eleanor of Aquitaine to secure coinage for his release. Whether you think Richard a great king or not, probably depends on your belief as to what a King of this period should be focused on. If you think Medieval Monarchs should be sword waving, campaigning against Capetians and crusading, then undoubtedly, Richard is the best. If you believe that by this period Kings should have an understanding of the nuances of economic policy and try to improve the quality of life for the masses, you may find him wanting.

Regardless of your opinions though, the nation love and respect The Good King Richard. Behind him, is left a vacuum of such immense volume it threatens to suck the entire Plantagenet empire into it.

Extracts from *"Lament for King Richard Lionheart"* written in 1199 AD.

By Gaucelm Faidit
Translated by A.Z. Foreman

It is an awful thing: the greatest pain

And purest grief that I have known to sting,
The ache that squeezes me to tears again
Is mine to sing and tell while I can bear it.

The father and the captain of all merit,
Courageous noble Richard, England's king
Is dead. My God, the loss and harrowing.
The words are strange to say, harsh to the ear.
The heart is hard that takes this with no tear.

My lord and king! May God the true forgiver,
True man, true life, true mercy and true Sire
Grant you in death the pardon you require.
May He forget your failings and your sin
May He remember all you did for Him.

Chapter 26: King by Default

One of The Lionheart's final lucid acts, before ceding to advanced stage septicaemia, was to, with shaking hands, pen a letter. This letter was sealed and stamped with Richard's official emblem. It was handed to one of his most trusted servants who was also a devilishly fast and competent rider.

This servant spurs his horse onwards and Chalus castle is swiftly left behind. Every town the servant rides through, he will dismount for only the briefest of respites. He will seize the opportunity to drink deeply from his water canteen and swop his horse out for a fresh one before riding hard again. He doesn't eat, nor does he sleep.

As the servant rides, Earl William Marshal is busy entertaining nobles at Vaudreiul Castle. The squires and younger knights look on him in awe, the hero of a thousand battles stands before them, to say he is a legend would not be an exaggeration.

Marshal's story was deserving of the meteoric rise he has commanded and the office of Earl he now possessed.

Despite this being Marshal's fifth goblet of wine, he is somehow neither ruddy of complexion, nor slurred. The fifty-three year old Earl is telling a story and all press closer so as not to miss a word, "Every time we manage to get a ladder up against the wall, the Capetians push the bloody thing down again." Marshal takes a large swig before discretely placing his wine on the table behind his back.

In a conspiratorial whisper, he continues, "Finally, one of the ladders sticks and two of my boys fight their way up the walls as the cursed Capetians rain arrows, missiles and all manner of hell down upon them. They are courageous though and will not be deterred, they manage to pull themselves over the wall and though the two of them fight more like two hundred men, they are greatly outnumbered and do not stand a chance!" The entire hall has fallen silent, everybody wants to listen and even those who have heard the story before, wish to show respect to The Great Knight. The people adore him.

Richard's servant rides through the night. This is a perilous business. Had he hobbled his horse, fell from the saddle or even died riding like this, it would not have been unheard of. The message the servant carries is important though and time is of the essence, his risk is a calculated one. The horse's hooves skid across the damp grass but the stallion's footing stays true. Even the equine knows this is a noble quest of the highest order and will not wish to be found wanting.

"Now, there was not a chance in Hell, that I was going to leave my boys up there to get hurt!" the assembled assortment of knights and nobles cheer Marshal for this sentiment. Marshal is stood atop the feasting table by now, all eyes are on him.

He continues, "So, I bolt across the battlefield in full armour and shoot up the ladder, like I have a rat up my arse." Marshal comically mimes an exaggerated, high-kneed awkward running style pumping his arms like a mad puppeteer which causes empty plates to dance about the table and laughter to erupt across the hall.

"Somehow, I make it, but when I reach the top, I realise I may have made an error of judgement…Now, it's probably escaped your attention, but I'm not as young as I once was…" this invokes more mirth from his audience, "and after running across the battlefield, the climbing of the ladder, I'm exhausted, I'm bloody knackered." Marshal theatrically demonstrates the deep pants of breath he had drawn after his run, heaving his great shoulders high and low to demonstrate his point. "To make matters worse, half of their damn army have seen my stupid assault and are now charging, twice as hard as they were before at me and my boys."

Richard's servant arrives at Vaudreiul Castle, the guards at the gate cross their halberds to stop him, "Dismount, state your business."

There is hurried conversation and Richard's servant throws his arms in the air, frustrated, before dismounting and rifling through his saddle pack. Eventually, he finds what he was looking for. The guards recognise The Lionheart's Seal and stand down immediately.

Marshal is reaching the climax of his story, he drops his voice dramatically causing all gathered to lean closer to listen, "I think that's it, I'm done for, I'm about to be captured, at my age! I look over my shoulder though and there they are, the rest of my boys are with me." Marshal goes on to name a number of the knights that had followed his charge personally. Each man present he names flushes with pride, for being accommodated by Earl Marshal is a great accolade.

Marshal rounds off his tale, "Do you know what I learned that day? I learned that nobody, and I mean nobody, messes with The Bloody Plantagenets!" Marshal roars the final two words amidst a great din of approval in the hall. Men are banging their goblets on the table, stamping their feet. Marshal sits back in his chair and smiles contentedly.

Richard's servant rushes through the claustrophobic, close stone passages of the castle that are lit by flickering torchlight. In the distance, he can hear the sounds of merriment. Richard's servant hears a great crescendo of cheering in the feasting hall and hurries towards it. He collides with a serving wench, her tray of chicken legs flies into the air before crashing to the stone floor with a clatter. The servant neither slows to apologise nor offers to help her.

Marshal wasn't sure what he intended to do with his life now the The Capetians were all but done, he did know this though, he was finally ready to let his saddle sores heal. He also planned to leave the fighting to younger men. King Richard was only forty-one, there was no reason he couldn't rule for many years to come. People respected and feared the man enough, Marshal predicted that The Plantagenet empire was about to enter a period of unprecedented stability, prosperity and peace under The Lionheart; the likes of which it had never before seen. Marshal would be a part of it, he decided, but a small part, to retire would be a great adventure indeed.

An anxious servant hurrying towards Marshal interrupts him from his reverie, a letter is clutched in his hand.

Upon hearing the news of Richard's demise, Marshal finds himself in a role that he is unused to. As the son of a minor knight, who was once given up as a hostage and written off as collateral damage, he is shocked to find the fate of the entire kingdom rests almost entirely in his hands. Whilst Marshal has been close to every major event in History to date in our story, he has largely been tossed about by the winds of circumstance and change. Yes, he had mopped Young Henry's feverish brow in his final hours but had been unable to save the man, he may have covered The Old King's retreat but he couldn't help the patriarch retain his crown, he did help restore the Plantagenet empire from the Capetians and yet still, Richard was dead.

Marshal is a lowly house knight no more though, by this point in our tale he is nobody's pawn. Marshal is an Earl of the realm, a fearsome warrior and a legend in his own right. He has his own knights under him and an entire household that answer to him, Marshal commands as much influence as anybody alive in the Plantagenet empire. Not only is Marshal permitted to have an opinion on whom the next King should be, he can probably decide it. Earl William Marshal stands in the shoes of King Maker.

From the smoke and confusion, two candidates emerge. Marshal has concerns about both. There was John, and perhaps it's a generational thing, but Marshal had never quite understood him. Marshal knew more about the rivalry that ran in the blood of the Plantagenet brood than most, but John's plotting against Richard whilst he rotted in prison had seemed a cheap move. That being said, John knew his way around government. He knew who to ask to get answers, he knew how to raise an army. John was needlessly cruel and not always entirely effective, but he was young, perhaps, if given a chance, he could be a great King?

The other choice, was Arthur. Arthur was the son born posthumously of Geoffrey after he died in a jousting accident. Whilst there was nothing wrong with Arthur per se, he was only sixteen. He was a kid, how would he stand up to the pressures of leadership?

Say Arthur was to become King, there would be no period of transition for the boy, he would face challenges immediately. Philip would be keen to undo all of The Lionheart's campaigning from the last four years and would raid Normandy, Pope Innocent would throw his weight around demanding Crusades left and right. Once they smelt weakness, every Baron would test this new administration's resolve.

John or Arthur, Arthur or John? The names dance around Marshal's head like lovers, twirling in dance about a midnight fire. Marshal takes a crown coin from his pocket. When you are facing an impossible choice with a binary outcome, there are worse things you can do than place it in the hands of fate. As the coin arcs and spins catching the light mischievously, you will know, in that very moment that the coin turns with absolute certainty what you want it to land on.

Marshal does not need to see if the coin lands heads or tails, for deep down, he has already decided. Marshal will support John. He will be advised by his fellow Earl and long-time friend, Sir Hubert Walter, that he will regret this decision for the rest of his life. When Marshal makes a decision though, he doesn't question it, he commits to it absolutely. Marshal sets off that very evening, to pledge his allegiance to the new King John.

John sits in the grand dining hall of Fontevraud. To a casual observer, he is alone, but tonight, John dines with the ghosts of his past. He hums softly to himself and pours from a carafe of wine. News has reached of his elder brother's death and John is not in the least bit surprised. Why would he be? It was written in the stars he would take the throne. How else could you explain it? Three elder brothers parting like the sea for Moses to clear the path for John to sit upon the throne, if it had not been pre-destined it would be absurd.

John raises a glass in mocking salute to the ghost of The Old King.

"How are you Father? Are you proud of your youngest son?" In anger, The Old King splutters in disgust. His translucent face glows red, he cannot bring himself to say a word to his formerly favourite son, who's betrayal had left him with no reason to carry on.

"Nothing to say to me Father? No advice, no congratulations?" John asks mockingly, swilling his goblet idly.

The Old King has nothing to say that is repeatable, he clutches at his stomach.

John's oldest brother, Young Henry, pours himself a goblet of wine and approaches the new monarch. Though this was supposed to be a casual evening, he is in full armour regalia, his teeth glisten white and his hair is perfectly coiffured.

"You need the love of the people, John. Don't dismiss the common populous, they are your most valuable asset and your greatest responsibility. You cannot rule without their love and adoration," pontificates Young Henry pompously.

"I can't rule, without their love and adoration?" John cocks an eyebrow quizzically.

"You need the people and the people need you," surmised Young Henry.

"I just think it is a little rich, getting advice on how to rule from you, someone who had all of the advantages in life. You were the oldest son, the heir apparent, how could you screw that up? You had so many chances, so many opportunities to be someone. In nine hundred years, how do you think you will be remembered? Henry the Great? Henry the Feared? Unlikely. If you are remembered at all, it will be 'Young Henry', a foggy character of whom people aren't sure if he is Henry II, Henry III, or even a king at all? So," continued John, "I will politely decline your advice, thank you, and I will not covet the adoration of the people." For the second time this evening, John has rendered one of his deceased family members speechless.

Now it is the Lionheart's turn, "Well little brother, glad to see things going right for you, I always believed in you," Richard points East. "To business, Jerusalem is prime for conquer, with Saladin dead, The Holy Land is in disarray. Here, I have drawn up battle plans for how best to advance on Jerusalem."

"I wasn't planning on going to the Holy City," John advises.

"You weren't planning on going to the Holy City?" The Lionheart looks appalled and throws his arms in the air, he is completely disgusted, "Why ever not?"

"Well, why would I?" John asks confused.

"What do you mean?"

"I have a great empire that covers all of England, more than half of France, the Channel Islands, I was going to just focus on that. I'll repeat my question, why would I want to go to Jerusalem?"

The Lionheart looks flummoxed and scratches his head, "It's just a thing, really, isn't it, a thing that people do."

"Not really. Nobody else here has done it," John gestures towards The Old King and Young Henry who awkwardly mumble their agreement.

"So," continues The Lionheart, "you're just going to focus on running a cross-channel empire, foreign policy, internal economic balancing and strategic expansion, that kind of thing?" asks Richard, his face clearly showing he thinks that sort of business beneath a King.

"Yes," John replies

"Righto. Very good then."

Marshal pauses for a moment at the entrance to the dining hall.

John, who he will now pledge his support to, sits alone, his eyes are closed and he is humming softly to himself, he is grinning like a Cheshire cat. Marshal sighs and walks slowly into the grand hall. He prays he has made the right decision.

Marshal's backing John's was important, but it didn't change the fact Arthur was Richard's heir and legally speaking, next in line for the throne. At sixteen years of age, Arthur was untested, but that didn't rule him out. Powerful men were lining up behind him. These largely fell into one of two camps. The first wished to follow Arthur because they didn't believe in John, the second believed getting in with the young king early would further their own interests. A heavyweight residing in both camps, was Philip Augustus.

With Richard out of the picture, Philip was seriously threatening most of Northern France and Arthur would soon have to make a stand against him to defend his lands of Brittany. It was a fight Arthur would never have been able to win without significant support and so a peace treaty was drawn up. Wise as this decision may have seemed at the time, siding with Philip was a statement. Arthur may not have completely understood what his handshake with the Capetians signified, but he had just ostracised himself from his entire family.

Shock waves of this alliance rippled across Europe, but in reality, it shouldn't have been unexpected. It is no exaggeration to say Philip has been playing this game for as long as he has been on the throne. First there had been Geoffrey (Arthur's Father), he was appointed Chief of Staff for Philip and was all but ready to rebel against The Old King before dying unexpectedly either in a jousting accident, or being smote by God. Closely followed was Richard, Philip succeeded in turning him against The Old King and sparking a civil war across the Plantagenet empire. Then, of course, there was John; as Richard languished in jail he successfully made him turn traitor against his own family and finally now, there was Arthur.

Arthur may not have understood what the truce he signed with Philip truly signified, but Philip did. He wasted no time and sent messengers far and wide, declaring his new best friend Arthur as the rightful Plantagenet King. He also announced John a fraud, a charlatan and declared his lands in France forfeit.

Any hopes Arthur may have harboured of appeasing both his Uncle John and Philip Augustus, were done. He had now well and truly picked a side. It was time for him to commit. As young as Arthur is, he knows that power is born from holding key castles and imprisoning important hostages. From his position in Northern France, it was not difficult for him to swoop into the castle of which Eleanor of Aquitaine resided and seize his own grandmother as a hostage. It was a low move and John was furious to hear of his mother being treated in such a way.

John descended on the castle with everything he had and the attack was a spectacular success. With minimal loss of life, John seized back the castle and took his nephew hostage. There are conflicting reports as to whether John starved his nephew Arthur to death in a cell, or beat him until his heart gave out but either way, Arthur will never be seen or heard from again.

Chapter 27: The siege of The Saucy Castle

With Arthur out of the picture, John has just succeeded in inheriting the largest empire in Europe. The kingdom has largely been restored to its former glory by The Lionheart in the four years running up to his sudden and unexpected death.

Up against John, is the standard enemy, the Capetian King Philip Augustus. Only a year actually separates John and Philip, but it feels like more. Their experience base, maturity and aptitude for Kingship are wildly misaligned. Philip has been king by this point for nineteen years, he had been instrumental in defeating The Old King, fought competently in The Third Crusade and had spent the last four years getting beaten by The Lionheart but with each painful defeat, Philip had been learning.

It would be dangerous to underestimate Philip at this stage, he has taken the Capetian dynasty from being a gnat, nipping at the flanks of the Plantagenet elephant to being a serious contender.

We rejoin our tale at Chateau Gaillard, the unconquerable castle Richard had built to choke off the aortal route into Rouen and to forever demonstrate his dominance over The Capetians. Chateau Gaillard, which literally translates as, "The Saucy Castle" was truly like no other. No expense had been spared during construction and The Lionheart had taken a personal interest in every detail.

The Lionheart declared upon completion that it was an unconquerable castle and you can see why he thought so, The Saucy Castle was a masterful blend combining both the pinnacle of Medieval castle building technology with the natural advantages offered by the geographical surroundings. Would-be attackers were forced to approach from an open Southern advance, their way towards the castle would be blocked by the wide and fast-flowing River Seine.

Invaders scratching their heads at this point, would be relieved to see a manmade bridge that would take them across to a small, landmass in the centre of the river. Unfortunately, they would then spy a defended fort on this landmass itself. Should they be able to overcome this they would be rewarded with yet another bridge, taking them to yet another island. Exacerbating the situation, this second island also had a castle sat upon it. Should an invading army be able to defeat both of these defensive fortifications, they would have earned the right to cross the final bridge.

After these initial labours of Hercules, invaders would then be confronted by the most expensive castle built to date. To even have a chance to take the Saucy Castle, you would need to beat two other castles first. Richard had every right to be proud.

Philip disagreed with The Lionheart though, he didn't think it would be any picnic to conquer but he thought he had spied a weakness, he didn't think it was unconquerable. Philip you see, had no intention of fighting through two fortified castles before engaging his main target, he planned to bypass the first. He aimed to achieve this by sailing boats up The Seine laden with bridge building gear, thus allowing his armies to envelop the fortifications on either side of the river.

How could a man of The Lionheart's considerable experience not have anticipated this when he built the damned Saucy Thing? The answer is, of course he had. A wooden barricade had been set up down river, well within shooting range of the castle walls built to prevent just such an assault.

Not to be deterred, Philip stands before his men delivering a speech and looking for volunteers.

"I need a group of men, who are able to swim." A number of men raise their hands, by no means a majority though. Even amongst veteran sailors, being able to swim is not a prerequisite to their trade. Across Philip's army there is less than a third who feel confident in their ability to stay afloat in water.

"They will need to swim out into the inky black, ice cold, fast flowing waters of The Seine in the dead of night." Looks of both confusion and alarm are exchanged between the ranks of men with their hands held aloft, many drop their arm.

"You will be required to swim out to a wooden barricade and hack it to pieces using an axe, all whilst keeping your head above the surface by treading water." There are now only three hands still aloft.

"People will be shooting at you whilst you do it." No hands now remain in the air.

"Actually, it's probably easiest if I just pick some people for it," decides Philip.

Unbelievably, Philip's scuba squadron pull it off. Casualties are heavy, but it wasn't as bad as you might have thought. Yes, they are chopping away at the barricade in full view of the fortifications, but equally, it's pitch black and the targets bob up and down unpredictably, pulled this way and that by the fast currents of The Seine. They scurry like beavers, frantically deconstructing a dam. One minute, they are atop the blockade, the next, they are back in the drink and ten metres downstream. The only target is their flailing arms frantically fighting the current. Picking them off is a tough shot for even master archers upon the castle walls.

After a few hours of this assault, the wooden barricade is held together primarily by the force of the water that rushes through the gaps as opposed to the nails that once secured the beams. The attack barges cast off from their moorings upriver and row hard, the tug of the undercurrents spur them forward. The first barge builds up speed, faster and faster, cutting through the water. "Brace!" screams the Captain.

Men dive about the deck, grasping frantically for fixings as the ship's bow hurtles towards the barricade. With a thunderous crash, the lead barge smashes through the blockade, for a heart-stopping moment, it looks as though the barrier will hold and it has all been for naught. With an almighty creak, groan and roaring splinter though, Philip's first boat makes it through. The rest follow easily. Smashed wood washes to the embankment in the ships' wake.

The barges are unloaded. A bridge is built at lightning speed even whilst the men shield themselves from projectiles raining down. To the defenders, who watch the efficiency with which the attackers are executing their training, it feels like they are facing the ghost of The Lionheart and in many ways they are. Philip Augustus has spent more time in the war room with The Lionheart than anyone else, ever, on both sides of the table.

Philip Augustus smiles as he watches his soldiers do exactly as they have been commanded to, for he understands the importance of discipline within an army, the diligence with which his men perform their duties is not chance, it's a result of rigid training.

The Capetians are now on both sides of the river. This is not checkmate, not by any stretch of the imagination, The Capetians still have a hell of a way to go. None of the fortifications have fallen and The Saucy Castle can happily be supplied up the rear as it were. What exactly, Philip intends to do next remains unclear. When word reaches King John who is many miles away, he finds it difficult to quantify how significant an advantage Philip has won that night at the un-takeable castle. He certainly isn't supposed to be on both sides of the Seine, but how important could his new position really be?

John plays it back and forth in his mind, yo-yoing between convinced he has lost everything, to thinking maybe it wasn't so bad. John lacks the military experience to put this into perspective, he calls for Earl Marshal.

Marshal assesses the situation and confirms that yes, Philip's success in surrounding two sides of the castle was indeed, extremely serious, it was likely the beginnings of a siege and it was one he didn't think they could win.

John listens to Marshal's summary with a growing, apoplectic horror. Though the feeble, early morning rays have not yet heated up the King's bedchamber, his skin is slick with sweat. He feels sick. He is firing questions at Marshal, desperate to provoke some kind of reassuring response from the old Earl, "Can they be beaten? Will we defeat them? The castle walls are some of the highest in Europe aren't they?"

This is the first Plantagenet King I have served under, Marshal thinks, that asks more questions than he answers. It becomes clear that the best course of action is for Marshal to depart for The Saucy Castle immediately and lead a relief force to end the siege. As Philip's forces are split across two sides of the Seine, a two-pronged attack seems logical. A land force and a naval fleet attacking in synchronisation would yield the greatest chance of success.

This plan threw up more questions which was something John was quick to point out, "Who will lead the naval force?" Not Marshal, that was for sure, he was no mariner.

In the end, a naval mercenary captain by the name of, Lupescar the Wolf, was chosen. His résumé was up to scratch. He had commanded large armies with plenty of ships, he loved boats and had a ton of experience sailing, he was the man.

If you are going to let a wolf loose in your kingdom though, you can't get annoyed when he eats a chicken or two and Lupescar was eating everything. Every farm dwelling he passed, every undefended village, would be ransacked by the Wolf and his men, regardless of whose side they were on. Livestock were slaughtered, artefacts stolen, daughters and wives raped. The Wolf was not a nice man. Taking the decision to elevate him to Head of the Admiralty was an unpopular choice with leadership and laypeople alike.

Marshal advises John the best strategy to relieve this siege would be to attack under the cover of nightfall but the Wolf vetoes this idea. The Wolf claims The Seine would be too difficult to navigate in the blackness. If you can't attack at night, you do the next best thing, at first light it was agreed the two armies would strike the Capetian forces either side of the river.

Marshal waits, in the darkness, with his men. He shakes his head ruefully contemplating how a few short months ago, he had been planning his retirement under The Lionheart. Marshal hates waiting. His limbs are heavy and he feels weak and lethargic. Marshal has seen enough action though to know that this is an illusion. When the time comes, he will give a good account of himself, but by the gods he hates this waiting.

Finally, Marshal is granted his reprieve. He watches the first rays of sunlight emerge over The Saucy Castle's turrets, he breathes a sigh of relief, the waiting was over. Silently, Marshal raises his fist high into the air. The signal is picked up by lieutenants across his army who do likewise. The cavalry respond, they thunder down into the unsuspecting Capetian troops.

Initially, the battle goes exactly as planned. The sieging army were not prepared for this and are disorganised. They panic. A small rabble of men try to put up a defence but they are routed almost immediately by the venom of the attack. Trapped against the fast flowing water of the Seine, The Capetians are left with only one option open to them. They pour, en masse, over the hastily constructed bridge they had made to the other side.

The men on the castle walls cheer wildly. Marshal joins in their exuberance for he knows that The Capetian troops will only be met by death and carnage on the other side of the river at the fangs of the Wolf.

Except, they aren't, at the other side of the bridge. The Capetians are organising into defensive lines. Frantically, Marshal scans up and down the river, where the hell are you Wolf?

The Capetians were preparing a counter-attack. They heavily outnumber Marshal's force and they march across the bridge, confident in their ability to see them off. Marshal's men stutter and baulk, though they hold for a moment, they will not be able to for long.

"Wolf, where are you?" Marshal mutters, shielding his eyes against the rising sun and staring up and down the Seine, mentally willing his naval support to sail into view. The Leading Capetians have reached the other side of the bridge by now and begin putting Marshal's men to the sword. Capetian archers have also crossed and are raining death down, it's becoming a massacre. Marshal's men begin to run.

Marshal considered charging in but has not lived for so long nor survived so many battles by being rash or hot headed. Marshal can read the ebbs and flows of a battle in much the same way as you are reading this book and he knows the battle is lost. He turns and rides off into the countryside.

As Marshal and his men turn tail and run, the Capetian troops cheer. Their cheers give way to confusion, for around the meandering river bend, the first of The Wolf's naval fleet lazily drifts into view. The Capetian commander cocks his head in surprise. Lining each side of the river are thousands of his archers, fully primed and ready to fire. This literally could not have happened at a better time. The Capetian leader gives the order and The Wolf's fleet is defeated violently and swiftly by a deadly crossfire.

As The Capetians erected trebuchets, belfries and dug defensive ditches, it was abundantly clear that they were here to stay. Inhabitants of the nearby French village, Petit-

Andelys, who had sought shelter from Philip's army in The Saucy Castle were sold out and told to leave. These non-combatants would be a burden and eat up valuable supplies. It was a dark decision to make.

At first, Philip reacted chivalrously to the trickle of refugees pouring out of the stone behemoth and granted them free passage to the countryside. As the trickle turned into a stream and then a torrent, Philip changed his mind. His sieging army interlocked shields creating a wall as real as the stone ones the villagers were trying to escape from. As they turned to re-enter the great castle, that route was also denied to them. The doors were locked.

The unarmed villagers were left in no mans' land. Open to the elements many fell victim to exposure and starvation, more to the incessant stream of missiles being exchanged between the ramparts and the attacking army. As the Plantagenet defenders nobly ready themselves to defeat the old Capetian enemy, they are haunted by the ghosts of the very subjects they are supposed to protect who starve and rot below them.

The Saucy castle will last out for a further six months, before falling into Philip's hands.

Philip will identify the castle's Achilles heel and exploit it. Not wishing to apportion blame, but on the West side of the fortifications King John had seen fit to erect a Chapel, this will prove to be a catastrophic error. The chapel was built into the wall and its unbarred window offered a tantalising target to the inner bailey.

A Capetian force scaled the wall and gained access to the church. Here, they made such a din that the defenders panicked. The defenders, convinced the attackers were already inside, retreated swiftly and formed up ranks. Meanwhile, a crack team of Capetian soldiers crawled up, hand over foot, through the horrors and excrement of the latrine long drop for the central bailey. They will gain access to the inner walls and unlock the gates for the main army.

The centrepiece of the Plantagenet empire was lost.

Shortly before The Saucy Castle falls, John, who has been holding base in Northern France, announces he must leave For England immediately. The purpose of this trip is to host a strategy meeting. John reassures all barons residing in Northern France that he will return on swift winds with an unbeatable army. These promises are undermined somewhat when every conceivable valuable in Rouen Palace, from the silver cutlery to the artwork, was loaded onto John's ship sailing for England. John's decision to take his wife with him, Queen Isabella, also spoke volumes. King John fleeing sent a loud message to all that he no longer believed his position in France tenable.

The Plantagenets are unable to resist the Capetian hurricane that blasts over them. Rouen falls, Normandy surrenders, Brittany is seized, even Aquitaine succumbs. Philip Augustus secures his place in the pages of History as one of the most successful Capetian Kings ever. As for John, he is bitter and twisted at his loss and whilst he hides behind the safety of the frothy swell of the English channel, he swears revenge, he swears that he will restore The Plantagenet empire to its former glory. As if further proof was needed that The Plantagenet star was dying though, it is at this moment that the Queen Mother Eleanor of Aquitaine passes away.

Eleanor dies at the monastery of Fontevrault, Anjou, there is no hint of foul play. She had retired to the abbey to preside over it as Warden some years earlier and she liked it there. Eleanor liked it for a number of reasons, the great tapestries made her feel part of a bigger picture and she thinks the gardens pretty, this is not why she stays though. Eleanor likes it here, because it is in this very building the remains of her son Richard have been interred and it is here she feels closest to him.

The night Eleanor died, she awoke with a dry mouth. Rolling across her straw mattress, she reached for a ladle that had been placed by her bed for this very purpose. A smugglers' moon struck her room at an acute angle. The mercurial lighting bounced mischievously off the water in the pail and threw her reflection back to her. Not her reflection, at least not quite, staring back at Eleanor was a fourteen year old version of herself. The girl in the pail's beauty causes a raspy gasp to catch in Eleanor's throat.

The girl's wide eyes shine with innocence, hope and longing. Young Eleanor yearns for romance and adventure. She does not yet know how things are, just how they should be. She is plotting a course to the brightest star and plans to travel there in style. She wants everything that life has to offer, she longs to walk the streets of Jerusalem on an Easter Evening, to wake up on the side of the mountainous Alpine range on Christmas day. Young Eleanor wants to travel, she wants to see the world and experience everything. She doesn't just want one great love but two, maybe more. Young Eleanor plans to be a lady of mystery, mystique and sensuality. Her lovers wouldn't be boring either, her romances would burn white hot with a fire that could forge iron.

Young Eleanor wants to be a Queen, not in the sense of being married to a King, she wants to be a Queen in her own right. She wants the people to respect her, to adore her and to obey her. She wants to be loved and feared and able to make decisions. Her tutors kept explaining to her that women didn't lead, that their role was to make babies and manage the household, it was a lesson Eleanor would never even try to understand.

Young Eleanor also wants to be a mother. Though she knows it is greedy to wish for anything other than a healthy baby, deep down she wants a boy. She wants a son that is both romantic and fierce, noble yet ruthless in the pursuit of ambition.

If it seems like Young Eleanor expects a lot from life, she does, but she also has a lot to give. She is incredibly smart, not just book learning, she also understands people in a way few can emulate. Energy is a resource that, even as she grows older, she never runs low on. Young Eleanor is a remarkable lady and though she does not yet understand quite how much so, she will come to.

The reflection in the water is shattered into a thousand, shaking droplets, when a single tear leaks from the eighty-two year old Eleanor's eye and rolls down her paper skinned cheeks to drop into the bucket. It is not a tear of sadness though, it is one of joy. Everything Young Eleanor had ever hoped for and more came true over the life of this remarkable Queen.

Eleanor of Aquitaine lies back in her bed, and shutting her eyes for the final time, she thinks of Richard.

Chapter 28: Blood in, Blood out

King John's decision to leave mainland France and run across the Channel to the safety of England, has left Earl William Marshal and a number of the other Barons in a compromising position. For men of power such as these, who governed land both in Northern France and England, they now have two different kings they are required to answer to. With no relief force forthcoming from King John and the withdrawal of his protection, Marshal and the Barons are left with no other choice. They are forced to pay homage to Philip Augustus. They try to asterisk this with the proviso that they are only doing this for their lands in Northern France and their commitment remains to John for castles they command in England. It's a seriously messy business and completely unprecedented, it was also never going to work. After all, what was to happen if King John and Philip fell out? Which they do, immediately.

For King John cannot bear to crystallise his losses in France by accepting them and instead pledges to chase them. This takes the form of a diligently prepared naval fleet, a fully resourced army and a convoy of flat packed siege engines. Problems start on this campaign, however, before it begins. The main issue is that a significant number of The Barons want nothing to do with it, why would they? They have land on both sides of The Channel, all they would accomplish by supporting King John would be the endangerment of their French interests for little or no upside.

John is bewildered and frustrated by the lacklustre action his Barons demonstrate at mobilising beneath his banner. He has lived his entire life in the Plantagenet court and has never seen anything like it. The Old King would have glared at them until they complied, The Lionheart would have committed some kind of atrocity to bring them into line, even Young Henry would have inspired them into action. John isn't sure what to do.

Bring the leader into line and the rest will follow, John reasoned. In front of the entire court, he rakes Marshal over the coals, admonishing him for his treachery in paying homage to Philip Augustus. Marshal, who had hoped the King might see reason, is stuck. No argument he is able to voice can make John empathise with the impossible situation he had found himself in. Marshal protests that he has not committed treason and that being the liege of both King John and Philip was entirely plausible and they could make it work. The argument was going round in circles. Marshal fell back on his old favourite, "Trial by combat then, let's do that!"

Marshal has a fearsome reputation, but by this point in his career he is by no means unbeatable. He is fifty-nine and though still strong as an ox, he has a gut that protrudes past his belt line, he is slower than he once was and his right knee shakes if called upon to support his weight. These are weaknesses an accomplished fighter would both notice and exploit.

There are a number gathered in the very room that could probably have beaten him, but nobody wanted to. People like William Marshal, he's a good guy. A soldier that had stood shoulder to shoulder with his men in the trenches and come out good, a decorated Earl with lands and power. What wasn't to like?

Seething, John looks imploringly about the court for his champion, a vein in his temple pulses visibly, silence meets him. Marshal, understandably at this juncture, decides it would be politic to retreat away from John's immediate presence and wrath. Marshal sets sail for Ireland where he has lands and is far enough away to be out of sight and out of mind of the increasingly unhinged King John, at least that's what Marshal hopes.

Earl Marshal, who has by now served under four different Kings and a Queen, decides the fighting, jostling for position, influence and favour required to make a career in the Plantagenet court, was a young man's game. Marshal wants to strike out on his own. He gathers up his wife, key nobles and his son John Marshal and sets his eyes West. Marshal has a claim on the Irish lands of Leinster, county Kildare, through his wife Isabel De Clare. Ireland had a lot of potential, but was also largely a law unto itself with each individual baron wielding considerable power autonomous to any central figure of authority. The De Clare family had been absent for some time from the region and re-asserting power would be a task in itself. Though this would be dangerous, compared to fighting under the incompetent King John's banner against the wolfish Philip Augustus, it seemed a walk in the park.

Marshal should have known better though. King John is not going to let him get away that easily. At the last possible moment, John sends a messenger to Marshal rescinding the earlier permission he had granted for the expedition. John was after all, technically speaking, High King of Ireland. It was a title he had not had a chance to explore or enforce to date and he felt Marshal carving out part of the country would undermine him. He also didn't like Marshal turning his attention West when John wanted all momentum hurtling Southwards towards France.

By this point though Marshal has spent a lot of money, time and effort preparing his expedition. He also believes for him and his family to be safe, he needs to establish a powerbase far away from the shadow of King John. Putting the Irish sea between himself and the angry monarch seemed a very shrewd move. Despite John's latest directive, Marshal sets sail anyway. It isn't treason thinks Marshal, it probably isn't even illegal really, he does, after all, have a signed document granting permission for him to sail over to Ireland. That John had rescinded this document at the eleventh hour was neither here nor there. Marshal tells himself that he is operating in a "grey area," somewhere between squeaky clean and belligerent disobedience.

Somebody who doesn't believe Marshal is operating in a grey area, is King John. He believes his behaviour to be in direct contradiction of an explicit crown directive. John wastes no time seizing Marshal's lands across England and Wales to demonstrate his displeasure. Marshal wasn't too concerned about this, for he had enough occupying him in Ireland. He had fallen foul almost immediately upon landing of a local bully by the name of Fitzhenry. Fitzhenry was the big dog in Ireland and did not take kindly to another Rottweiler turning up and trying to eat from his bowl.

Fitzhenry was no stranger to combat but Marshal felt with his own experience and resources, he probably could have beaten him in a campaigning season. To openly declare war against him though, would certainly not be operating in a grey area, it would be out and out treason for Fitzhenry is John's man. Instead, Marshal sets about pulling political levers in a bid to undermine Fitzhenry. The lesser lords of Ireland believe Marshal represents a great new hope for the land and love him for it. Marshal encourages a great majority of the lords to write a letter to King John complaining about the unfairness of Fitzhenry and expressing a desire to unseat him.

Marshal may have been one of the greatest warriors of this period but he is an average politician. He has not read the situation well, nor has he understood that King John and Fitzhenry have been in constant communication over recent weeks. John had been waiting for an excuse to summon Marshal back to England and this was it.

Marshal is panicked, he does not know what will await him when he reaches the court of King John. He is also fearful to leave Ireland whilst Fitzhenry covets his land. There is little he can do though, there is no misinterpreting King John's summons and disobeying would be treason.

Marshal prepares to set sail for what he knows is a trap.

Before he does though, he gathers all of his men loyal to him and implores them to stay so. In his absence, his pregnant wife Isabella and John of Earley, a loyal baron of note, will lead any defence should it be required. When Marshal sets sail for England, he is more scared he will never see his family again than he ever has been riding into battle. This was a world he did not fully understand and one he cannot recall asking to be a part of. He has always tried to serve The Plantagenet family loyally, do what was best for his own kin and keep the soldiers under his command alive and paid. He is not used to this murky world and nor is he used to being on the wrong side of the crown's law.

Marshal was right to be worried. The hearing, regarding the letter sent to oust Fitzhenry, is farcical. It essentially turns into a bidding war and it is one King John decisively wins. He offers boons, grants and tax breaks for all of the minor lords of Ireland in return for their fealty, something they eagerly take with a shrug to Earl Marshal. Marshal has gone from having the support of most of Ireland, to being completely alone. To make matters worse, Fitzhenry's request to return to Ireland is immediately approved, predictably, Marshal's is not.

Fitzhenry wastes no time setting sail for Ireland and makes arrangements to seize Marshal's lands. He also has an ace up his sleeve, clutched in his grubby little mitts is a letter from King John. It requests, in no uncertain terms, the presence of John of Earley in England. Earley was the knight left behind to manage any military matters in Marshal's absence, losing him would throw any attempt at resisting Fitzhenry into disarray. In short, Marshal was screwed.

Marshal follows King John's travelling court of which he now has no formal part to play in. He is a castrated dog on a leash. He is treated like a leaper, nobody speaks to the hero of a thousand battles nor acknowledges his existence. The great warrior draws comfort from the stars, for he knows that the pin pricks of light against the black velvet he gazes upon are the same as those his wife, Isabella, also looks up to of an evening. He prays she is alive and well, for no word has reached him from Ireland since he arrived at the court of King John.

Marshal did note, with more than a little interest, that in all of his time travelling around with King John, he had not seen his right-hand man Earley arrive at the court as per the summons. Not that this necessarily meant a lot, the season had turned and crossing the Irish sea would be difficult, if not impossible. Had Earley wished to acquiesce with King John's request but been unconfident in making the crossing, he may have just surrendered to Fitzhenry. That would probably have been sufficient to appease King John until The Irish shipping lanes opened once more next Spring.

It was the not knowing that Marshal found the hardest. Eventually, King John rode alongside him in the column and decided to put him out of his misery.

"Hello William, how are you? Are you enjoying being part of my court?" asked King John provocatively.

"Aye. I am," Marshal wears his stoicism like armour and gives his King as little as possible to manipulate him with.

"I suppose you would like some news from Ireland?" King John smiles evilly.

Though Marshal tries to betray nothing, he is not a good actor, his face contorts as though his very heart has been squeezed at the mention of the land his beloved resides in, "Aye. I would. I truly would." Marshal's eyes shine both with hope and fear.

"There was a bloody battle for your lands, Marshal. Your wife is under siege as we speak and she is losing. Your ally John of Earley is dead." King John continues smiling widely as he looks upon Marshal's crestfallen features, delighted at the effect the news he has imparted is having on the old Earl.

Marshal knows without John of Earley to keep his men

united and fighting, his castle will soon fall and the capture of his wife was inevitable. In some ways, he hoped she would surrender now, for that would surely garner more favourable terms from the vindictive Fitzhenry. He suspected she would not though, these lands were hers by ancestry and she had always been a fighter. She would not give them up easily and she lacked the military experience to know she was beaten.

Marshal is in turmoil, he requests once more to return to Ireland, this is again refused. Marshal endures the coldest, darkest Winter of his life. It is far too late in the season by now for word to reach him from Ireland's shores, so he is left with his own imagination to conjure dark narratives of what has become of his wife and friends. Marshal becomes numb to the world and clings to his routine like a drowning man to a life raft. He wakes, he trains, he rides with the court and he falls asleep each evening with the aid of three or four large goblets of wine.

Even the arrival of Spring, does little to thaw the icy tendrils that have wrapped around his great heart. Spring does, however, see the shipping lanes reopen. Word finally reaches Marshal from Ireland. It turns out the King had been entirely untruthful with his earlier update. Upon receiving the summons to King John's court, Earley and a group of other senior officials who had also been sent for, refused the crown's request. They would not forsake Earl William Marshal.

The defence mounted by Marshal's wife, Countess Isabella, Earley and their band of loyal lieutenants proved so solid in fact, that Fitzhenry was soon retreating across the country and Marshal's men were on a counter-attack of their own. Lords that just a few months previously had been ready to sell Marshal out for the prizes offered by John, could now see with clarity that this war was only going one way. A lot of these men decide to re-join the Earl's family which further tips the balance in his favour.

King John eventually summons Marshal and imparts

this update to him. Earl Marshal pretends it is his first time hearing it and expresses shock at the turn of events. He even goes so far as to advise that when he left Ireland, he had no idea anybody coveted his lands nor would anyone make a move against him. Marshal's diplomacy in not mentioning King John's vindictive lies of a few months earlier serves him well.

King John advises Marshal may return to Ireland and Fitzhenry's wings are clipped.

Chapter 29: The church bells fall silent across England

So focused have we been on Marshal's struggles for his land, family and introspective turmoil, we have had little chance to ask what exactly it is that John has been up to during his incessant roaming about the country? Well, the ice that began to crack during the reign of King Richard, is now collapsing all around us. The nation is bankrupt. John's focus should be on some kind of sustainable quantitative easing and a nurturing, economic recovery plan, but it isn't. All he is interested in is winning back the lands in Northern France he has lost. John's obsessed with it, it occupies his every waking moment, it is his Jerusalem.

The tried and tested method of raising money for a Medieval King is taxation from his own barons, but that's the problem, none of them have any confidence in him. King John is swiftly learning that the business of Kingship is a paradox in itself. You are both a leader and a servant, free yet shackled, a peer whilst somehow peerless. In short, like many senior managerial positions that exist today, it's all about people. You've got to understand what makes them tick. You have to build your own brand and pit it against those you find yourself surrounded by on the chessboard of life. It's important to understand who you can intimidate, who you should placate and who can be inspired to follow you. John doesn't get this, not at all, not even close.

John can't extort, charm or coerce money from his barons, so he needs to find some other way. He sits in church at Mass, though his mind is elsewhere. What to do, what to do? John drums his fingers on the shelf in front of him whilst simultaneously stroking his chin with the other. Money making schemes are flying through John's mind.

His initial thoughts are to sell something, for John was very into this and whilst his brother The Lionheart had joked about selling London, John would actually have done it. He sold governmental titles, administrative positions and even the charter for the not-yet-founded city of Nottingham. It's a good strategy for quickly acquiring liquid funds, but it's also short sighted.

Money in the bank is essential, however, an organisation such as the Plantagenets wasn't judged primarily on their cash reserves. Potential investors placed a higher weighting on how much revenue the estate generated per annum. If you would like to hire mercenaries on credit, or to borrow from another sovereign state, they wanted to know how much money you would earn next year. They *got* that you didn't have cash in the bank now, hence the loan application.

With the loss of Normandy and John selling off everything in England, the Plantagenet revenue stream which was once akin to the mighty Mississippi river, was becoming the bloody trickle of an elderly man with a kidney stone.

With little left to sell, John began to look at other options. He had not inherited a fiat (faith) currency, so in theory at least, it was impossible to debase his own money and thus swiftly raise funds. The Crown Coins that circulated about the country had a set weight and therefore an inherently fixed value. This had all been cemented way back during the Norman conquest of 1066, William the Conqueror times. The weight could neither be altered, nor changed. The Plantagenet empire prided itself on its sterling coinage and enjoyed the stability this afforded to the money in circulation. During the early years of John's reign though, something strange began to happen. Rogue batches of bad coinage began to pour into circulation at an alarming rate.

These so called, "weak pennies" had silver shaved

313

from the edges, making them a shade lighter and thus less valuable. John was quick to blame counterfeiters for this practice of coin clipping, but rumours ran rife that the crown itself was responsible. Merchants demanded more of these weak pennies for their goods and this, coupled with a succession of poor harvests, caused inflation to rocket. Goods were doubling in price almost annually. John was eventually able to arrest this spike by threatening the confiscation of any coins found to be underweight, but his foray into the world of currency creation was over. It was back to the drawing board for the King.

If he shouldn't sell anything else and he couldn't dilute his own coinage, John needed to make his assets work harder for him. Instead of dwelling on what he had lost, John considered what he did have. High up the list, was the King's Forest. The notion of this had been established by William the Conqueror who had so loved the deer roaming in the New Forest outside Winchester, he had declared the land to be under royal jurisdiction. The King was allowed to rule with absolute power under these trees and could dish out punishments arbitrarily without the need for trials.

Beautiful as the New Forest is, many residents of England felt they could deprive themselves of the sight of sweeping beech trees so as not to fall foul of the King's law. This got harder though for the Royal Forest seemed to be ever changing and without borders. By King John's time, in fact, over a quarter of the country had been labelled as the King's forestland.

King John would have his bully boys and enforcers out in great numbers patrolling these "forests" and penalising the most trivial of infractions. This did generate income, but it also cost him heavily. The cost John is incurring in alienating his own people is far greater than the coin raised by his extortionate practices. The lay folk hate him.

John scratched his head, raising money should not have been so hard. Medieval Europe's mode of government, the Feudal system, was one of the earliest and biggest pyramid schemes ever conceived, it was also one that John happened to sit atop. The Old King understood this and was a master at it, he would relentlessly roam his kingdom showing his face. He would demonstrate to towns, villages and cities throughout his lands that the Plantagenets were the ultimate brand. Those that did try to fight it were dealt with swiftly and loudly to spread a message, the machine rumbled on.

Whilst the Old King viewed ruling as a lot of hard work, chronic hypertension and ultimately died at war with his own children of a stress related ailment, John viewed it somewhat differently. He considered ruling to be soft cushions, exotic prostitutes and the right to get drunk and beat a man to death before lunch. King John does not possess the raw mettle and work ethic to make the machine run.

John is snapped out of his reverie when he notices everybody in the church stand up around him. He joins them. John has not been listening to the priest delivering Mass at all. Metaphysically, he has been walking down a thousand different avenues of money-making schemes and has found them all to be dead ends. John watches the altar boy walk slowly across the front of the church in the finest robes of silk. John scrunches up his face, think John think!

What else is left to sell? Focus John, you're a smart man, you have the answers

The altar boy stoops, for a moment John thinks he is hurt, but then he sees that he is just picking up a prayer book placed upon a low shelf. It has gold leafed pages and the front cover is embossed with rare gemstones. The altar boy goes to sing but is chastised by the priest, "Candles boy, they've gone out." A plume of smoke confirms the all-seeing eye of the almighty's agent on earth is correct.

I've sold government titles, I've sold land, I've sold options for cities that remain unbuilt. What else is left of any value in my empire?

The altar boy must stand on tip toes, to reach his lit splint up to the fine wax candles in their silver candelabras. He shoots a nervous smile at the organist, who prepares to play the largest and most grand of its kind in all of Europe. The altar boy would sing pitch perfectly, with all the grace and goodliness of a virgin swan, but the King is not listening.

How could I be so stupid? I'll sell the goddamn church

For a moment John panics, he has said goddamn within hallowed walls, was he to be struck down by lightning or afflicted with an ailment? There was no sound of thunder and he didn't feel queasy, although his heart is racing and his palms are sweaty.

"Goddamn," he whispers it looking furtively left and right, "Goddamn." This time he says it louder, "Goddamn" finally he shouts it and stands up in triumph. The altar boy and the priest falter, as King John strides out of the church clicking his heels.

John's decision to sell licenses and positions within the church, will put him on a collision course with one of the most dangerous and influential medieval Popes that has ever lived. John is about to go toe to toe with Pope Innocent III.

So far in our story, we have seen Popes able to exert little power or influence over monarchs residing across Europe. In The Old King's time we saw the Pope beg and plead for him to take the cross, something of which he never bothered to, even after allowing Archbishop Becket to die under his administration. We saw the church's poster boy, Richard the Lionheart returning home after three years of crusading, blood, sweat, tears and tarantulas, having invested

316

untold resources and manpower whilst personally risking his own life be afforded zero protection on his return journey. It's easy to see why John wasn't scared of the Catholic church.

He should have been treading more carefully though, for Pope Innocent is of a different breed entirely to those that have gone before. To say he was ambitious, would be an understatement. Whereas Innocent's predecessors had gone by the title of, "Vicar of St. Peter," Innocent feels his star shines brighter than this and declares himself instead "Vicar of Christ."

Innocent is not the leader of the church, or Rome, or even Christian Nations, no, he believes he has been advised directly by God that he should be leader of the entire world. It's always nice to have one of these, "told-by-God-to-rule-the-world" nutters around, you just never know what they're going to do next.

We start to see that this pontificating Pope packs a punch when he manages to seat his man, Otto IV as Holy Roman Emperor. In the incestuous world of leadership that prevailed over twelfth century Europe, Otto was actually a nephew of King Johns, not that this made much odds and John certainly couldn't expect any favourable treatment from this quarter. Otto was happy to be in the pocket of the Pope and was not about to put himself out for England.

Though devout, Innocent was never one to be quietly content knowing he was humbly doing God's work. Innocent wants formal recognition in a tangible sense on Earth and isn't prepared to wait for his reward in an afterlife. He has become a serious political player on the medieval European stage claiming fiefdoms over Portugal, Spain, Hungary and England. These nations will ultimately end up paying both homage and an annual sum to Rome, interestingly though, the annual sum is not overly onerous. Innocent seems less concerned about the actual financial benefit of this fiefdom arrangement than he does the message paying a tariff sets. He is basically saying don't forget, you may be King in your own country, but you are forever in my pocket.

John's taxation of churches and monasteries was a welcome financial life-line, raising somewhere in the region of 100,000 marks per year. To put this into context, this is around two thirds of The Lionheart's ransom. Even with this extra money though, without the support of the Barons, John is still very much on the back foot against The Capetians, to make matters worse, tensions with the church are rapidly escalating over these new taxes.

It is at this time that Archbishop Hubert Walter dies. He has cropped up a couple of times so far, he was the Earl who advised Marshal that he would come to regret supporting John's claim for the throne and he also assisted Eleanor in raising Richard's ransom. Whilst there is no hint of foul play relating to his death, it is not quick or pleasant for the career statesman. He is thought to have died from a carbuncle of boils that went untreated on his lower back. Treatment would have been unpleasant, no doubt involving rusty, heavy point needles heated white in the flames of a prayer candle, but it would also have been preferable to the long, drawn out death caused by the infection spreading into his bloodstream and shutting down his vital organs.

Surely, an Archbishop can have little to fear beyond the ethereal veil? When Walter approaches the pearly gates and St. Peter weighs his heart, how could a man who has dedicated the last decade to leading the church in England be found wanting? We should bear in mind though, Walter has spent far longer than a single decade playing the game of thrones with the Plantagenets. His career has left him with more than one regretful action and betrayed friend. Concerned for his immortal soul, as Walter feels the end drawing near he is determined to make amends and appease his guilty conscience.

In the synoptic gospels, Jesus stated that it was more

likely for a camel to fit through the eye of a needle than a rich man go to heaven. A learned Archbishop like Walter wasn't going to be caught out by this. He went into a stage of uber repentance, giving away all his worldly possessions to his cloister. The monks found themselves confused, they didn't know whether to shun luxury, as their vows suggested they should, or, obey an Archbishop in his dying wish. It was a tough question, particularly as Walter seemed so determined to pass on these fine garments, jewels and golden furniture to them. The Monks conferred and decided that yes, it was probably best to accept all of the nice things that Walter was bequeathing them, he was the Archbishop after all.

As the monks whispered final rites and internally wondered what to spend their new found fortunes on, King John arrived. It was always a bother when he turned up. You had to wear clean robes and make sure you got out the nice plates. John and his retinue were also well known for putting a serious dent into the cellar brewery. The monks of many cloisters brewed their own beer for a number of reasons, it was sterile, it was good for the economy of the church and it was a ton of fun. Having a working brewery in the cellar gave the monastery a frat house vibe and discussing the heavier themes of the Old Testament with a bit of a buzz, was the only way many of the younger clergy members felt it possible to engage in such debates.

They needn't have worried though for John wasn't in a drinking mood, "Sorry, got to dash, this is just a quick visit, I don't have much time, I suppose none of us do when it comes down to it, mind you, that's more your bag than mine I guess?" King John laughed good naturedly. The monks had never seen King John laugh good naturedly before, evilly yes, maliciously sure, but not good naturedly. It was extremely disconcerting.

King John truly is in an excellent mood though, the death of Archbishop Walter, who was The Lionheart's right-hand man and friend to Earl Marshal was fantastic news.

King John felt oppressed by grown-ups who commanded that sort of gravitas and was delighted to learn he was now dead. He feels that his harness has been removed and he is free to do whatever the hell he wants, there I go again, he chuckles, blaspheming on hallowed ground.

The reason for King John's visit is twofold, firstly, he immediately confiscates all of the windfall will and testimony payments made by Hubert Walter.

"Now, what need would monks have for gold, jewellery and fanciful frocks?" John asks rhetorically with a wicked wink. The King also needs to initiate the process for selecting a new Archbishop of Canterbury.

"It needs to be both fair and democratic," King John declares to the assembled, "Each of you gathered will cast one vote and each shall be deemed equal, as indeed you all are in the eyes of the Almighty. One soul, one vote, it is the only way." The monks look relieved, the Archbishop of Canterbury is an important position and there were a number of good candidates to consider, this would require some thought.

King John continues, "An Archbishop can only ever be successful, if they are supported by the Lord's agents on earth as a collective, that is why your support and vote is so necessary. I shall require you all to vote for my main man, John de Gray," King John's voice reaches a crescendo as he declares his name, like the announcer for a prize fighter stepping into the ring. Join points excitedly across the room to a beaming and attractive Monk dressed in white robes with a perfect smile. Gray strides into the crowd, using his chiselled jaw like a snowplough he scatters aside minor Monks and bee lines for the senior management of the church.

If this doesn't seem particularly democratic, that's because it isn't. King John wants his man Gray on the seat as Archbishop so, from a domestic standpoint at least, the church can't challenge his authority. Gray isn't a terrible choice, he just isn't being put forward as a choice.

Yes okay, The Old King had got away with putting Becket on the seat and The Lionheart had done a similar thing with Hubert Walter, but there was a difference, both of those former Kings were liked to some degree and feared to a whole other level. Little Johnny lackland didn't command the same respect.

Whilst on the surface the monks smiled and acquiesced as to how great a leader Gray would undoubtedly prove himself to be, behind closed doors, they decide to push back. Secret meetings are held and a new candidate is put forward, Archbishop Reginald. No longer would the monks allow their most senior Archbishop to be in the Plantagenet's pocket. Going against the King of England would be dangerous, but given the current climate, not impossible. Due to the shifting political tectonic plates there was now a power higher than King John, not God, well, sort of God, a more tangible and mortal version though who directly responded to messages, there was now a Pope Innocent III.

Upon hearing the monks have gone behind his back and told "Daddy" (Pope Innocent), King John is livid, he's spitting nails. These are *his* subjects and they are answerable to *him*, nobody else, certainly not some prat in a pointy hat presiding halfway across Europe. John takes deep breaths, inhaling slowly for five seconds and exhaling for ten. It isn't enough, he can't stop shaking and tears of rage run down his ruddy cheeks, his balled fists tremble.

Not for the first time in this book, a member of the ruling Plantagenet dynasty will, in anger, send a column of armed thugs dressed as knights to Canterbury cathedral.

The monks picking fruit in the gardens of Canterbury Cathedral see the dust clouds kicked up in the distance from the unit of knights riding towards them under the shadow of the red lion rampant flag. Hurriedly, they gather their baskets, their brows are creased with worried lines and they shuffle as fast as their dusty joints will allow.

Some of the monks who watch King John's men approach, are the same as those who witnessed Archbishop Becket slashed mercilessly down, unarmed at the altar, even those who had not personally witnessed this atrocity are painfully familiar with the story.

It's every bit as bad as the monks' feared. John's men burst into the monastery, naked blades held aloft, "traitors to King John, traitors!" They bellow. The monks can smell alcohol on their breath and they are rounded into the centre of the nave. There will be no hiding in the shadows of the cloisters for any of them this time for they are all considered answerable for judgement, not by God, but by the men of the King.

"Please, good Sir knight," begins a senior monk speaking softly. The room falls silent so he continues, "Though my bones are dusty as Saint Cuthberts and my eyes fail me, I still know a good heart when I see one. I sense in you much kindness, honour and…" He is cut off as he is backhanded across the face by a gauntleted fist that shatters his jaw.

"Traitors, we will burn down this cathedral with you all inside, if you do not leave immediately." The monks are happy to comply and hurry away from the soldiers. Sixty monks flee for the safety of France and little hares are set running across Europe towards Rome.

When Pope Innocent hears, he is not best pleased, "What the Hell is wrong with this goddamn family?" His assistant knows better than to call him out on his blaspheming.

The cream of the English churches' executive team has fled to France. This leaves Christendom's middle management team that do remain in England, in a very difficult position. They should probably tell King John they don't agree with his actions down in Canterbury, but that seemed like suicide and suicide was a sin… They decide, after much deliberation, that they should probably do nothing. "Don't rock the boat," is a sentiment nodded at a lot during the meeting. Many of the Monks even felt there was probably a proverb somewhere hidden away amidst one of the lesser known Matthew's or Mark's that said a very similar thing. There is palpable relief across the room as the Monks decide to do nothing.

Their relief is short lived, for a letter soon arrives from Pope Innocent commanding they behave very differently. It says something along the lines of, "Prepare yourself for persecution, all of Christendom across England must immediately go on strike conducting no religious services and all Church facilities should close immediately".

Prepare yourself for persecution? Was this guy for real? He sits on a beautiful white horse over a thousand miles away, eating caviar with a silver spoon whilst he shouts at us to charge forward and attack? John will kill us, he is unhinged, he cares not for tradition, sensibilities or the authority of The Pope.

Equally though, Innocent's letter had made it very clear that this was a directive and not up for discussion. To buy some time, the monks write back throwing as much confusion as is possible into the mix.

Hello Pope Innocent III,

We hope that you are well.

Fantastic initiative oh most Innocent of Innocentists, it is a plan that could only spell success your Popiest of Pontificators. We are (w)Holy behind you!

Before we begin though with directly confronting King John, a course of action we can hardly wait to take, can we quickly clarify a few points:
Will this ban on services include weddings?
Would be able to conduct last rites?

Does the strike include Wales?
We have pre-ordered 6 months' worth of
communion wine and are unable to back out on the
contract, are we able to still bless and distribute this?

The questions go on…

Yours Faithfully (!),

Team Monks

Throwing a number of cross departmental questions into any multi-national organisation, even today, will cause chaos. Back in medieval times when all correspondence was conducted by letter and the average response time was over a month, this bombardment of different issues raised in separate letters sends the Papal team into a spiral.

Innocent wasn't born yesterday though, he knows what the Monks are up to. He pens the final response to them personally confirming that yes, the strike will indeed stand in Wales and makes it crystal clear that they should be getting on with this nationwide spiritual lockdown. He pens another note, this time to the leading barons and noblemen of England. He outlines in this that the King is sick in his mind and that indulging his whims or demands was enabling the cancer to spread further. He also patiently explained that he, Pope Innocent, was the panacea for this sickness. Essentially, he is advising the barons and noblemen that they should rebel against King John. The tone of the letter is not admonishing nor damning, it is the letter of a disappointed parent. Innocent even goes so far as to expresses that he loves King John and looks forward to welcoming him back into the flock soon. Taking the moral high ground is a pre-requisite for the job of Pope.

On the 23rd of March 1208, the strike of the clergy goes ahead. Church bells across England fall silent. Heavy oaken doors are pulled tightly shut, wedding services cancelled and loved ones no longer permitted to be buried in hallowed ground. An unhappy coincidence of note is that eight hundred and twelve years later to the day, 23rd March 2020, churches will again be forced to close across England due to coronavirus restrictions.

During King John's time it is important to remember that every single citizen was a devout believer in God, this was an incredibly distressing turn of events. Should you have the misfortune to die during this period, you would reach the pearly gates only to find St. Peter slowly shaking his head.

Members of the clergy up and down the country met in empty churches and drank heavily from the communion wine. They winced in preparation and wondered how King John would take their action. Badly, that's how King John takes it, extremely badly. Which isn't really a surprise, the Plantagenets are not known for their calm temperament. Whilst this is extremely disruptive to the nation, it doesn't seem to have come as a surprise to King John who is ready with his riposte.

From the coast of Northumberland down to Land's End, armed men crash their way into churches across the country seizing all valuables and evicting the occupying Monks. The roads are lined with travelling clergy desperately clutching whatever meagre belongings they have been able to salvage. These refugees are dragged from horses and left battered and bloodied on the floor, their valuables stolen. It is open season on the church.

The Monks who have been thrown out of their vicarages and monasteries, will eventually be permitted to return to their own homes, as rent paying tenants of course.

As much fun as John is having turning this situation to his advantage, there are greater ramifications to being excommunicated than John may have at first realised. Technically, with King John now divorced from the Catholic church, the vows of fealty made by barons and noblemen across the land, no longer stand. They are free of any obligation to serve him or obey his commands whilst he remains ostracised from the church.

King John was certainly feeling as though he had a lot on. His country was in financial ruin, Philip Augustus was rumoured to be planning an invasion of England, the Barons and Earls of the nation were refusing to back his war with France and now, apparently, God hated him too. John breathed deeply, he prided himself at being able to juggle a lot of balls at once but this was getting ridiculous. What could possibly happen next? Well, it is around this time that John becomes a father.

It is widely agreed that the first three months of parenthood are the hardest. It isn't that any of the tasks required to keep a tiny human alive are in themselves complex, a baby's needs are fairly basic; cleaning, eating, sleeping. The challenge lies in the relentlessness of the demanding little bundle of joy you have brought, kicking and screaming, into the world. The sleep deprivation doesn't help. It gives an otherworldly twilight-zone edge that permeates into all aspects of life, this is coupled with the upheaval of every convention, habit or routine you previously held dear. Not that this is really the case for King John though, as a normal medieval man, it is unlikely he would have been in any way involved in midnight feedings or the changing of nappies.

It is difficult to say with any certainty, what form family units took in the medieval times. Records just don't exist on this sort of mundanity. We can pick up a few clues though and unsurprisingly, it doesn't scream love and unity.

Paternal relationships with children were relatively non-existent, with mothers bearing the majority of the heavy lifting. Fatherhood, at least for the Plantagenets, seemed an endeavour embarked upon for dynastic reasons as opposed to any form of pleasure. These were brutal times and with child mortality rates sitting around half, spending time getting to know the child too early in their life may have just been considered a bad investment of energy.

Even romances seem two dimensional. Young Henry escaped his father's camp so many pages ago to kick start the first rebellion, carelessly leaving behind his wife to face The Old King's wrath. The Lionheart jilted Philip's sister to be with Bear Spear, which sounds like the stuff of fairy tales but was it? He barely spent any time with the lady and when he was dying it was not her he sent for but his mother, he sent for Eleanor.

Our book opened with the controversial gifting of various lands and titles to the seven year old John as a wedding present to mark his betrothal to Isabella, Countess of Gloucester. Both were too young to actually get hitched at this point. The knot was tied around fifteen years later in a grand wedding ceremony. Two young people getting married as their eyes shine with hope for what is to come, who could object to that?

The Archbishop of Canterbury at the time, Baldwin, that's who could object. He objected on the grounds of them both being a great-grandchild of Henry I. This made them second cousins and therefore they resided in a bit of a grey area as to whether this was too close or not in the eyes of the church. John was keen to alleviate the Archbishop's concerns and listened calmly to Baldwin, nodding at just the right moments and looking thoughtfully at the senior clergy member. John reassured Baldwin that he would write to the Pope post haste and secure a letter of support for his marriage, thus securing its legitimacy. It was good being the son of the King, you could do things like write to the Pope. A quick letter, that was all it would have taken. Considering Richard was soon to join the crusades, the Pope was bound to grant him this boon, it was basically a done deal.

The only thing is, John never got round to sending the letter. It could be that he forgot, John is quite a busy schemer and a spinner of many plates, more likely though is that the illegitimacy of his marriage was his safety net. Should a higher profile potential bachelorette come into view, or, if John just got bored with his current wife, he could pull the rug from under everybody's feet declaring the marriage to be illegitimate. Which is precisely what he did.

A year after becoming king in 1200, John annulled his marriage with Isabella of Gloucester on the grounds of consanguinity. Confusingly enough, John's new wife will also be called Isabella, maybe he had a tattoo or something.

John is in his mid-thirties when he begins his second marriage whereas (new) Isabella was just a twelve year old girl, she may have even been as young as ten. This was weird, even for the time period. Although betrothals could happen at any age, marriages would typically wait until a lady was of child-bearing age. Considering John and new Isabella's first child does not arrive for another seven years, it is unlikely she had reached an age of sexual maturity when they did marry.

Whilst there were some tactical land advantages to their union, there were far more pitfalls. She was already betrothed to one of the influential Lusignan clan members and they were furious at being scorned in such a manner. They appealed to Philip Augustus who had also fallen prey to the Plantagenet Kings' wicked, wandering eyes. This served to further shake the Capetian hornet nest and catalysed armed conflict between the rival nations.

Considering the ramifications of leaving his original Isabella, this may, creepily, be our first example of one of our protagonists marrying for love.

Chapter 30: The Magna Carta

The Western face of Lichfield cathedral is adorned with a sculpture of King John. In this depiction, John holds a quill aloft for he is busy making History. He is judiciously and with great dignity, signing new legislature that will forever separate crown, church and state. King John is signing the Magna Carta. The quill that he holds is wildly out of proportion to many of the swords wielded by other monarchs on the Western Wall which conveys the message, rather literally, that we are now entering a period of our History where the pen will prove mightier than the sword. No matter our opinion on King John, we should always retain the image captured on Lichfield cathedral's Western Wall of him serenely, signing a document guaranteeing basic human rights to all of England.

The issue is, it didn't happen anything like this, John signed the document kicking and screaming. It's even up for debate if the Magna Carta even comes close to deserving the infamy it commands.

The beginning of 1213 opened as bleakly as any for King John. He was caught in a noose that he could feel tightening around his neck. The barons at home hated him for his extortionate taxation and planned rebellion against him. Pope Innocent was also unhappy as he didn't feel the King was upset enough about being excommunicated. In a bid to further turn up the heat, Innocent was petitioning Philip Augustus to begin a Holy War, not against the Saracens in Jerusalem but this time, against England.

With these all too real threats running rife throughout his Kingdom, the last thing John needed was imaginary ones adding to his woes, but this is what he got. Peter of Wakefield, druidic mystic from the North with a penchant for prophecies, predicted the King's spectacular fall from grace. He advised John would lose the crown before the fourteenth anniversary of his Coronation of that very year, it was written in the stars, by the 27th of May John would be gone.

John was fairly nonplussed by this ghoulish Nostradamus, but he was still a Plantagenet and would not put up with people prophesising his downfall. Wakefield was thrown in the dungeon. John did, rather sportingly, agree not to have him killed until the anniversary of his coronation had passed so Peter could be proven wrong.

Not long after this, John finally manages to roll double sixes. His naval forces, under the command of his half-brother William Longsword, fortuitously encounter the majority of Philip Augustus' ships anchored outside Boulogne. With most of the French army busy besieging the Count of Flanders, some fifteen hundred Capetian war galleys bob, up and down, innocently and harmlessly in the water. They are defended by only a skeleton crew, it was unbelievably good luck.

Over three hundred ships were seized by the English forces with hundreds more scuppered to prevent them falling into enemy hands. Cargo ships that were carrying supplies for an entire army were ransacked. Philip was forced to abandon his siege in Flanders and panic marched back towards the coast. The English scarpered, reaching the safety of their vessels just in time. The harbour was so full of debris that Philip was unable to give chase.

King John needed that, finally he had something he could communicate out to the nation that was positive. His run of good fortune didn't end there though. Later in that very same year, John managed to reconcile with Pope Innocent and was welcomed back into the flock. He publicly surrendered his crown and stepped down as King of England, before accepting Kingship once again however this time, as a vassal of the Pope. John once more had the support of Rome who now threatened Philip with excommunication, should he go ahead with the planned Holy War against England.

There were other conditions. John had to withdraw his support for Archbishop Gray and accept Innocent's candidate, he would also have to pay 1000 marks per annum to the Pope. This was a paltry sum and instead of representing real compensation, was just further symbolism of John's submission to Innocent. What wasn't paltry though by any means, was that John would have to pay reparations for the thieving his men had committed on the monks and the church, an investigative team was set up to ascertain exactly what sum these damages had run to.

The anniversary of John's coronation came and went. The King made a show of hosting a large public party. If he was concerned about the prophecy proving true with concealed daggers amongst the crowd or revolutionaries within his ranks, he didn't show it. Once Peter of Wakefield was proven false, both he and his son were dragged behind horses and hanged for inciting dissent. Sticklers for detail often feel this treatment a little unfair for Peter of Wakefield. The King did, after all, lose his crown to Pope Innocent before the fourteenth anniversary of his coronation. Granted, it was a symbolic surrender however had John not done this, chances are he would have lost it to Philip Augustus in a manner that would be impossible to deny.

Something else undeniable though, is that John has just secured two massive wins over as many months. He intends to trade on the back of these to get what he really wants, support from The Barons for his war against Philip Augustus. John has expressed desire to win back his continental lands since he was crowned, by now, he's completely obsessed with it. John has been tied up with domestic affairs, but that doesn't mean he has been idle on the international stage and he believes he has spied an opportunity.

Philip is a great King, there's no denying that, but he

is also fast becoming a victim of his own success. He has expanded his borders exponentially in almost every direction, understandably, this has pissed a lot of people off. John manages to tap into this ill-will and successfully creates a web of disgruntled leaders surrounding Philip. Active members of John's allied forces include Holy Roman Emperor Otto, The Counts of Flanders, Boulogne, Brabant, Holland, Lorraine and Limburg. This heavyweight coalition boasts 25,000 soldiers, Philip's boots on the ground number just under 15,000.

King John and Otto decide on a strategy so dastardly, it's just delicious. John would launch from Southern France and power up into County Anjou, the lost homeland of his ancestry. Once this had been secured, he would strike further North into the Capetian heartland. This would force Philip's hand, he'd be left with no other option, he'd have to ride out. John's soldiers would then, slowly retreat, like a dog licking its wounds and in doing so they would tease Philip's men further from the capital. It would be at this precise moment Otto would spring into action. Just as the Capetian troops were securing themselves against a rallying attack from the South, Otto would hammer down thunder from the North.

Whilst the plan sounded good on paper, it was terribly complicated. Should there be even the slightest deviation from the initial blueprints, communication lines over these kinds of distances would be redundant. In short, the right hand would not have a clue what the left was doing.

Things begin well for John. He powers up to Anjou exactly as planned, however, before he is able to invade he is diverted to a nearby, rebellious castle that requires quelling. The castle is under the stewardship of the Lusignans, they were still angry about John having married the lady intended for Hugh Lusignan. Eventually, The Lusignans see sense and realise that before their small castle stands no paltry attack force intended for them, instead, it is an army equipped to seize all of France. Hugh himself talks his family down from fighting for his honour and they are forced to join John. The King of England successfully storms Anjou and prepares to springboard into Normandy.

John's forces laid siege to the castle of Roche-au-Moine, deep within the Loire Valley. This proves a little too close for comfort for the King of France. Philip began to ride hard to challenge John and lift the siege. It was all going exactly as John and Otto had planned. As Philip left his homeland behind and approached the borders of his capitol though, he had an eerily intuitive change of heart and turned back. Philip sent word for his son, Louis VIII of France to ride South and engage with King John in his stead. Philip and the majority of his army would remain in Paris.

John is spooked. The plan was to faux limp away from the entire Capetian forces, not an expeditionary one. The Plantagenet army sieging Roche-au-Moine outnumbers Louis, John could probably win if he wanted to risk a battle but to get snarled up in a conflict for a castle of mediocre importance wasn't the plan. John tries to psyche out the castle defenders, erecting a gallows in clear view of the battlements, but it doesn't work. Word has reached them that Prince Louis is on his way and they will soon be liberated from the siege of this weak, English King. As Louis draws closer, John's nerve fails him and the hearsay proves true, he retreats from the castle. Cumbersome wagons and siege equipment are left behind in panic.

It's easy to laugh at John for this latest humiliation, but we shouldn't underestimate the achievements he has made thusly in the campaign. He has won back Anjou, that's massive. If he turned back and went home now he would be returning victorious. Someone who might disagree with that statement however, is Holy Roman Emperor Otto. Otto was relying on John drawing the Capetian forces away from Northern France, a task John has just happily abandoned. This is, of course, long before the days of communication technology, so Otto has no idea the English King has pulled back.

Otto roams Northern France looking for a fight and Philip does a similar thing. Although both men want the same outcome, they want to do it on their own terms. They jostle so that the sun might be in thine enemies' eyes or the slope of a hill with their own cavalry. The endgame is inevitable yet somehow, Philip is startled when the two forces come within ten miles of one another. He beats a hasty retreat. Otto gives chase but it is a Sunday and therefore battle is unlikely, it's not definitely off, but unlikely.

The blood is up in Otto's men and they pursue the Capetian King like wild dogs. By the time word reaches Philip he has calmed down enough from his initial surprise at being so close to Otto's forces that he is able to think rationally. He was outnumbered which was bad and could well portent defeat, equally though, to be caught fleeing would spell certain disaster. When Philip actually thought about it, there was no decision to be made. He pulls up on his reins and calmly organises his men into ranks to receive his pursuers.

When Otto and the coalition forces explode over the horizon, it is clear they have become consumed by the hunt. There is no semblance of order and not a shred of discipline has been maintained, they are a rabble, it is now Philip's turn to advance. Otto's coalition have the numbers whereas Philip's men have the training and discipline.

The Battle of Bouvines, as it will come to be known, is particularly hellish even for Medieval times. Contemporary accounts recall the sickly, stench of rotting flesh under the beating summer sun, the scream of dying horses and the taste of blood on the wind.

Both leaders were very much in the thick of the fighting. Philip was captured at one point, before dramatically being rescued by his lieutenants, Otto manages to get through three or four horses himself. William Longsword, the hero of the recent naval victory for John, has

334

his head caved in before being captured by a local bishop with a mace by the name of Philip of Dreux. It's mayhem. The dust and sand kicked up makes it impossible to read the ebbs and flows of the battlefield and eventually, it all becomes too much for Otto. He flees, whilst some of his men fight on they are severely disheartened at being abandoned and it is a token show of resistance.

This battle has been described as one of the most important that English folk have never heard of. Whilst it may be poorly chronicled in the British Isles, the same cannot be said for France. Philip's victory on the 27th July 1214, reshuffled the card deck for Medieval Europe. It cemented the changing of the guard that has been underway for the past decade and ushers in a golden age of prosperity for The Capetians.

More important than that though, Philip has created a country. Had he lost on that hellishly hot summer day in France, European maps would be unrecognisable today. Had Philip lost The Battle of Bouvines, Western France would be controlled from England and Northern France from Germany. Philip Augustus, the first man ever to refer to himself as The King of the French has created his own garden of Eden, he has created France.

Things are less positive for King John. Following this loss, Philip demands the return of the recently won lands of Anjou. John is heavily outnumbered and has no choice other than to surrender his recent windfall. John retreats to the Southernmost tip of France where he still controls a few acres of land. He concentrates his forces here and digs in. Philip weighs it up, the risk reward ratio just doesn't balance. Philip probably could win these extra couple of territories if he wanted, but it would take a lot of effort. Besides, he had just united a number of different nations under a single flag, he decided it best to consolidate these regions and ensure they all coherently pulled in the same direction. A cease fire is drawn up with John.

There is now nothing to keep John in mainland Europe, it is time for him to return to England and face the music. He had left as the man with the plan, he returns a mere shadow of his former self.

Handling the English Barons on the back of this latest catastrophe was always going to be challenging. It's unclear exactly how John should have played it, but probably not like this. John decided to go on the attack. He called out any Barons he felt had not amply supported him. John demanded money in lieu of their own absence during the great battle. The Barons countered with the argument that there had been no great battle as far as they could tell for John had retreated from the advances of Prince Louis.

The reaction John is facing is not a result of this singular failure, it's accumulative. The leadership team are sick of his persistent failures and demand change. Inconspicuously and unbeknownst to John, letters are being exchanged between leading English Barons and Philip Augustus. People want change and the heroic, successful Philip of France is an attractive choice.

As was typical for King John, his problems were being compounded by the church. To lift the country's excommunication, John had signed England up to be a vassal state of the Vatican. This had attracted a largely symbolic ongoing annual charge of 1,000 marks. What was not largely symbolic in any way however, was the reparations John was also expected to pay back in full for all of the looting his men had committed against the church during those lawless months.

Bean counters across Europe had been furiously crunching numbers and still hadn't managed to arrive at the final figure, the number was looking insanely high though. John doesn't want to pay these ballooning funds and nor can he, equally though, the thought of an unholy union between the church and Barons keeps him awake at night.

It was clear to all that the relationship between crown,

church and country needed redefining. As is often the way, inspiration on how things should look for the future was influenced heavily by the past. When Henry I, grandfather to The Old King, first ascended to the throne some one hundred and fourteen years ago, it was amidst a backdrop of turmoil and outcry. The former King William II had been intensely disliked. William was considered by all to be a tyrannical ruler who relished in performing acts of cruelty. No tears were cried when one of his own soldiers 'inadvertently' shot him in the back with an arrow during a hunting accident. When Henry was crowned, leading Barons of the country sought reassurances that such dire conditions would not play on repeat.

Henry was happy to fulfil their request. He understood that in this situation, an almighty gesture was required to win back support. During Henry's coronation of 1100, he wilfully signed The Charter of Liberties. He signed the document very casually and with little negotiation, for he has no intentions of keeping to it. How could he possibly have known, that over a century later, his great grandson would be presented with this very contract and ordered to reissue it to the nation.

By this point, some of the document was irrelevant. There was an amnesty on goods stolen from Henry I providing they were promptly returned, there was a forgiving of debts for the deceased King William, there were, however, some clauses that were certainly not irrelevant and caused real concern for King John.

There were some general and probably to be expected concessions towards The Barons on matters relating to inheritance, marriage freedoms and management of The Royal Forest. Most alarming by far though, was a clause specifying that all oppression that had become a force for evil across the country should be challenged. This would be difficult for the King to uphold, for John himself was the cause of much of the evil and oppression.

If this charter had already been signed a century prior, what was the problem with John re-issuing it? After all, surely these agreed principles were already a bedrock of the English legal system? Unfortunately The Charter of Liberties, despite its impressive name, began to gather dust in a drawer almost immediately after being signed.

All of the Kings since Henry I but before John had heavily outweighed the youngest Plantagenet in political clout, military resources and economic health, to the point they were able to simply ignore the promises that had been made, after a while, people stopped bringing it up. That it has been dredged from the sludge pits of the past is testament to the alienating nature of John's rule.

The Charter of Liberties was only the starting point for what the Barons were demanding though. The campaign of culpability being levelled against the King, has by now gathered such momentum it has morphed into something entirely new.

The Unknown Charter is referred to as such in recognition of it not resurfacing from French scholarly archives until the late nineteenth century. This manuscript goes much farther than The Charter of Liberties ever did and further even than The Magna Carta will when they get round to writing it. It forbids the King from demanding shield payments in lieu of National Service and it clarifies that no military support will be given for campaigns as far South as Anjou. It reigns in the unchecked power John's ancestry have formally ruled with and requires approval to be sought from The Barons for pretty much anything The King could want to do.

Unsurprisingly, John really doesn't want to sign this. With neither party willing to back down and their demands worlds' apart, civil war was looking inevitable. It is a war John doesn't believe he can win and he will do anything to slow the axe that is falling towards his neck.

On Ash Wednesday 1215, in front of a room full of

witnesses, King John takes the cross and pledges to lead a Crusade in the Holy Lands. Whereas The Lionheart had sewed a red cross upon his tunic which was the symbol favoured by French Crusader Knights, John instead took the Black one that was associated with English nobility. Through the collapse of his continental interests, John has, in his own way, given birth to a nation too. The English Channel will prove to be a cultural divide far greater than the twenty-one mile stretch of water at its widest point. John has made England an island.

Whilst Pope Innocent is excited about John's pledge, the Barons are dubious. They have seen first-hand how much a crusade costs and highly doubt that England can afford it. They also want answers to the demands they have placed before the King. The Barons refuse to be diverted and go on the offensive. They seize the castle of Bedford and lay siege to Northampton. John is aware of the powder keg his throne sits atop and has been preparing himself for many months. He has siege engines ready, columns of knights and a seemingly endless sea of mercenaries. This was going to be a closely contested conflict.

Up until now, The Baron's War has largely been contained to Northamptonshire, all of that was about to change though when the rebel Barons invaded London. Assisted by sympathisers to their cause, the gates were raised to let in the revolutionaries whilst most of the residents were preoccupied attending Sunday Mass. Capturing the city of London was a coup for the rebel forces, not just for the momentum it contributed to their cause but also in a far more tangible manner. The majority of the King's wealth that he was using to prop up an entire eco-sphere of sell swords, mercenary crossbowmen and pikes for hire, was concentrated in London. John would not be able to make payroll and with that, his campaign was over.

Less than a month later, King John will be forced to sue for peace. During the negotiations it will be stipulated he must sign the infamous Magna Carta.

Today, original copies of the Magna Carta can be seen in seventeen different locations across England and two abroad. Sites in England include Lincoln Castle, The British Library, The Bodleian Library…they're in the kind of places you'd expect them to be. If it's a prestigious, historic seat of power and you paid a lot for parking, there could well be a page or two of the Magna Carta residing within.

Should you visit Lincoln Castle, which holds one of the originals, you'll see a small crowd of cardigan wearing admirers of the manuscript, gathered around its glass encasement. They speak in hushed whispers to one another and are in a state of reverent awe. To behold this cornerstone of British legalese that defines the very basic rights of common man across the country, truly is a privilege.

For every cardigan wearer you count though, ten more people pass by without affording it so much as a glance. They are to be forgiven. Firstly, it is hardly front and centre even within its own home at Lincoln Castle. It resides in the subterranean, *David P J Ross Magna Carta* Vault. That the Magna Carta is mentioned after David Ross, co-founder of Car Phone Warehouse, speaks further volumes as to its relevance today. Historians are similarly stumped as to how important it actually was, whilst it is nice for the Englishman to have his own version of the Declaration of Independence, it is unclear how relevant it was back then, or if it carries any weight today.

Sinead Quinn, owner and proprietor of Quinn Blakey Hairdressing recently invoked the power of the ancient Charter, as did a bookshop in Nottingham, a London gym and a children's indoor play centre in Liverpool. These entrepreneurs were citing the document of 1215 as a defence against refusing to comply during the UK's nationwide lockdown mandated in response to coronavirus. It's unclear the exact articles these owners were referring to as nothing is written within the Charter itself about hairdressers or pandemics. The only clause that could perhaps be construed as relevant for Quinn's defence, is article sixty-one.

This legal direction interestingly declares that if wronged by the crown, a council of twenty-five barons are permitted to rebel against the monarch in power. Though this grants flexibility to a council of Barons, it does not extend the same power to the population at large. It is this kind of small print that made The Magna Carta not a champion for the people, but an extension of already weighty rights for the elitist.

To date, Quinn's Hairdressing has been fined £27,000 for non-compliance with UK Government Lockdown Laws. To put this into perspective, this is an eye watering £9,000 more than the businesses' Net Assets as declared in their 2019 unabridged accounts.

One thing that is undisputable about The Magna Carta though, is that the list of witnesses to King John's humiliation is vast and impressive. It's a who's who of key government cogs, dissenters, assenters, wonders, blunders, rising stars and falling apples, it is both the cream of the crop and the scum on the Thames. It doesn't take long, as you scan down the list of names, to spot a couple of familiar ones. Hugh de Neville is there, the chief Forester who declared all of Essex to be a fully taxable forest. A few lines under Huge Hugh, is the fan favourite, heavy hitter but considered positively ancient for the period at sixty-nine, it's the scrawled signature of Earl William Marshal.

Hugh de Neville has witnessed many signings of Great Charters, but never one that felt quite like this. For one thing, King John isn't signing it. He is sweating profusely, reading the contract over and over, turning back and forth from page one to the final thirtieth, he tries to get up to use the privy but is snarled back to his seat. King John knows he is beaten, for now, but he has seen enough days to know the weather will turn. He spends as much time looking at the document as he does glaring out at the assembled and internally vowing their downfall.

Hugh is distracted from watching the King by a humongous snore and grunt from the seat beside him, it reverberates across the chamber causing all to turn and stare. The protagonist of the unintended interruption awakes with a snap.

"What in the hell of all things was that?" he barks, eyes wild, hand reaching to his side for a sword that is not there.

For many, Hugh thought, such a display would have attracted ridicule or even punishment, but not for Earl William Marshal. The man is beloved and his stories are legends from a golden era gone by. Though his tales are fantastical, there are few who doubt they are true. Marshal commands the hearts of the men. Hugh has nothing but respect for him. That's why, when he hears Marshal muttering something, he leans in closer, "What did you say Earl Marshal?"

Marshal was one of the men you could count on a single hand who has stayed loyal to John throughout the short Barons' War, even so, as a leader of men himself who had fallen prey to John's cruelty he did not view the Charter as a bad thing.

"My favourite passage, is that the ruling bastards," Marshal often forgot that he was, in fact, one of the 'ruling bastards' these days, "cannot take horses, carts or wood without the consent of the owner, it's revolutionary!"

It is, thought Hugh carefully. Marshal had picked out a good section to enthuse on but Hugh has his reservations, "Do you not worry how it will be enforced though, Earl Marshal?"

"How it will be enforced?" Marshal is confused by the question, "The King commands great armies, how could it not be enforced?"

"Aye, that he does, but the King is also the most prevalent offender for taking men's horses, carts, wood or whatever the hell else he desires!"

The divide between Marshal and Hugh sums up the Magna Carta. There are the undertones of a foundation so noble that a nation could be built upon it. Use of vocabulary such as, "every free man" or, "no man shall be," feels inclusive and reads more like an election speech than a medieval contract. Whilst the clauses do spell out human rights so basic they are taken for granted today, in the thirteenth century, they are ludicrously unenforceable when the main signatory has no intention of upholding these.

With so much uncertainty as to whether the Magna Carta is priceless or scrap, can anybody truly place a value on it? Apparently so, The Hereford Cathedral recently insured their copy for a premium of £24 million. There are some issues with this valuation though. Firstly, the whole document is shamelessly self-serving for the Barons who already have life pretty good. Yes, they are trapped in the pyramid scheme that is the Feudal system, but aren't we all? At least the barons have nice castles to reside in, land, peasants they can extort to death.

The Barons place paramount importance on first-world problems that affect them and them alone. This is evident throughout the document; issues such as the king taking hostages from them, emergency taxes, that kind of thing, are all over the Magna Carta. Granted, there may have been some trickledown economics that would benefit those at the bottom, but the returns diminish with each layer and by the time it reaches the peasants at the bottom, any gains would be negligible.

Somehow, whilst largely being too right wing and elitist in many of its sections, it also manages to be too liberal in others. The charter outlines that a panel of barons will sit in judgement of the King in his every action, should they find him wanting, they will have the jurisdiction to seize his lands and other assets. Come on, King John is a weak monarch but this was never going to happen. Just a few chapters ago we were seeing The Lionheart raping and kidnapping wives of those who disobeyed him, to envision a symbolic head of state who has no real executive power at this period in History, is madness.

Once you have identified one spurious clause within a contract, it will not take you long to find a second, a third usually follows. By this point, the legal document in general is considered to be distressed, or nonsense. After all, if there is a single leak in the four thousand four hundred and seventy-eight words that make up the Charter, how an earth can it be considered watertight? Best to scrap the whole thing…and scrap it King John does, immediately.

Chapter 31: No pigs were harmed during the writing of this chapter

John was confident his signing of the Magna Carta would spell an end to his conflict with The Barons, whilst having no real repercussions on how he ran the country. He envisioned the contract sitting quietly in the background, much as The Charter of Liberties had for his great-grandfather. The Barons didn't see it this way though, they refused to disarm and insisted on invoking their right to question his every decision.

Outmanoeuvred in his own country, John seeks help from overseas, he writes a letter to The Pope. Innocent receives the correspondence and is happy to assist the newly sworn Crusader King. The Pope writes to all Barons across England advising them the contract they have shackled their ruler with is illegal. The Pope tells them that their actions could undermine the efforts of all of Christendom to reconquer Jerusalem. The Barons aren't buying this whole Christendom thing. John has only agreed to lead a Crusade because he has no other options and now he was clearly holding The Pope to ransom. Well, if King John can look outside his own borders for allies, so can we, think The Barons.

With the scrutiny we have placed upon the signing of The Magna Carta, like a ship passing in the night, we have missed the departure of a memorable player that entertained us during the early pages of this book. Six months prior to the signing of the Magna Carta, William the Lion, King of Scotland, passed away in his sleep. The Scottish King, in his younger days, had yearned to liberate the lands of Northumbria from The Plantagenets and wrote a number of letters on that very subject.

Following the failure of the First Rebellion, unable to punish his own brood too severely, The Old King focused much of his vengeful malice on William. William was bound to a series of humiliating treaties, the primary one being that The Scottish Church would be unable to appoint their own Bishops. This may not sound a lot, but it was, it severely hamstrung Scotland in their bid for independence and it was a blow that William felt personally.

Following the death of The Old King, William campaigned against the religious injunction, whilst simultaneously appealing for a slice of his beloved Northumbria. William succeeded in lifting restrictions on the Scottish clergy when he managed to strike a deal with the cash strapped Lionheart, during his Crusading years. Despite making numerous offers, Northumbria remained a dream unfulfilled for The Scottish King.

William the Lion died in the city of Stirling of natural causes at the grand old age of seventy-one. He enjoyed a staggeringly long innings as ruler of Scotland sitting on the throne for a total of forty-nine years, his reign remains record breaking. He is the longest serving King of Scotland prior to the country joining Great Britain.

His sole son and successor, Alexander II, inherited a throne of opportunity. The lengthy reign of William the Lion had birthed a period of stability in Scotland, meanwhile, South of the border, confusion and chaos reigned.

Alexander didn't feel that alone he packed the punch required to knock the English King off his feet, but he knew a man who did. Alexander wrote a letter to Philip. It took a while to receive a reply for Alexander was not the only one writing to him right now, Philip had a very full inbox. The Barons across England were looking to import a "ready to assemble" royal family and wanted The Capetians. After all, Philip had already proven he was extremely effective in developing his own dynasty's interests, he commanded one of the largest empires in Europe and he had always wanted to defeat the Plantagenets. He was clearly their man.

In many ways, Philip was their man, but he was also an old man. Philip had recently celebrated his fiftieth birthday. Although this is hardly a penultimate anniversary today, Philip had way exceeded average life expectancy for the period (thirty-one). Philip also respected that the decisions he made today, would not affect his tomorrows. After all, it wasn't *he* that would have to govern England, it was his son.

Prince Louis VIII, Philip's son, was well up for the challenge. The Capetians had been invited by leading barons and the neighbouring nation of Scotland to invade, what could possibly go wrong? Philip briefed his son extensively on the slipperiness of the Plantagenets. If Philip had any concerns about delegating the invasion force, he gave no sign of it.

May 1216, saw Louis sail into Dover. Though his men readied themselves for a beach landing under assault and a deathly rain of arrows, no resistance force bothered to meet them at the infamous white cliffs. Suspecting a trap, the Capetian soldiers disembarked carefully and crept loosely up the beach. When it became clear that no hostile welcome party was there to greet them, they began to cheer and laugh. After not losing a single man, they began to march upon London.

Louis had prepared his men for this seventy mile hike to be hell. He had explained to them, it would be gruelling and they would be harried by guerrilla warriors for every inch, yard and mile they seized. This just wasn't the case though. Louis' men encountered a few roadblocks on the way to London who turned and ran immediately when confronted by superior numbers. It was all disconcertingly easy for Louis.

Over the next two months, with minimal bloodshed and no serious battles of note, Louis will be welcomed into both the capital city of London and the historic seat of power, Winchester. He will be declared King of England. Barons across the land and Alexander of Scotland himself, queue up to bend the knee to the new Capetian King.

Everything is caving in around John and yet he cannot even draw strength from the country's support structure. His paranoia by now is all too real, The King of England trusts nobody. Even Eustace the Mercenary Pirate Monk defaulted from the Plantagenet King and allied with the Capetian One. Conflicting reports fly in incessantly, this Baron has defected, that Lord was seen with so-and-so. The situation is impossible. Having lost both London and Winchester, John does not even dare to reside in England, instead, he is lying low in Wales. Wales is largely controlled by the fair and stalwart, Earl William Marshal.

Despite his former cruelty towards the elderly Earl, John is afforded the same unerring loyalty Marshal has always pledged to The Plantagenets.

Securing London and Winchester were certainly big victories for Louis, but he hasn't finished the job yet. In his eagerness to reach London, he had marched straight past a whole host of hostile castles. Cutting the head off the Plantagenet snake by securing their two main cities was smart, but the pressure was now very much on to use these power bases to consolidate their position. Louis doesn't though, he seems reluctant to leave London.

Sensing his son's invasion has become rudderless, Philip pens a jesting letter to Louis chiding him for coming all the way to England and not even taking the time to invade Dover Castle. Philip doesn't shout or threaten, but his son listens to him, The Capetian King has a very different management style to The Plantagenets who have taken centre stage over these pages.

Dover Castle is an important strategic stronghold and Philip was probably right to point his son in that direction, that being said, it is no easy task. The defenders of Dover

Castle are well stocked and professionally trained. They formidably rain down death upon the attackers and to make matters worse for Louis, roaming guerrilla warfare bands across Kent strike the attackers with persistent, hit and run raids. The siege lasts for three long months and the defenders show no signs of breaking. Louis eventually cuts his losses and returns to London with his tail between his legs.

Another military success John will enjoy, is at Rochester castle. As he is fleeing Capetian troops he finds the garrison of the castle have turned coats and joined the Capetian Prince, John takes the time to lay siege to the fortifications. The walls were not well staffed but that wouldn't be the case for long. Reinforcements had been sent for and the sound of horses' hooves thundering across the bridge that spanned the Medway river would soon sound the death knell for John's sieging army.

Except, the bridge was no longer there. John had taken a series of wooden galleys, lit them alight and sent them crashing into the timber bridge. The defenders were alone in facing the wrath of King John.

John writes to local landowners requesting a swine of pigs be sent to him post haste. Upon their arrival, the hogs are butchered so as to provide barrel after barrel of pig fat. The gelatinous, gloop stinks and sweats in the midday sun as it is hauled to the frontline of the siege. Next, come the sappers, they dig under the towers of Rochester castle, packing into the tunnel the foul-smelling lipids.

A single lit split is all it takes and the fatty fuel fires up. The tunnel beneath the tower is transformed into a hellish inferno. Sections of the wall and the tower itself collapse with a pained roar of the Gods.

King John captures Rochester castle, he erects a giant gallows ready to hang all inhabitants. At the eleventh hour he is convinced this would be a bad move for it would be setting a precedent were he himself, or his men, ever to be captured. As much as John wants to kill every living soul within the now crumbled walls self-preservation wins through in the end and he settles for just killing a single, randomly chosen unlucky defender. In what must be an example of King John's sense of humour, he has a monument erected for the pigs that were slaughtered during the siege.

Spurred on by his success in Rochester, John rides hard and attempts to lift the siege of Windsor. He marches South with his armies but at the last minute, his nerves fail him. He gets within twenty miles of The Capetians before bottling it and scarpering North.

It may not have been quite so simple as that. There is also the possibility that he had spied an opportunity. King Alexander of Scotland was rumoured to be travelling through Cambridgeshire over the next few days, capturing him would certainly have been a huge coup for this seemingly cursed English King. To be fair to John, capturing the King of Scotland had swung the tide for his father before him in the first rebellion all of those years ago.

Whilst John prowled Cambridgeshire hunting for any whiff of Alexander, he was brought surprising and concerning news. He had indeed successfully broke the siege of Windsor Castle, for the army that had once coveted its grand battlements now sought a greater prize, they were now hunting him. John flees Cambridgeshire and The King of Scotland succeeds in evading capture, travelling unmolested throughout England back to safety.

John rides hard North to escape Louis' men and aims for Lynn. If ever there was a location in Albion where mother nature's veins run close to the skin and you can hear the beat of her heart, it's here. Rivers such as the Great Ouse, Witham, Welland, Nene, all flow many hundreds of miles past countryside cottages and through great towns, they power watermills, get fished in, swam in, played in, drank, boiled and gargled. These rivers swell and subside, they roar and ripple. As if through some unspoken agreement, they all unite at this precise point before together drifting lazily through the sludge of The Wash and out towards the final horizon, the deep unknown of The North Sea.

It is these arterial waterways and ready coastal access that interests King John, the fact that Lynn is an affluently booming trade hub also helps.

The city had enjoyed wealthy patrons since the times of King Henry I who were financially incentivised to see the city grow, it also had the natural advantages of being able to pan-mine salt from the Wash. These miners knew they would never strike it super rich from this activity, this wasn't gold rush America and The Wash was not the Klondike. The key difference was that supply of salt in The Wash was abundant, twice per day, every day, as regular as the tide the sludge was saturated with the stuff. Supply may have been high, but so too was demand. Any food that was spoilable had to be smoked and salted to preserve, this made the market massive. This wasn't a licence to print money, but it was a steady earner and Lynn grew ever more prosperous as a result.

John believes the South lost to him for now and intends instead to set a base of power up in the North. As he arrives into Lynn though, he is exhausted. He has ridden hard for weeks that feel like years. The pressure has been intense. We all deal with stress differently, for John, he has been drinking heavily and for some reason, eating a potentially dangerous amount of plums.

When he arrives at the local inn, he doesn't even bother to mock the bartender's beard. The Innkeeper is shocked for John is white as a sheet and shivering uncontrollably, judging by the sounds and smells coming from his arse he is also suffering serious diarrhoea. The King does not entertain that evening in the common room, he stalks straight off to his chambers and orders wine to be sent upstairs to him.

Whilst The King will be seen throughout town over the next few days, it is not a display of strength. He cuts a vampiric figure, pale and gaunt with black, haunted eyes. His

351

loosely fitted robes blow freely on the coastal breeze as he negotiates the distribution of various supplies he wants sending North. Despite still suffering from a sweating sickness and knotted bowels, after less than a week, John decides his work in King's Lynn is done. He declares he will travel to Lincolnshire to meet with potential allies and stir up barons still loyal to him for a final showdown with Louis

The quickest way to Lincolnshire is through the swampy Wash and King John is certainly in a hurry.

Chapter 32: Who the Hell is Edward Morris?

The spectacular Norfolk Wash should be considered one of Britain's natural wonders. The wide, meandering curves carve a lazy path through the marshland meadows. Splinter streams split off from the main river bends, which, in turn, give birth to their own little trickles. Beautiful as it is, as crucial to our fragile eco-sphere as it may be, The Wash is also terribly muddy.

It's the kind of mud that grasps desperately at your ankle, pulling you down towards its jaws. It's the kind that treacherously transform from terra firma, to a terrible sink hole in but a single step. More than one walker has been pitched knee deep into the frozen filth of The Wash and many have tales to tell of losing their footwear. Generally speaking though, that's about as bad as it gets. You'd be seriously unlucky to get taken out by a sinkhole in The Wash, to be in danger of such a feat you'd need to weigh as much as a luxury SUV, or, a drove of fully treasure laden donkeys.

"King John, are you sure you want me to send this drove of fully treasure laden donkeys across the mouth of The Wash?" incredulously asks the King's manservant, who feels this may be some kind of test.

"Aye," John nods in a distracted fashion. It was clear he wasn't listening. John feels ostracised, exiled to the wilderness.

King John and his mounted men peel away from the fully laden wagons and ride a different path. The horses would be hobbled were they to travel at any speed through the swamp and they know it will be quicker for them to circumnavigate The Wash. With a whinny and a nervous stamping of feet, the lead donkey reluctantly plods forward pulling his cargo behind him.

Perhaps we can excuse John for not mentally operating at full capacity, for unbeknownst to him, he does not have long left on this Earth. He has suffered from the disease of Kings, gout, for a long time and it is flaring up painfully. Whilst the gout is certainly debilitating and slows him down, it isn't this that will get him. His feverish stomach upset has advanced, he has passed blood and mucus in his bowel movements for the last three days, he has told nobody.

We have witnessed the horrors of dysentery already in this novel with the passing of Young Henry. We concluded the disease could have been transmitted through any number of unhygienic actions from drinking dirty sewage water, personal contact with somebody who had not sufficiently washed their hands after popping to the privy, that kind of thing.

Dysentery, as a disease, is non-discriminatory. A king is equally as likely to be afflicted with this potentially lethal ailment as a pauper. Yes, a king may be more likely to receive a higher quality of doctor than a commoner, but in the thirteenth century, that wasn't saying a lot. We've seen it happen, but many find it hard to accept that at such a pivotal moment in History King John simply died of dysentery. Conspiracy theories began the rounds.

Just like with The Lionheart, poison was tossed into the mix. Those who follow this line of thinking believe that King John was poisoned by a frog, yes, a frog. The small amphibian is said to have been milked, unsure exactly what that entails, and the poison poured into John's wine by an anonymous monk. The ever-suspicious John, wilily told the monk to drink the wine first, which he duly did. John was alarmed to hear a few days later that the monk had died, by this point though, it was already too late.

Another theory is that the death was caused by outrageous self-indulgence on the part of King John himself.

After suffering from the early stages of dysentery, an ailment that a young, healthy man such as himself may have been able to shake off, John refused to acknowledge his condition. According to contemporaries upon falling ill, he quaffed heavily on cider and even worse than that, he ate an inordinate amount of plums. The cider isn't judged too negatively by writers of the period, the plums though, that was considered a problem. Exactly what constitutes an inordinate amount of plums remains unspecified, for it to be so remarked upon though suggests it was a lot. Generally speaking, a diet high in fibre is great for regularity and gut health. However, if you find yourself experiencing the runs, fibre should be cut back, way back. Medieval quacks didn't have a complete understanding of food groups, but they did seem to know that excessive plums would exacerbate heavy diarrhoea.

The final cause of death sometimes attributed to John, is that he may have eaten a dodgy lamprey. Lampreys are the same jawless bastards that did in for The Old King's grandfather, that's right, John may be the second King in this book to die from eating a lamprey. I mean just how good are these cartilaginous parasitic eels? Apparently, they taste like squid and are considered a delicacy in France. Whilst a number of recipes are freely available online for preparing lampreys, the safest option is probably avoidance.

King John will leave behind both a lasting legacy and a hell of a mess. Before we unpick the aftermath of his passing though, let's look at what happened to his treasure. Last time we saw all the jewels, holy relics and golden cutlery he'd been able to grab from his palace before going on the run, they were being casually waved across the swamp lands of The Wash strapped to the back of a train of donkeys. What happened there?

Predictably enough, the convoy gets into trouble almost immediately. The wheels start to be sucked and slurped at by the sinking slosh. Men leap down from atop the wagons and horses cursing, they are surprised when they land to find that they themselves sink knee deep into the slime. With grunts and groans, they wrestle their feet free and make their way to the back of the baggage train. At the beginning they just push.

These men are no lily-livered weaklings. They are hardy soldiers of strength, heroes of a hundred battles. They were strong to the core and confident they could get the wooden wheels rolling in no time.

Their pushing is of no use though. The men can't get any purchase on the slippery mud. Their heels glide backwards whilst they heaved, meanwhile the wagons move not an inch. They decide to strip a tree of its branches and use them for leverage. The thinking behind this plan is that by wedging these under the wheels, the resulting friction would get the convoy moving again. A quick search around confirmed that nothing could grow in this wasteland that is washed out by salt water twice a day.

"Why don't we dismantle one of the wagons for wood instead?" Asked one of the soldiers.

Good idea.

Plank by plank, nail by nail, the man begins to deconstruct the leading wagon. Its cargo is distributed across freighters further back in the line with spare capacity. The great beams of wood are piled up neatly, ready to wedge beneath wheels of wagons that have been rendered immobile. The problem though, is that this all takes time. By now, the sky is darkening and the tide is approaching. The waves are lapping at the donkeys' feet and they do not like it. They are scared. One tries to bolt, tethered to an unmoveable burden though he slips and breaks his leg. His bleated screams unsettle the men who are equally uncomfortable by the rising water levels. The donkey's throat is slit.

Finally, after what feels an age, the beams are wedged under the wheels of the first wagon. Men return to the rear to push and not a moment too soon, for by now they are almost ankle deep in the swell.

"Heave, heave, ho!"

It's working, the lead wagon begins to roll forward across the plank, first one foot, then two feet, three feet, four but then disaster. The wheels slip off the side of the board and sink back, even deeper than before, into the mud. The waves are lapping higher and the animals are besides themselves with terror, the men are not faring much better. The situation is desperate. Any rational commander could see that the convoy was not salvageable and difficult decisions needed to be made, fast. The donkeys are cut free. The men flee for safer, higher ground. Whatever they are able to steal is taken and anything too large to loot, or too sacred to steal, will be dispersed across the marshy seabed.

To date the treasure has not been found, at least, it probably hasn't. There's an elusive figure in the metal detecting world who goes by the name of Edward Morris. Google "Edward Morris Metal Detecting" and he'll come up, not that Edward Morris is his real name, he's the Banksy of this world. Morris flies under an alias for if the story he tells is true, it's paramount he preserves his anonymity. Should you decide to dig deeper than a casual web search you'll find that many have solid suspicions as to his identity, even so, we'll respect his privacy.

Out detecting one day, Morris hears the familiar beep beep beep from his instrument that never fails to set his heart a-racing. It's why he does what he does, come rain, snow, or whatever the hell else the English weather can throw at him, Morris will be out there hunting for finds.

Morris moves his detector back and forth, he is trying to confirm the exact location of his hit. He is tingling all over. What have I discovered? What great treasure have I unearthed? Could it be an ancient Roman coin or a lost pendant of Queen Boudicca…yeah right. Morris knows what his find will be, it'll be a bottle cap. It's always a bottle cap. The Norfolk countryside soil was saturated with the bloody things.

Once he hits a depth of about four metres though, he strikes…rust. A rust sized spherical object, about the size of a golf ball, lies at the bottom of the hole. Morris doesn't think on it further. A rusty golf ball was slightly better than a bottle cap, but only just.

The rust sized golf ball sit on a shelf in Morris' garage for many months, forgotten. Unrelated to the rust ball, Morris visits a tarot card reader. The foreteller of fortunes first demonstrates her authenticity by referencing a fall that Morris had suffered in his childhood, this proves her legitimacy, in Morris' eyes at least, he was ready to listen. The psychic went on to rather cryptically, advise him that he needed to work out a puzzle. Intrigued, Morris returns to his rusty golf ball in the garage, could this be the puzzle the wise woman alluded to?

Whatever Morris discovered that day staring at the ball of rust, convinced him that he had figured out the mystery. Morris vehemently believes that he knows the exact location of the sunken treasure of King John.

Why the need for all this subterfuge, why not just go public with it? Well, Morris has advised in various interviews that the land is owned by a private company, it is for this reason he is understandably secret about the exact location of the find. After all, it was he that got up early on Sunday mornings for years, he was the one who endured the rain, the cold and people sniggering at him for his anorak hobby. He watched the fields change with the seasons, all the time he wore his big earmuffs and waved his silly little metal stick. No doubt teenagers mocked him, he must have trod in cow manure, he would have endured finding bottle cap after endless bottle cap.

The American existential psychiatrist, Irvin Yalom, had a rather unique and crushingly beautiful philosophy surrounding death. He is credited with saying that we all die twice, once in a physical sense and again when nobody alive remembers us. Like a candle blown out in a darkened room, when that last person whispers our name for the final time, that is the true moment our flame will burn out.

If this is the case though, then John is not truly dead at all, for he lives on in many people's memories. King John's name is uttered with a greater frequency than perhaps any other monarch in this book. He enjoys a legendary legacy in modern psyche forever immortalised as "The Bad King John". He is the only English Monarch of his name, for no descendants would ever curse their child and future King with his moniker. Is this fair though? Should we really portray John as some kind of beard tugging, empire wrecking cartoon villain?

Disney certainly thought so. In 1973, Wolfgang Reitherman, one of the infamous "Nine old Men of Disney," did just that. He created an animal version of Robin Hood. Hood himself was cast as a wily and cunning fox, ever ready to duck and dive. Reitherman's Hood is a trickster, a geezer and magnetically charismatic. Little John, presumably in a comedic twist of irony, is far from little, he is a giant bear.

Interestingly King John is cast as a lion. This seems to be a nod to the three lions that flew on the Plantagenet flag. John is a lion in features alone though, he is portrayed as an over indulged, greedy and vindictively childish feline. He will count coins with a miser's glee whilst spooning with sacks of money in his royal bed. He is cruel. He will savagely and routinely beat his underlings.

Even the great bard, William Shakespeare, struggles when he wrestles with the subject of King John. The play that he will float out there of the same name dropped like a lead balloon. It has been placed as his third most obscure play with a measly 2% of those asked confident they had read the script.

We have heard from two great institutions so far, The Walt Disney Company and William Shakespeare, let's hear from one more when considering John's legacy. British publicans contribute a whopping £23 billion to the UK's GDP. Bars also generate somewhere in the region of £13 billion in taxes and provide just shy of one million jobs. Hospitality is a significant gear in the English economic engine. What do the barkeepers of the country think of King John?

They don't like him. Whilst hundreds of pubs bear the title of other Kings and Queens of England, John has only one or two that bear his name.

Perhaps we are being unfair to him and should cut him some slack? After all, he inherited a kingdom riddled with debt, was surrounded by discontent Barons that wished to undermine him and he played upon a board against the highly competent Philip Augustus and Pope Innocent III. John didn't just catch a hot potato, he caught one that was lined with plastic explosives, broken glass, filed down nails and deadly anthrax. It would have taken a leader of exceptional foresight to navigate this unsolvable maze. It would have taken The Old King, or maybe Richard.

Primogeniture makes a mockery of Darwinism. Whilst John may have had many talents, these would undoubtedly have seen his career plateau far below the seat he sat upon during his life. His role as King, during one of the most turbulent periods of English History, was not a kindness for the people he ruled over or John himself.

Finale:

Completing a historical book is, in many ways, as challenging as starting one. There are no obvious beginnings to the story you are telling and you never feel you have reached a definitive end. To confound the situation further, everything is intrinsically interlinked. Just because John is dead, does not mean the consequences of his actions won't live on. The narrative you have told is a straight line without a beginning or end. There is a lot of important events that occurred before page one and there will be plenty that follow the final full stop.

Whilst it's difficult to know where to finish, it isn't impossible. Like staying at a party for too long and looking around, bleary eyed, to sadly realise you recognise nobody; this is where we now find ourselves. The Plantagenet family that launched our story so many pages ago, are all dead. Their star that burned so brightly has gone supernova and imploded in on itself. They are basically done. An empire that once stretched from Scotland all across much of Europe, is now restricted to a few isolated pockets of resistance across England.

Mopping up these final dissenters might take the best part of a year, maybe two, but in reality it would be a formality for The Capetians, they had won.

"Not so fast," growls the Great Earl Sir William Marshal, "one more time, just one more time I will ride into Hell for this accursed family."

With a creak of his knees and a windy wheeze, Marshal pulls himself up into his saddle and rides hard towards the city of Lincoln.

Further Reading

What's that you say? You've still not had your fill of The Plantagenets and want more? I get it.

There are obviously hundreds of works available, but, as a start, check out the titles below. They have been helpful for me in the putting together of this book:

Eleanor of Aquitaine by the wrath of God, Queen of England, Alison Weir (1999)
King John, Marc Morris (2016)
Lionheart, Stewart Binns (2013)
Saladin and the Fall of Jerusalem, Stanley Lane-Poole (2002)
Normans and Plantagenets, J. Ewing (1930)
The Greatest Knight: The remarkable life of William Marshal, The Power behind five English Thrones, Thomas Asbridge (2015)
The (True) Story of Eustace the Monk, Kathryn Bedford (2012)
Two Medieval Outlaws Glyn S. Burgess (1997)

Prefer your History with a dash of lemonade and a slice of laughter?

Plug in your headphones and give *The Rex Factor Podcast* series one, reviewing all the kings and queens of England from Alfred the Great to Queen Elizabeth a listen.

More of a visual learner eh? That's okay, we've got your back... *Britain's Bloodiest Dynasty* with Plantagenet enthusiast Dan Jones is well worth a watch.

Dying to know what happens next? Keep an eye on www.casual-historian.com for latest news and updates and to sign up to The Casual Historian Newsletter.

About the author

Alan McLean was born in Nuneaton and completed his studies in the historical city of Lincoln. He has worked in industries as diverse as Education, Signage, Cleaning and even Chimney Sweeping. Employed as a freelance writer for international ghost walking company, Mysterium Tours, McLean found himself exploring the darker chapters of European History.

McLean's unique writing style makes the Past accessible by boldly embellishing interesting details, whilst simultaneously glossing over the mundane. His debut novel, "A Casual Historian presents The Early Plantagenets" is a book for people who like to buy History books but never normally finish reading them.

During the day, McLean can be found walking in the Staffordshire countryside with his wife Laura and his Border Collie, Loki. By moonlight though…expect to see this dark author prowling the marshlands with a shovel, looking to unearth skeletons from days gone by.

Printed in Great Britain
by Amazon

72101445R00220